JAPANESE AND EUROPEAN MANAGEMENT

JAPANESE AND EUROPEAN MANAGEMENT

Their International Adaptability

Edited by
Kazuo Shibagaki,
Malcolm Trevor,
and Tetsuo Abo

UNIVERSITY OF TOKYO PRESS

Publication assisted by a grant from The Japan Foundation.

CONTENTS

v

PREFACE

This book arises out of the annual conference of the then Euro-Japanese Management Studies Association held at the new and splendidly equipped Sanjo Conference Hall, University of Tokyo, in September 1987. The theme was 'The International Adaptability of Japanese and European Management'. The Association itself had grown out of an initial international meeting of researchers, managers, and scholars, held at the Free University, Berlin, in 1984 under the aegis of Professor S.J. Park, to whom the credit for the initiative that led to the founding of the Association is due. For the Association's members, the Tokyo conference, as the first to be held in Japan, was a valuable opportunity to strengthen Euro-Japanese links and to promote collaboration on work of mutual interest. It was also at this meeting that the Executive Committee decided, in view of the increasing importance of the Pacific region as a whole and of the Association's own expansion and the interest of its members in comparative studies, to change the Association's name to Euro-Asia Management Studies Association.

For publication purposes, the editors have grouped the papers under three main headings, rather than follow the order in which, for various reasons, they were presented at the conference. The intention has been to follow the logic of starting with the general and conceptual issues, before dealing with the empirical accounts of specific cases giving details of how far Japanese management abroad and, in a smaller number of instances, European management in Japan have been showing themselves to be internationally adaptable or not.

On behalf of the Association, I should like to thank Professor Shibagaki, Professor Abo, Professor Kudō, and their colleagues for their work in connection with ensuring the success of the conference, which was appreciated by all who attended. To Professor Shibagaki and

Professor Abo, and also to the ataff of University of Tokyo Press, are due special thanks for all the painstaking work involved in preparing this volume for publication; and to the Japan Foundation for supporting it financially.

We look forward to future conferences and to the continued expansion of international comparative work on Asia and the Pacific region.

Malcolm Trevor
Chairman E-AMSA

INTRODUCTION

Kazuo Shibagaki
University of Tokyo

This book is based on the papers submitted to the fourth International Conference of the Euro-Japanese Management Studies Association (EJMSA), held in Tokyo in 1987. However, this book is not simply a transcript of the proceedings of the conference. Each paper was revised for publication, supplemented with footnotes where necessary, and presented in an academic style. As background to this book, it may be worth explaining the intention behind the organization both of the EJMSA and of the Tokyo Conference.

Since the 1970s, especially the latter half, the expansion of Japanese enterprises into Western countries rapidly increased with the intensification of trade conflict and the rise of the yen. The enterprises that went abroad have taken a variety of forms, such as subsidiary, local corporation, and joint enterprise, and most of them tried to introduce, in varying degrees, 'Japanese management' to the local areas. This has given rise to many types of conflict in industrial relations. The European researchers and businessmen who had been closely observing these firms held a workshop entitled 'Transferability of Japanese Industrial Relations' in Berlin in 1984. This was the beginning of the EJMSA. In the following year, 1985, a second workshop, entitled 'Internationalisation of Japanese Enterprises' was held in London. It was on this occasion that the group formally became an academic association. Then, in 1986, there was the Rotterdam Conference, entitled 'Industrial Cooperation between Europe and Japan', which was followed by the Tokyo Conference. In the first three conferences, numerous empirical studies were presented on the character of Japanese enterprises in Europe and the problems they faced in local areas. Furthermore, research topics broadened from particular to more general issues, as one can note from the shift in the contents of the themes cited above.

The organizing committee for the Tokyo Conference was composed of the following members:

Kazuo Shibagaki	Institute of Social Science, University of Tokyo, Chairman;
Tetsuo Abo	Institute of Social Science, University of Tokyo, Secretary;
Akira Kudō	College of Arts and Sciences, University of Tokyo, Secretary;
Hiroshi Itagaki	College of Liberal Arts, Saitama University;
Toyokichi Onizuka	Faculty of Management, Hōsei University;
Masaru Sakuma	Institute of International Business, Kanagawa University;
Mie Sugai	Japan International Cultural Institute;
Tatsuji Suzuki	Faculty of Economics, Niigata University;
Yoshiaki Takahashi	Faculty of Commerce, Chūō University;
Yoshiya Teramoto	Faculty of Economics, Meiji Gakuin University;
Moriaki Tsuchiya	Faculty of Economics, University of Tokyo.

The theme of the Tokyo Conference, 'Comparative Studies on International Adaptability of Japanese and European Management', was selected with two points in mind. First, since this was the first EJMSA conference to be held in Japan, it was hoped that besides taking up the issue of Japanese enterprises in Europe, we would be able to look at European enterprises in Japan; through a comparative perspective, we could gain a deeper understanding of both. Second, on the basis of the numerous empirical studies presented up to now, we hoped to be able to theorize about Japanese multinational enterprises. What is meant by 'theorization' here is, rather than to simply delineate the characteristics of Japanese multinational enterprises that are distinct from those of their European counterparts, to clarify the basis of that distinctiveness. In order to make this point clear, it is obvious that we must examine the so-called Japanese management, the characteristics that make Japanese mutinational enterprises distinct, and the factors that gave birth to that distinctiveness. There are, perhaps, both universalistic factors and those peculiar to Japan, and it is by identifying them that we are able to understand the international adaptability and limits of Japanese management. The term 'adaptability' may be interpreted here not only in the sense of 'passive adaptation', but also more positively as 'applicability'.

The principle task of the conference was to analyse characteristics unique to Japanese management. Diverse elements were pointed out, even though they were mainly representative of large enterprises: from lifetime employment, seniority wage, and enterprise union to groupist and egalitarian personnel management and employee participation in management at various levels; on-the-job training, in-house education, and the 'bottom-up' style of decision making; and further, in the area of an enterprise relations with the outside, extensive utilization of the sub-contracting system and 'enterprise alignment' (*keiretsu*). The problem is that in order to explain the basis of these, the cultural peculiarity of Japanese society is frequently brought out. Of course, it is not meaningless to explain economic or management phenomena in cultural terms. However, in the case of Japanese economic phenomena, this approach often tends to become excessive, and as a result, there is a tendency to explain everything in terms of Japanese culture, even when they can be explained by economic logic alone.

There is no doubt that the relatively superior performance of Japanese economy or the success of its management system is due to certain elements unique to Japanese management. This is particularly evident in the manufacturing industry, especially in the assembly-type mass production machinery industry, which made its appearance in the twentieth century: the automobile, electric-electronics, and precision machinery, industries, for example. What made this success possible, in my understanding, is not Japanese culture, but the economic system, especially the characteristics of the labour market and the capital structure of enterprises.

To state briefly, the peculiarity of the labour market is the formation of a wide and deep internal labour market and that of the capital structure of enterprise is what is referred to as 'corporate capitalism' (*hōjin shihonshugi*). I shall not go into the subject of the internal labour market, since already a great deal has been said about it. Corporate capitalism refers to a system in which large enterprises are the great stock owners of nearly all corporate entities: individuals with large stock ownership are exceptional cases. Such enterprise groups as Mitsubishi or Mitsui are comprised of associated companies that own one another's stocks. Under this type of capital structure, the corporate stock owner does not interfere in the management of the enterprise, except under the most unusual circumstances, and the management of the enterprise is normally run by a manager who is promoted internally from an employee's status. This can be considered the most extreme form of managerial control. It is from this fact that the argument such as 'capitalists do not exist in contemporary Japan' is born. Be that as it may, what I would like to stress here is that both the internal labour market and corporate capitalism are systems that can be explained in terms of economics.

Why is it that these systems were possible in Japan and not in other countries, for example, in Western countries? Or why does it create conflict when transferred to other countries? Here again it would be easy to rely on a cultural explanation, which for me is too simplistic. The answer lies not in cultural differences. Rather, it is due to the near absence of cultural resistance in the case of Japan upon the formation of a new economic system demanded by the production structure of new industries, while there is the presence of a strong resistance in the case of Western countries.

The culture of a country or region is generally conservative in character, for it normally includes social consciousness deriving from religion, ethnicity, social status, and class. In contrast to this, economic activities are productive and therefore are innovative in character. When we take up the question of culture in relation to the economy, we should examine the negative influence of culture on economy rather than emphasise the positive and innovative aspects. In other words, we should ask whether or not and how and how much culture acts as an obstacle to economic innovations. If we ask the question this way and examine the cultural roots of the economically rational character of Japanese management and establishment of the internal labour market or the corporate capitalism underlying it, I must say that the presence of the type of culture that could prevent the formation of such a new economic system was not very strong. Or, to put it more strongly I would say that there was no such culture in Japan. Conversely, we may say that in the case of Western countries, the culture that was already formed by the nineteenth century acted as an obstacle for economically rational innovations demanded by the new industries that appeared in the twentieth century.

There were 82 participants in the Tokyo conference, including 17 individuals from abroad (the UK, the FRG, France, Holland, Israel, Korea, and the USA) and 5 foreigners residing in Japan. The conference was held on September 29 and 30, 1987, at the Sanjo Conference Hall, University of Tokyo, thanks to the cooperation of the Institute of Social Science of the University of Tokyo and financial support from the Japan Society for the Promotion of Science and the businessmen's group, Nobara-kai.

Part I
Japanese Management and International Adaptability

THE EMERGENCE OF JAPANESE MULTINATIONAL ENTERPRISES AND THE THEORY OF FOREIGN DIRECT INVESTMENT

Tetsuo Abo
University of Tokyo

Introduction

Since the 1970s, the foreign direct investment (FDI) of Japanese firms has been expanding at a more rapid pace than that of other developed countries, and there are increasing concerns about the great influence this will have on international and domestic economies. The important point here is that this impact from Japanese multinational enterprises (MNEs) is not simply of a quantitative nature. This investment not only substitutes or partially supplements the FDI of the US and European MNEs, but also involves qualitative issues in the activities of MNEs. We shall illuminate some new aspects of FDI to which not so much attention has been paid. This discussion will also provide an opportune time to reconsider the mainstream theory of international direct investment which has been principally based on the experience of American MNEs.

Some Japanese studies on FDI take large American corporations as the model for their research. Their efforts seek to introduce and apply to Japan the American or Western type of theories mainly based on and developed from American MNE models. Needless to say, this process has played an important role. However, we are now faced with immense new problems which will not allow us to rely on theories purely based on the American model. Some of these problems are related to the principal issue of how and to what extent the technology and know-how stemming from 'Japanese-type management' can be adapted or transferred to foreign countries where cultural climates are quite different from Japan's.

In regard to this point, we have available the results of studies like M. Y. Yoshino's, which take into account this particular element in a theoretical framework based on American models. But these problems are

3

not so simple that we can deal with them within the context of established theory. By looking at established theory, of course, we can suggest to what extent the Japanese-type MNE is universal or particular. Here, however, 'particularity' does not have great meaning; in other words, it is only a residual from the examination of 'universal' elements. Therefore, it will be difficult for us to develop a new point of view or useful theoretical framework to analyse the Japanese-type MNE on the basis of that 'particularity'.

However, I will try to take this particularity into consideration not only to show the difference of the Japanese MNE from the Western model but also to show the special implications of this difference in terms of the advantages of the Japanese MNE. I shall also ask whether this particularity actually has any universality in terms of the human factors related to management organization and practices. I will postulate that the web of human relations in East Asian countries is more adaptable to the steady and bit-by-bit changes in production processes at the present stage of industrial development.

Application of the American model

T. Ozawa's approach is representative of the type which illuminates a characteristic side of the Japanese type MNE by applying the MNE theory based on the American model (1). His theoretical framework is, in short, a combination of the international product cycle theory developed by R. Vernon and others and the Hecksher-Ohlin international trade-investment theory. Ozawa mainly discussed the Japanese FDI, which was made from the latter half of the 1960s to the early 1970s in developing countries, particularly in East Asia. In this period of time, Japanese small- and medium-size and labor-intensive industries, such as textiles, electronics and other miscellaneous industries, became very active in overseas production in order to take advantage of lower wage cost abroad under the 'threat' of new competition arising from NICs (Newly Industrialised Countries). This is a typical pattern in the product or 'industry' life cycle theory.

But here, what I want to pay attention to is principally another aspect of Ozawa's argument. This argument states that 'Japanese-type management' is making best use of its relative abundance of labour as a comparative advantage of production factor endowment compared with other developed countries. In this way, Japanese firms are modifying Western technologies in matured industries into a more labour-intensive type and, by taking advantage of the resulting benefits, are expanding their overseas manufacturing activities in the developing countries, where labour supply is more abundant. This idea comes from the Hecksher-Ohlin theory and its successor, A. Mandel's, that international capital investments as well as foreign trade should take place on the basis of the difference of international comparative advantage determined by the condition of production factor endowment, such as capital and labor. Ozawa's new idea is that Japanese firms act as 'interceptors' and transfer Western technologies in forms that are applicable to these countries where sufficient labour is easily obtained.

On the other hand, the limitation of Ozawa's analysis of the Japanese MNE in its entirety is also clear. First, the expansion of Japanese MNEs to developed countries since the latter half of the 1970s is far beyond the scope of his analysis. For example, auto, electronics, and chemical industries, which are among the major Japanese manufacturing investors in the USA and Europe, cannot find more abundant and lower wage labour there. A more important point, however, is that it is essential to take into account the qualitative difference of management and worker when we do comparative research on the local production activities of Japanese and Western MNEs. Ozawa speaks only of the quantitative difference of production factor endowment (2).

K. Kojima also developed his own idea of the Japanese-type MNE but this has an aspect common with Ozawa's, and, in fact, both influenced each other to a considerable extent (3). The theoretical framework of Kojima's approach is also based on Hecksher-Ohlin's comparative advantage theory of trade; and he strongly supports overseas production by Japan's comparatively disadvantaged industries in developing countries by introducing a 'Japanese-type product life cycle theory'.

The real uniqueness of Kojima's thesis, however, is to put forward the international division of labour based on comparative advantage through the implementation of the FDI in the comparatively disadvantaged industries. Here he criticises American type monopolistic, large MNEs which substitute their local production for foreign trade by making use of their higher level of technology and large scale of capital. On the other hand, he eagerly recommends the Japanese type of MNEs to transfer their technologies, which are closer to the local developing countries' level, and create a comparative advantage and competitive power of export in the local industries so that these processes can contribute to the new development of the international division of labour.

This is not simply a comparative analysis, but a normative opinion of Kojima himself. Whether we may or may not agree with his standpoint, the most important problem for us is the fact that there is no space in his model for the FDI of Japanese firms in developed countries. The local production of Japanese auto firms in the USA, for instance, according to his opinion should not be carried on because it is not necessary for those firms to run a risk under such circumstances when they can export favourably, judging from the ideal principle of comparative advantage theory that production should be preferred in the country with the lowest cost. But, surprisingly enough, this assertion was made in April of 1981 when the 'voluntary' restriction of Japanese car exports to 1.68 million units had already started. He seems to be too optimistic about maintaining a free trade world in the present climate. However, especially in the world after the oil crisis and the breakdown of Pax Americana, nationalism has been becoming more or less dominant over the efficiency-orientedness of the market economy, despite increasing economic interdependency between national economies. Therefore, there is no approdriate choice other than FDI for manufacturing firms to take place under the contradictory relations mentioned above. If all Japanese firms had heeded Kojima's advice, they would have been much more seriously opposed by Western countries when they entered the US market following frictions in the trade war.

Although the above two approaches can be said to succeed in examining a salient feature of Japanese MNEs, principally within the framework of neo-classical theory, its perspective is obviously limited to FDI in developing countries. The reason for this is not only the fact that Japanese FDI in developed countries came later but also a limitation of the perspective of the analytical framework itself.

Explanations from the Marxist or dependency theory

How have Marxist analyses been able to keep up with neo-classical ones in this field? There are many genealogies in Marxist capital export theory, but not much stock of research on Japanese FDI has been accumulated. Consequently, there have been only a few noteworthy papers which deal with Japanese FDI in developed countries.

What is common to many of these theorists is what the author calls the 'excess capital theory approach', which has great merit since such a viewpoint enables one to examine the dynamic expansion of Japanese capital export since the latter half of the 1960s, especially in the

1970s, in relation to the transformation process in the entire economic structure of Japanese capitalism. However, the term 'excess capital' is very controversial since both the concept and its connection with capital exports are not so clear-cut, and in the actual research by most Marxist and dependency theorists, the process and background of the structural change have not been successfully analysed, and only the exploitation of low wage costs and plentiful materials in developing countries is emphasized. The latter fact is, of course, important in relation to the rapid increase of the wage level in Japan, which is a sign of the changing domestic economy; however, such a phenomenon can be seen in any developed country.

The real question of the Japanese MNE, however, comes about after these kinds of macro-level points of view complete playing their role. Then the micro-level or firm-specific aspects and management-level elements must appear to be more crucial factors. The reason why at the end of March of 1987 the cumulative amount of Japanese manufacturing investments in Asia (US$8.3 billion, or 29.5%) is ranked second behind North America (US$9.9 billion, or 35.1%) by just a small margin would be due not only to wage costs and geographical location, but also to the 'closeness' of cultural distance, especially a similar quality of labour. The nature of people in East Asian countries, in general, has many features common (but not entirely the same) to Japanese in terms of group orientedness (less individualism), flexibility (less demarcation), and skill with their hands, so that the local application of Japanese management is much easier than in Western countries.

In these respects, S. Fujiwara is among the few researchers who have deliberately gone into the issue of the qualitative aspect of capital-labour relations, i.e., the problem of 'Japanese-type industrial. relations', from the economics point of view (4). He is correct in pointing out that production process technology and production organization are a competitive advantage of Japanese manufacturing firms over US firms and that the key factor in deciding the transferability of Japanese technology to the USA is Japanese-type industrial relations, including the sub-contract system. His field of vision is broader than usual in that he lays stress on the difficulty of transferring Japanese type industrial relations and estimates that the major practice of Japanese firms in the USA should be active capitalisation of microelectronic technology, such as the introduction of robots.

Even so, his analysis of Japanese industrial relations and Japanese MNEs is limited. He emphasises that the principal feature of Japanese industrial relations can be understood in enabling the increase of labour intensity which is brought about by the introduction of Japanese-type process technology. This is a sort of balance of power theory on the understanding that the main factors which influence the difference of industrial relations between the USA and Japan is that of the degree of development of the trade union movement. In this context, the difference of industrial relations is still regarded as quantitative. Therefore, if the recent changes in US unions' attitude, i.e., a change towards a more cooperative relationship between management and the UAW in the automobile industry, comes to stay, Japanese-type management methods and technology will be transferred without much problem. In his understanding, the objective of introducing automated process technologies into US plants is to minimise the resistance of American unions. But as an effect of such automation, it is more important to make a wide dispersion in the sense of togetherness, quality, and dexterity among American workers. This is the question of the quality of workers and one of the major reasons for the conspicuous development of the mass production systems in the USA for the first time in the world.

Application of the Japanese management theory

We have seen that the emergence of Japanese type MNEs made it clear that the theoretical frameworks of conventional economics are not sufficient to illuminate this new type of MNE. The point is how we can integrate the new point of view that stresses the qualitative difference of management and labour into the existing framework. It is also suggested that such concerns and viewpoints have been awakened by the process and intellectual product of Japanese management arguments.

Now I will inquire into the main points and implications of arguments about Japanese management in relation to the Japanese type MNE. It is interesting to note that foreign researchers like M.Y. Yoshino and M.H. Trevor are more distinguished than their Japanese counterparts who have examined Japanese management in connection with the international expansion or foreign production of Japanese firms. There are, of course, many Japanese researchers who have analysed Japanese management itself, but most of them have responded to the upsurge of interest abroad and, for the time being, are concentrating their major concern on the domestic background of the particularity of Japanese management.

Yoshino's research is the most prominent and most neatly applies

Japanese management arguments to Japanese MNE research (5). Though depending on an American model as the theoretical basis, he has produced a good account of the uniqueness of Japanese-type MNEs. According to him, one of the salient features of the overseas expansion of Japanese firms is export-orientation supported by the activities of general trading companies, but later, after various kinds of 'threats', there has been a drastic change in overseas production. Needless to say, movement from export to local production is generally seen almost everywhere, but much more smoothly, just as the product life cycle theory tells us. Yoshino's important contribution was to make clear the special implication of 'forced' local production of Japanese firms in close connection with his superb analysis of Japanese management.

As for the background of Japanese management, homogeneity, and group orientation, which are socio-cultural characteristics of Japan stemming from geographical and historical conditions, are pointed out. The conspicuous features of Japanese management methods are mentioned as follows: emotional and cooperative human relationship without contracts, flexible decision-making methods, decentralisation of leadership depending less on job classification or position. Although each one of these indicators may not be originally his own, his capacity to grasp the overall character or implication of Japanese management is so unerring that his approach to Japanese MNE arguments can be quite insightful. If the particularity of Japanese management is deep rooted in the socio-cultural background, then it would have to face serious problems and tensions in bringing these methods into a different type of society. He shows this concretely on the basis of his field surveys on Japanese management subsidiaries in Thailand (1973): the advantage of Japanese management rests with each employee or their human relations, depending on day-to-day experiences and mutual understanding, so that it is not easy to list such practices in a manual, as American firms do.

From this understanding, he raises an essential question about the overseas production activities of Japanese firms: 'The question remains, however, can the Japanese management system adapt itself to accommodate heterogeneous elements and still function effectively in the international marketplace?' (6). His focal point here is the possibility of a trade-off relationship between comparative advantage and Japanese management methods.

Yoshino established a milestone for MNE theory by incorporating a kind of 'soft', factor which comes from Japanese management theory, into the 'hard' framework based on the Western model. However, his theory still has a limitation mainly resulting from the subject itself: an empirical study of Japanese MNEs in East Asia up to the 1970s and a theoretical model based on American experience. In his book in 1976, he did not foresee the massive expansion of Japanese FDI in developed countries, probably because of Japan's technological lag behind Western countries. It seems, in Yoshino's understanding, that as the comparative advantage of Japanese management is closely connected with Japan's particularity, such advantage would not be able to surpass the Western-type universality. More recently, he has proposed the overseas production of Japanese firms in developed countries in the coming ten years (7). Yet, how has he been able to solve the question mentioned above?

M.H. Trevor's book is an earnest piece of research on Japanese MNEs in developed countries, which is substantiated with reliable case studies of Japanese firms in the UK (8). As for the theoretical framework to analyse MNEs, based on managerial organisation theories, he also takes up principally the American model but adds some other models of developing countries. The latter enables the applicability of his framework to become wider.

Trevor emphasizes the importance of the implication in 'five per cent difference' of Japanese management referring to the words of Takeo Fujisawa, a co-founder of Honda Motor Co.: 'Japanese and American management is 95 per cent the same and differs in all important respects'. His main concerns are how this difference of Japanese management adapts in its internationalisation, a concern which is basically common to Yoshino's and, to some extent, Ozawa's. After having examined comprehensively major arguments on Japanese management and produced a number of case studies, he concludes the essential characteristics of the Japanese MNE as 'reluctant', just as expressed in the title of his book, since the particular nature of Japanese management causes tensions in the societies of host countries. In the mature developed countries like the UK, the inflexibility of demarcation underlined by the 'that's not my job' consciousness is a serious obstacle for the application of flexible job organisation and all company-level cooperative aspects of Japanese management. Also, the operation of Japanese organisation largely depends on 'implicit communication and shared values', and the tension arising from this should be higher for British white collars than blue collars because the former want to have the reasoning explained (9). Thus, he insists on the applicability of Yoshino's thesis to developed countries, pointing out that an adjustment of Japanese management methods would be necessitated in the UK, with the result that the efficiency attained at the parent plants more or less decreases.

On the other hand, Trevor demonstrates his critical point of view on Japanese management more strongly, as is generally seen with many European researchers compared with Americans. While he recognises that Japanese management is a well-organized combination of competition and cooperation, he takes into more consideration its measures for controlling workers for the reason that the balance of power between management and workers is favourable for the former. This is true, but a problem would be that too much emphasis on the 'hard'-oriented balance of power aspect may detract from the merit of his approach to Japanese management understanding principally illuminated in the socio-cultural context. In my understanding, a more essential criticism of Japanese management should probably be on the impact which both management and workers together have outside the company, such as the problems of family, education, social relations, international trade friction, and so on, rather than inside.

At any rate, Trevor has covered the limitation of Yoshino's thesis and widened the range of its applicability to developed countries. Moreover, extending the scope of view of Japanese management to East Asian NICs, he even mentions the possibility of a 'Pacific Century' approach focusing on the second wave in comparison with Max Weber's thesis of the first wave of the Industrial Revolution in the Western countries. This question, so far, has not yet been answered by Trevor. The point is, again, that the theoretical framework for dealing with the particularity of Japan or Asian-type management practices has not yet been fully developed. Also, one should mention that Trevor's case studies are limited to the UK or Europe.

Among the several studies by Japanese scholars of Japanese MNEs in connection with Japanese management, that of K. Yasumuro is especially stimulating. His book has similar concerns to those of the above two researchers: to examine international management behaviour by looking at the conduct of Japanese MNEs in East Asia (10). He grounds himself theoretically in a broad survey of related arguments abroad and in Japan.

It is particularly suggestive that Yasumuro refers to E.T. Hall's concept of 'context' for comparative culture. Hall says that culture has a programming function of processing complicated information among people and considers 'context' or 'culture in which people are deeply involved with each other' (11). According to his understanding, Japan is a highly contextual society because it has a culture in which, under the condition of good communications between its constituent members, the programming to determine human relations in society works efficiently. On the other hand, the USA, for example, is a low-context society. Yasumuro applies this characterisation of Japanese society to the concept of Japanese management and explains that in Japanese firms, since various kinds of information about the members, such as values, norms, and so on, have been input beforehand into their organisations and since well-informed insiders (Japanese) can easily foresee each other's behaviour, these organisations work very well with a minimum of messages. This means, however, that when such an organisation is introduced to a low-context society, the 'outsiders' (native people) cannot enter easily into the organisation's human relations, making cultural friction unavoidable.

This is the same as arguing that the problems of Japanese management and its international transfer are cultural. But Yasumuro does not deal with Japanese culture and society simply as a peculiarity but as something comparable by using the analytical tool of 'context'. The possibility of using this common measure in order to show an aspect of culture which is essentially a qualitative difference as a quantitative difference may enable us to provide a clue for objectively analysing the question of the international transferability of Japanese management. At the same time, of course, there are limits to translating qualitative differences into quantitative ones. I wonder to what extent Yasumuro is aware of this difficult problem.

For, on the one hand, he finds from his questionnaire survey the important fact that as the overseas transfer of Japanese methods possibly results in a large reduction of their efficiency, there is a tendency for overseas plants to strengthen 'direct control' over local practices by many Japanese expatriates. On the other hand, he suggests that 'manualisation' of the overseas management of Japanese firms take place in order to implement the localisation of personnel. However, as Yasumuro himself recognises, the difficulty of manualisation is the distinguishing feature of a high-context society, so the question is also whether Japanese local plants can still retain their advantages of Japanese management through the localisation of personnel ('indirect control').

The implication for the development of a multinational enterprise theory

It was previously argued that the most important impact of the Japanese MNE on FDI theory was to have shown the limitations of MNE theory based on Western models and the necessity of explicitly taking into account the qualitative aspect of capital and labour which is virtually abstracted from the traditional theory of economics. Some suggestive pioneering studies in this field have already been done, but much remains to be done in the way of systematic insights into the implications of the theoretical challenge of the Japanese case within the framework of economics and social science, as well as empirical field research. The following are some comments on the theoretical framework and methodology with which we should implement our research on Japanese-type MNEs.

In regard to the development of the MNE theory, two points should be taken up. First, we now have a new question regarding the substantial elements of technology, a fundamental part of the thesis of advantage which has been regarded as an absolutely valid proposition about firms since Hymer's model. It has been made clear that the level of technology, particularly process technology, is determined not only by such factors as the objectified plants and the small number of engineers who design and control them, but also more broadly by the adaptability to change, the sense of togetherness, and the quality, and so on, of shop-floor level workers, including supervisors, who are operating the lines.

Labour management policy, of course, can have a substantial influence on labour discipline, for instance. However, the fact that we can see the features of Japanese society mentioned above at many levels, e.g., both in blue-collar and white-collar workers and from small-size firms to large, from industry to industry, would show that such features should be considered to have a common background in Japan's socio-cultural constitution. Besides, this human-related aspect of technology which is based on the national differences is difficult to grasp in an objective form, such as a manual, even compared with intangible assets like managerial knowledge or know-how. So there are a great number of problems with the international transfer of this type of technological advantage. The fact that the foreign firms which have tried to imitate QC circle practices have seldom been able to give life to them may be partly because of this.

On the other hand, the applied production technology, such as 'light-thin-short-small' (kei-haku-tan-sho), though it may be a product of Japanese society and culture, has grown up under conditions that can easily be generalized as the environment of islands with a scarcity of natural resources. This can then be transferred internationally to a considerable extent. The transfer to the East Asian area, which was pointed out in Ozawa's argument, is one form of these types, and even to the developed countries in the resource shortage era. The initial success of local production of Sony and Honda in the USA and Europe is a representative case of this type, although the unique innovative technologies of these companies supported that success.

The second implication Japanese MNEs have posed is that as a determinant of FDI, the importance of location-specific factors are usually considered less important than ownership or firm-specific factors (12). The location-specific factors consist of the difference in wage costs, market size, the policies of local governments, and so on. Firms have to adapt to these economic and political climates, which are different from the parent countries, but here the differences are still quantitative. The traditional arguments principally presume homogeneous economic conditions and emphasise the aspect of one-sided control from parent companies which have advantages of capital and technology and which internalise or integrate their foreign subsidiaries either as divisions of parent plants or as only a part of the large organisation.

Based on an analysis of the historical development of American MNEs, I myself have stressed the importance of qualitatively different markets, plants, and political environments and consider that this aspect of localisation tends in many cases to contradict the aspect of 'control or integration' (13). Localisation has been paid attention to by others as well, though mainly by company officials and journalists either for propaganda or policy proposals, but not much by researchers. Their major concerns have been concentrated on the 'contribution' to the host countries by way of raising local content in human resources, parts and components, and ownership, etc. In my understanding, however, the meaning of localisation is greater than that of mere tactics or an appeasement policy in the sense that the local activities of MNE's subsidiaries have to adapt to the different ways of doing things or rules of the local markets and plants as 'local firms' as long as they do business in the host country. Consumers' tastes, the work practices of blue-collar and white-collar people, trade practices between companies, and the ways of behaving in political organisations all have their own historical and cultural backgrounds so that it would be extremely difficult for any foreign companies to change these local environments to fit their own customs. Many US MNEs have tried to apply their own methods, which were developed in the domestic parent companies to the host countries, but few have been successful for long, even in developing countries. Therefore, an MNE necessarily works with the tension between the need for both localisation and integrated control within its world-wide organisation.

This stress on location-specific factors is gaining new meaning, since the heterogeneity of the host countries, especially Western developed countries from the standpoint of Japan, is quite conspicuous, while Europe and Canada, which are the main areas for the activities of the US MNEs, are fundamentally the same as the USA. In this regard, M. Wilkins recently pointed out an interesting aspect (14): US MNEs have had sufficient preparation for their multinationalisation in the home society, where they can experience almost every kind of ethnic group and region, that for them differences in customs of living, values, religion, and language are much more 'familiar'. For Japanese firms, in contrast, these factors are 'unfamiliar' even in East Asian areas. In short, the development of Japanese MNEs has provided an opportune moment for clarifying a new point of view on MNE theory that the focal point concerning the relationship between firm-specific and location-specific factors must move further towards the localisation aspect.

Finally, it should be useful to show a working model in a joint field research project on the Japanese automobile and electronics plants in the USA (15). This is called an 'application-adaptation dilemma model'. Application and adaptation, to a considerable extent, correspond respectively to firm-specific and location-specific factors. Japanese firms in the USA have to pay a great deal of attention to the differences between Japanese and American cultures. However, the more extensively Japanese firms adapt to the local climate, the more difficult it may become to apply their human-related comparative advantages to their subsidiaries in the USA.

In order to evaluate how and to what degree Japanese management is applied or adapted, we have identified more than 20 principal elements or practices of Japanese management which are especially related to overseas manufacturing activities, e.g., job classification, job rotation, training, production control, turnover ratio, local content, ratio of Japanese expatriates and so on. The details and analysis of this evaluation are explained in Hiroshi Itagaki's paper in this volume. What I want to say here is that it is much more important to check the levels of these smaller elements on the shop floor or at workplaces than the stereotypical 'three treasures' of Japanese management: lifetime employment, the seniority system, and the company union. The main distinguishing feature of Japanese management is that by instilling identification with the company unity and flexibility based on 'workplace-oriented operations', Japanese firms have been able to achieve high quality and efficiency, most important in the manufacturing process, but also in sales divisions and in related parts and components makers. Thus this method may enable us to gain access to the point of contact between Japanese management and Japanese social constitution.

We have now come to the point of arguing the question of to what extent should we take into account cultural factors in proposing a theoretical framework of MNEs. Such a task is, of course, far beyond the scope of this paper. However, we may find that culture is not simply a residual after we take out the 'rational' factors, but an understandable factor which exerts a regular influence on certain functional levels of an economy. In this sense, some human elements in Japanese management may be necessary conditions for determining the ideal development of a specific type of industry in whose production processes the role of group-oriented human factors are particularly important. The question should be how can we take a specific culture into consideration at the historical stage of industrial development. How different and historically significant is the Japanese case compared with the first Industrial Revolution in the UK and the labour-saving and resource-consuming type of industrial development which followed it in the USA? This is not a question simply of pointing out the cultural differences between different countries but rather of implementing our theoretical analyses of the structures of management, industry, and MNEs on the basis of their cultural context.

Notes

(1) T. Ozawa, *Multinationalism, Japanese Style*, Princeton University Press, Princeton, 1979.
(2) *Ibid.*, pp. 206–11.
(3) K. Kojima, *Japanese Direct Foreign Investment*, Charles E. Tuttle Co., Tokyo, 1978.
(4) S. Fujiwara, 'Nichibei Bōeki To Taigai Chokusetsu Tōshi' (Japan-US Trade and Japanese Foreign Direct Investments in the US), *Economic Research Series of Yamaguchi University*, Vol. 20, 1981.
(5) M.Y. Yoshino, *Japan's Multinational Enterprises*, Harvard University Press, 1976.
(6) *Ibid.*, p. 177.
(7) In his lecture at the Epson Techno-Forum (July 26, 1985).
(8) M. Trevor, *Japan's Reluctant Multinationals*, Frances Pinter, London, 1983.
(9) *Ibid.*, pp. 178–79, 185–86. For a comparison of Japanese management with the British shop-floor level, see the systematic findings and insightful analysis in Ronald Dore, *British Factory–Japanese Factory*, University of California Press, 1973.
(10) K. Yasumuro, *Kokusai Keiei Kōdō Ron* (The Theory of International Management Activities), Moriyama Shoten, 1982.
(11) E.T. Hall, *Beyond Culture*, Anchor Books, 1976, p. 39 and Chs. 6–8.
(12) On these two factors, see N. Hood and S. Young, *The Economics of Multinational Enterprise*, Longman Group Ltd., 1979, Ch. 2.
(13) Cf. T. Abo, 'American Automobile Enterprises Abroad During the Interwar

Period : Case Studies on Ford and General Motors with Emphasis on the Process of Their Multinational Adaptation to Local Climates', *Annals of the Institute of Social Science*, No. 22, 1981, University of Tokyo.
(14) M. Wilkins, 'Japanese Multinational Enterprise before 1914', *Business History Review*, Vol. 60, Summer, 1986.
(15) See H. Itagaki's paper in this book. Also, Duane Kujawa and Mamoru Yoshida, 'Cross-Cultural Transfers of Management Practices: Japanese Manufacturing Plants in the United States', paper presented at the 1987 Annual Meeting of the Academy of International Business in Chicago. The authors are the American members of this project.

THE BRIGHT AND THE DARK SIDES OF JAPANESE MANAGEMENT OVERSEAS

Hideki Yoshihara
Kobe University

The Japanese production system transferred abroad

Japanese production system in foreign plants

At one time, the local production of Japanese corporations in foreign countries was concentrated in developing countries, for example, the Asian nations. However, since the second half of the 1970s, the local production of Japanese corporations in advanced countries (especially the USA) has been gradually increasing and has recently become common. In promoting overseas production, these enterprises have made it a rule to transfer their Japanese-style production systems to their foreign plants.

It is convenient to think of the integrated production system as being composed of three main elements, as follows: production equipment, production technology, and the organisational climate at the factory (1). Companies such as those producing electrical machinery, precision tools, and automobiles are usually called assembly companies. However, they do not involve just simple assembly processes, since important pieces of equipment used in the assembly operation are developed and manufactured by the same company. Such equipment made in-house is transferred to the overseas plant (2). In a similar way, companies make strong efforts to transfer to the foreign plants production technologies, such as systems and know-how for quality control and management of delivery schedules, which had originally been developed in Japan over the years. The QC Circle is an example of a soft production technology developed and enhanced by Japanese firms that has gained worldwide reputation.

In the transfer of the Japanese-style production system to overseas factories, one factor that cannot be overlooked is the effort to transfer the organisational climate. Egalitarianism, attention to detail, emphasis on teamwork, strong discipline, and the so-called 5 S movement are aspects of the organisational climate which Japanese companies try to introduce in foreign factories.

Let us use the 5 S movement as an example. The 5 S's are the initial letters of the following Japanese words: *seiri* (arrangement, adjustment, regulation), *seiton* (good order, proper arrangement), *seisō* (cleaning), *seiketsu* (cleanliness), and *shitsuke* (training, discipline), which together give rise to the name of this movement. The 5 S movement enjoys considerable diffusion at the plant level. This is because order, discipline, and cleanliness at the work site are basic prerequisites for manufacturing high-quality articles with high productivity.

Almost without exception, Japanese expatriates try to introduce and enforce these 5 S's in the workshop. They persuade and train local supervisors and workers to keep the factory floor clean, their tools and parts in their proper places, and so on. Also, a strict attitude is taken towards discipline at the workplace. Smoking in the workshop is prohibited, and so is drinking coffee or other beverages. Japanese plants overseas are well known for their cleanliness and rigourous discipline.

Good performance

Toyota Motor Corporation is presently producing passenger cars at NUMMI (New United Motor Mfg. Inc.), a joint venture with GM (General Motors). The joint venture uses an existing factory which originally belonged to GM. The production equipment is basically the same as that used when GM was running the factory, and the workforce also used to belong to GM. The only changes are in production management and quality control, which Toyota transferred from its Japanese plants. It is reported that average productivity at the NUMMI factory is twice that of GM factories. The results achieved by NUMMI are so extraordinary as to be considered 'a miracle' (3).

The case of this Toyota-GM joint venture is only one example. Japanese companies nowadays are spreading their production facilities to the USA and many European and Asian countries. There are many research reports dealing with the high product quality and high productivity of Japanese production systems in overseas factories (4). On the other hand, this author knows of no negative research results reporting, for example, that the Japanese production system is inferior to the local system; or that a company switched back to the local system; or that, as a result of having adopted the Japanese system, either productivity went down or the rate of defective products increased.

Demonstrating the exact relationship between a production system and its performance is very difficult. Even the previously presented NUMMI case is not based on exact measurement. But although there are problems associated with exact, measurable evidence, there is no doubt that the Japanese production system has achieved a high level of performance in Japanese plants located in foreign countries.

Reasons for international workability

M. White and M. H. Trevor, researching Japanese firms established in England, reported that British labourers appeared to accept Japanese work practices (5). Moreover, the authors maintain that the Japanese production system had the effect of waking up England's work ethic, which had been dormant for many years. Positive responses to the Japanese production system are heard from many workers in other places, such as the USA, Malaysia, Thailand, and Taiwan. Why does the Japanese production system awaken the work ethic of foreign labourers and motivate them to perform their jobs with higher morale? I would like to propose the following three reasons.

The first is that the number of opportunities for workers' participation increases. In American and European factories, as a general trend, workers are treated as though they were machines. Workers are supposed to be mere robot-like executors of the instructions given by their superiors and by specialists.

Under the Japanese production system, workers are not machine-like individuals doing their jobs, but are expected to use their minds while working. One of the features of the Japanese production system is the so-called bottom-up approach. Workers on the job site are encouraged to express their ideas and to make proposals to their superiors and the company's specialists, who, in turn, receive them constructively. Then, improvements in the work routine developed jointly by the workers, their superiors, and the experts are put into use.

Based on egalitarianism, efforts are made to reduce the differences between workers and superiors or specialists as much as possible. They all use the same cafeteria, choose food from the same menu, use a common toilet, etc. Every effort is made to give the worker the same treatment received by the specialist or supervisor. Moreover, once or twice a year, and in some places once a month, company presidents hold regular general meetings. During these meetings, overall business results as well as information on the environmental conditions surrounding the firm are presented to all the employees, including factory workers. This information sharing is also inspired by egalitarianism.

The second main reason is the style of leadership found among Japanese supervisors, characterised by initiative-taking and example-setting. White and Trevor write about these attitudes of Japanese managers. 'More generally, management behaved in a way which was highly consistent with the working practices demanded of workers. For instance, just as the latter were required to be highly quality-conscious, so the managers took a most active interest in quality problems and never allowed sub-standard products to go out to customers in the interests of expediency. In short, the Japanese-owned firms were characterised by a high degree of leadership by example' (6).

In many American and European companies, managers and engineers do their work in individual offices separated from the factory floor. They do not go into the factory often, and on very few occasions do they solve problems in cooperation with workers. On the other hand, Japanese managers and technicians are accustomed to solving problems at the factory in cooperation with workers. In Japanese factories, managers and technicians do not work in individual rooms. They work together in a room which is usually located in the center or in a corner of the factory. There are also cases in which desks and chairs are simply put in the workshop for them, with no partition panels. If a problem should arise which is unmanageable for workers, managers and engineers run to the spot and look for a solution. This is leadership by initiative and example.

A third reason for the international applicability of the Japanese production system is that it is a rational system which meets production needs. The strength of this production system is clearly displayed in plants where colour TV sets and automobiles are assembled. What are the conditions required to realize the mass production of technologically complicated products (such as colour TV sets and automobiles) with high productivity and a low rate of defects?

The first necessary condition is the existence of a cooperative relationship among the workers. Through good teamwork, productivity increases and the percentage of defective items goes down. As can be seen in plants assembling colour TVs and automobiles, workers do not perform their duties in isolation, but rather conduct their respective operations along the assembly line while relating mutually with many other workers. Whether or not good teamwork among many workers exists has an important effect on productivity and on the quality of the final products.

The second necessary condition is that workers, one by one, accomplish the work of their respective stations. Even if the job looks simple, it really demands both skill and attention from the worker. In order to mass produce high technology articles with high productivity and quality standards, the responsible accomplishment by each worker of his or her task is very important.

The third condition is the accumulation of small improvements. Colour TVs and automobiles consist of a large number of parts and materials. These parts and materials are often modified and improved upon, in some cases even daily. Equipment, measuring instruments, and tools and jigs used in the production process are replaced and improved upon quite frequently. Furthermore, production methods and organisation are not fixed, but evolve and improve as soon as better ways of doing things are found.

If one takes a close look at the different aspects of the production site, one might see that small improvements accumulate day by day, moment by moment, in areas such as product design, parts and raw materials, production equipment, production management, and quality control systems and processes. Through this assiduous accumulation of small improvements, high-quality products are manufactured with high efficiency.

There have been many cases of small improvements being realized from the ideas proposed by plant workers. Based on their daily job experiences, workers—rather than their superiors or experts and techcians—are often in the best position to think of and implement improvements. The Japanese production system encourages workers to ask themselves the following types of questions: How can we improve this production equipment? Or this product? Or this production method? Where and how can we change things so that the rate of defective items and the production costs go down? Under the Japanese production system, workers ask and answer these types of questions on a daily basis (7).

Impact of the Japanese system on local plants

As we have seen, the Japanese production system has produced excellent results not only in Japan, where the system was developed and advanced, but also in such foreign countries as the USA and in Europe and Asia. When transferred abroad, the Japanese production system seems to exert a positive effect on local related industries. Japanese companies located overseas often provide technical guidance to their local suppliers of parts and raw materials. Through this guidance, the Japanese production system permeates local firms operating in industries related to the supplier sector.

Furthermore, another effect is the competitive pressure that the Japanese companies put on local competitors to improve their production systems. Local manufacturers attempt to introduce some good features of the Japanese system, and, as a result, production systems in the local industry improve. This is an imitation effect (8). As Japanese companies spread their overseas manufacturing activities all over the world, it is possible to imagine that their presence will improve the world's production systems.

The frustration of local managers

Dissatisfaction with Japanese-style management

According to White and Trevor, who also conducted research on a Japanese trading company and two Japanese banks operating in the City of London, the response of office workers to Japanese-style management appeared to be less positive than that of plant workers. Japanese managers tended to get along better with blue-collar than with white-collar workers (9).

Dominique Turcq, a Frenchman, while working at Sony conducted an analysis of Japanese management by using the methodology of participant observation. In his book *L'animal stratigique*, he clearly describes the criticism local employees make of Japanese-style management. 'I often heard criticism in the sense that the Japanese raise objections, that communication with them is bad, that they keep exclusive information to themselves, do not delegate responsibilities, and constitute a closed group, etc.' (10). And Turcq continues: 'There exists a big status distance between the Japanese expatriates and the local subsidiary staff; this distance is similar to that which can be seen in a Japanese company between regular and temporary employees. There are absolutely no points in common between these two categories' (11).

According to Hayashi Kichirō, the following are the criticisms made by American managers working for Japanese companies in the USA (12).

- Objectives are not clearly presented.
- Important decisions are made by Japanese.
- If one is not a Japanese national, one cannot be promoted beyond a certain position.

- There are many time-consuming meetings; people not directly concerned with the problem at hand are also requested to participate in these meetings, which are extremely time-consuming.
- Americans cannot understand the logic behind the methods used by Japanese managers, and explanations are rarely offered.

Local managers of Japanese firms located in Indonesia and Malaysia also made the following critical comments.

- There is little delegation of authority, and local managers cannot make any decisions without prior consultation with the Japanese managers.
- Although there is talk about decision making by consensus, local managers are not included in the consensus-building process.
- The method of performance evaluation, compensation, and promotion is usually vague and difficult to understand.

Whether or not the above criticisms of Japanese management are true is not yet clear. Nonetheless, it must be emphasized that American, Indonesian, and Malaysian managers of Japanese companies have these kinds of complaints. They are more or less critical of Japanese-style management and thus become frustrated and unable to display their capacities to the fullest.

Local technicians and engineers engaged in research and development are also often critical of Japanese management. For example, a large Japanese manufacturer acquired an American company which had a large-scale R&D department. However, less than three years after the acquisition, many American technical people quit their jobs. Why? After the acquisition, the head position in the R&D department was occupied by a Japanese engineer. Japanese were appointed not only to the head post, but to many other key positions as well, and expatriates began to build a close relationship with the parent company's R&D department. This relationship soon reduced the Americans' freedom to conduct R&D in their way, and before long, many excellent technical experts and engineers had left the company (13).

Hosokawa Micron has 27 foreign subsidiaries, most of which are located in the USA and Europe. The majority of them are the result of acquisitions. One of the main objectives of these acquisitions was to secure good local talent (managers and engineers). After the acquisitions, local nationals rather than Japanese nationals were appointed as presidents of the subsidiaries, and management was conducted according to local practices. President Hosokawa Masuo explained this policy. 'Many qualified managers and engineers would quit the company after the acquisition if a Japanese were appointed company president and Japanese-style management were enforced'. In his opinion, Japanese-style management is often avoided by local managers, supervisors, and engineers (14).

Reasons for dissatisfaction

This author once addressed the following question to C.A. Bartlett of Harvard Business School: 'Assuming that you graduated from Harvard Business School, would you want to work for a Japanese company in the USA?' 'No', was his answer. This no was not an expression of his personal feelings, but rather his overall conjecture about the feelings and ideas of graduates from Harvard and other first-class American business schools. I continued, 'Why wouldn't you want to work for a Japanese company?' He gave the following reasons (15).

First, the initial salary is low and the pace of salary rises and promotion is slow. When one compares the initial salary at major American companies and consulting firms, the initial salary paid by Japanese subsidiaries in the USA is substantially lower. Furthermore, after joining the company, the pace of salary increases and promotions is slow. This is because the seniority system, a normal practice in the parent company, is more or less transferred to the American subsidiary.

The second reason is the lack of sufficient opportunities for promotion. Most of the presidents of these companies in the USA are Japanese nationals. In addition, many important positions, such as the heads of the finance and engineering departments, are also occupied by Japanese. Even if one is promoted, the idea of reaching, at best, the post of vice-president will not be attractive to graduates of Harvard, Stanford, and other first-class business schools.

The third reason is the Japanese language. Since the company is a subsidiary, communication with the Japanese parent company is inevitable. Often such communication can be carried out only in Japanese: communicating in Japanese is difficult for Americans. Moreover, for many business school graduates, learning Japanese is too great a sacrifice in terms of time and money.

A fourth reason is the lack of opportunities for participation. Important decisions are handed down by Japanese, while Americans cannot take part in the mainstream decision-making process. Final decisions are made at meetings, but these meetings are no more than simple formalities. Important decisions are handed down by Japanese after 5 P.M., communicating with the Japanese parent company. These are the feelings of many Americans. We are not concerned here with whether or not their view of the decision-making process is correct. The important issue is the perception of American managers regarding the decision-making process at Japanese companies.

And this situation is not unique to Americans. In France, the UK, Germany, and other European countries, as well as in the Asian NICs, many people hesitate to work for Japanese companies. Apart from the reasons mentioned above, the following four points were made (16).

The first is that the methods for performing the various jobs are not always easy to understand. The previously mentioned French researcher Turcq uses the concept of ambiguity as a key element in analysing Japanese management. Foreigners, in particular Westerners, dislike working in an ambiguous and opaque world.

The second point is that the foreign subsidiary has insufficient strategic autonomy. Foreign subsidiaries are thought of as simple implementors of the Japanese parent company's strategy. Subsidiaries cannot decide on their own strategies.

The third point concerns a violation of existing privileges. It has already been pointed out that one of the characteristics of the Japanese factory's organisational climate is its egalitarianism. For workers in general, egalitarianism is a positive thing, but for managers and engineers it often represents a sacrifice. The reason is that under Japanese-style management, they are deprived of the special treatment and rights they previously enjoyed. In companies following the Japanese way of doing things, they cannot expect to have their dining rooms, parking places, toilets, individual offices, etc.

As a final point, we may consider the low profile which Japanese companies have overseas. In the USA, there are people who cannot distinguish between Mitsubishi and Matsushita. Many companies which are well known in Japan as established firms are not famous to the same extent in the USA or Europe. For highly qualified local people who can find employment with world-famous companies, such as IBM, GE, or Philips, Japanese companies with their low profile are probably not attractive enough.

As previously mentioned, workers and first-line supervisors in Japanese foreign factories enjoy high morale. For them, there are many opportunities for participation and promotion. Also, due to egalitarian treatment, the distance between lower employees and managers and supervisors is reduced. However, as we have seen in some detail, these reasons do not apply to managers and technicians. Thus, they often feel frustrated and become unable to display their best capacities. Therefore, under the same Japanese management system in both cases, factory workers and managers and technicians face completely different circumstances.

Overlooking advantages of multinational enterprises

Little top-class talent in foreign subsidiaries

Few non-Japanese nationals have become presidents of Japanese overseas subsidiaries. Through study meetings in 1986 with businessmen, the author discussed local top management and internal internationalisation. Many of the issues raised were related to the fact that there were too few examples of local nationals becoming presidents of subsidiaries, that many companies were not strongly inclined to appoint local nationals as presidents, and similar concerns (17).

A survey done by the Japan Overseas Enterprises Association reports that of all Japanese subsidiaries located in advanced countries, in only 16.2 per cent have local people been appointed to executive positions. Also, interestingly, in as many as 79.5 per cent of the cases, the respondents predicted that in the future the president would also be a Japanese (18).

Aside from the presidency, will there be many cases of recruitment of other highly able and qualified local managers and engineers? Although no data are yet available, it is this author's observation that there are not many Japanese overseas subsidiaries where excellent graduates from renowned universities, such as Harvard, Stanford, and Cambridge, are employed.

We have already seen that high-level professionals and managers in the USA and Europe are not necessarily willing to work for Japanese companies. In addition to this fact, Japanese companies themselves do not actively attempt to recruit first-class foreign talent. When these two factors are taken together, the result is a scarcity of excellent non-Japanese being appointed to middle or top management positions.

There are many Japanese companies which may be characterised as multinational enterprises. Their business activities are spread over the globe, with bases in almost every country of the world. What are the genuine advantages of multinational enterprises compared with domestic companies? One important advantage is that multinational enterprises can recruit excellent foreign talent and utilize their capabilities (19).

However, in the case of Japanese multinationals, many local managers and engineers feel frustrated and cannot display their capabilities to the fullest. Also, there are few local nationals who reach the position of company president, and few graduates from top schools are recruited. Thus, Japanese multinational companies are not capitalising on the genuine advantage of multinational corporations, that is, the opportunity for utilising human resources in every country they operate in.

The situation of American multinationals

In Japan, presidents of many foreign companies are Japanese. Of 1,052 companies for which data are available, 699 (66.4 per cent) have Japanese presidents. Three-fourths of the 611 American companies (450 companies) have a president who is Japanese (20). These data are in sharp contrast with the small number of foreign nationals being appointed presidents of Japanese overseas subsidiaries. The general tendency is to appoint Japanese presidents in foreign subsidiaries located in Japan, while there are but few cases of foreigners being appointed presidents of Japanese subsidiaries abroad.

A representative American multinational is IBM, which has 31 R&D facilities, 10 of them outside the USA. Also, two out of the four laboratories devoted to basic research are located abroad, in Switzerland and Japan (21). IBM recruits not only top American human resources but also personnel of Swiss, Japanese, and many other nationalities. As another example, let us look at 3M, a multinational with R&D sites in 19 different countries. Out of a total workforce of 87,000 people, the company has 6,429 R&D employees, 1,200 of whom are foreign. At 3M, foreign scientists and technicians are an integral part of R&D activities (22).

New challenges for Japanese multinationals

Japanese companies began operating in foreign countries in 1951. After 35 years, Japanese firms have attained a high level of internationalisation. But, as we have seen in this paper, the multinational spread of Japanese companies presents both bright and dark aspects.

The bright side is the factory. The Japanese production system is successful abroad. Thanks to this system, workers and first-line supervisors enjoy high morale, enabling the factory to get good results, such as high productivity, lower costs, and a lower proportion of defective products.

The dark aspect is the office. The Japanese management system is not necessarily welcomed by office workers in banking, trading, and other service companies. In addition to the service sector, middle and top managers and engineers in Japanese overseas manufacturing companies have many complaints against Japanese-style management. The high frustration level tends to affect their performance negatively.

Since the fall of 1985, when the Japanese yen sharply appreciated, Japanese corporations have been actively promoting the multinationalisation of their activities. In order to be successful in this internationalisation process, Japanese companies have to keep the bright side as bright as it has been up to now. But, on the other hand, they must urgently find solutions to deal with the dark side. A careless transfer of the Japanese management system abroad must be avoided. Perhaps Japanese multinationals are facing the difficult problem of renewing their concept of multinationalisation (23).

Notes

(1) Yoshihara Hideki, "Taishū Dōin no Nihonteki Seisan System" (The Mass Mobilization Japanese Production System), *Kokumin Keizai Zasshi*, Vol. 154, No. 4, October 1986.
(2) Yoshihara Hideki, "Nihon Kigyō no Seisan Gijutsu no Kokusai Iten" (The International Transfer of the Japanese Firm's Production Technology), *Business Review*, Vol. 30, Nos. 3, 4, March, 1983.
(3) *Business Week*, April 27, 1987, p. 53.
(4) See the following references. *Waga Kuni Sangyō no Kyōryoku ni yoru Beikoku Sangyō Kasseika* (Activation of American Industry through Cooperation with Japanese Industries), Nikko Research Center, September 1981. *Waga Kuni no Taiō Sangyō Kyōryoku* (Japanese Industrial Cooperation with Europe), Nikko Research Center, August 1984. M. White and M. Trevor, *Under Japanese Management*, 1985. Yoshihara Hideki, "Kaigai Kōjō ni Miru Nihonteki Keiei" (Japanese Management in Foreign Factories), *Keizai Keiei Kenkyū Nenpō*, Vol. 34 (II), March 1984.
(5) White and Trevor, *op. cit.*, p. 130.
(6) *Ibid.*, p. 131.
(7) One of the most outstanding features of the Japanese production system is that it brings out workers' abilities and will. See Yoshihara, 1986, *op. cit.*
(8) The impact that local production of colour TVs by Japanese manufacturers in England had on this country's competitor firms and parts producers has been reported in *Waga Kuni no Taiō Sangyō Kyōryoku, op. cit.*, pp. 244–47.
(9) White and Trevor, *op. cit.*, Ch. 8.
(10) *L'animal strategique: l'ambiquite du pouvoir chez les cadres japonais* (Strategic Animal: the Ambiguity of Power among Japanese Managers), Editions de l'Ecole Hautes Ftudes en Sciences Sociales, Paris, 1985. Japanese translation, *Aimai no Kōzō*, (The Structure of Ambiguity), by Hayama Akira, Mainichi Shinbunsha, 1987, p. 171.
(11) *Ibid.*, p. 186.

(12) Yoshihara Hideki, Hayashi Kichirō, Yasumuro Ken'ichi, *Nihon Kigyō no Global Keiei* (Global Management of Japanese Management), Toyo Keizai Shinpōsha, 1988. See also Hayashi Kichirō, *Ibunka Interface Kanri* (The Management of the Interface between Different Cultures), Yūhikaku, Tokyo, 1985.

(13) Based on the author's oral survey.

(14) Based on the author's oral survey. Regarding Hosokawa Micron's international management, see also Ch. 8 (written by Yasumuro Ken'ichi) in *Hijōshiki no Keiei* (Unconventional Management) by Yoshihara Hideki, Yasumuro Ken'ichi, and Kanai Kazuyori, Tōyō Keizai Shinpōsha, 1987.

(15) During the fall of 1985, Bartlett spent about one month at the Research Institute for Econonics and Business Administration, Kobe University. At that time, he conducted research with the author.

(16) Based on various written materials and the author's oral surveys.

(17) Symposium Proceedings, *Gaijin Power o Keiei ni Ikasu—Genchijin Top to Uchi Naru Kokusaika* (Making the Most Efficient Use of Foreign Human Resources: Local Top Management and Internal Internationalisation), Kansai Economic Research Center, June 1987.

(18) *Kokusaika e no Aratana Taiō Iinkai Shōwa 57 Nenji Hōkokusho* (Committee for New Measures towards Internationalisation, 1982 Report), Nihon Zaigai Kigyō Kyōkai, March 1983, pp. 39–40.

(19) R. Vernon, *Sovereignty at Bay*, Basic Books, 1971, p. 333–34.

(20) Data are from *Gaishikei Kigyō Sōran* (General Survey of Foreign Companies), 1986 Edition, Toyo Keizai Shinpōsha, 1986.

(21) Mitsui Nobuo, 'Gijutsu Kaihatsu to Kokusaika' (Technological Development and Internationalisation), *Business Review*, Vol. 34, No. 2, 1986.

(22) Nonaka Ikujirō and Kiyozawa Tatsuo, *3M no Chōsen* (The Challenge of 3M), Nihon Keizai Shinbunsha, 1987, p. 106.

(23) See the following reference on the current and a new conceptual framework (paradigm) for the multinationalisation of Japanese companies. Yoshihara Hideki and C.A. Bartlett, 'Genchijin Top to Uchi Naru Kokusaika—Takokusekika no Shin Paradigm' (Local Top Management and Internal Internationalisation: A New Paradigm of Multinationalisation), *Sekai Keizai Hyōron*, June 1987.

THE GLOBALISATION OF JAPANESE COMPANIES

Akihiro Okumura
Keio University

Today, Japan's economy and its companies, as a whole, are in a phase of transformation. Traditional systems of economy and management, which have so far contributed to Japan's present success, are being challenged by a fundamental change of environment. There are several sources of this transformation. One big source must be globalisation. Although the internationalisation of Japanese companies has developed through direct investment and exports during the past decades, the notion of globalisation is regarded as new and different from the notion of internationalisation. The strong trend of globalisation of Japanese companies urges them to transform their behaviour towards a new style of management. This paper will focus on a conceptual framework for understanding the new wave of Japanese globalisation strategy and provide guidelines for Japanese global firms. Since practitioners and researchers of Japanese global firms have many problems to solve before entering the global age, it will be worthwhile to propose a conceptual model which will be helpful to them.

Forces for the globalisation of Japanese companies

Although the globalization of Japanese companies has gradually developed from the 1950s to the 1980s, the speed of globalization has drastically accelerated in recent years, particularly after the G 5 meeting in 1985. There are several sources governing the movements of Japanese globalisation. First is the fixing of a high yen value. The dollar has been fixed at almost ¥120, and some forecast that the value of the yen will rise to around ¥110 or ¥100. The high yen has a significant impact on the Japanese economy. Many companies which rely heavily on ex-

31

ports are damaged severely due to losing their competitive edge. Thus, Japanese companies began to transfer their plants to foreign countries, particularly to the USA and Europe instead of to ASEAN countries. Some practitioners began to be afraid of the hollowing out of the Japanese domestic market. Secondly, there is a heightening of economic friction. In the past, exporting literally meant internationalisation. However, nowadays, excessive exports are bringing about trade friction between Japan and the importing countries. This causes Japanese companies go abroad and build their own plants and subsidiaries in local markets. Thirdly, NIEs, such as Korea, Taiwan, and Singapore, are quickly catching up with Japanese companies, especially in labour intensive industries. Furthermore, even in some high-tech segments, such as chips, VCRs, and automobiles, Korean companies have become tough competitors for Japanese companies. This also drives Japanese companies towards globalisation. Fourth, the world economy has increased its homogeneity and diversification simultaneously. The world market is increasingly becoming similar in terms of purchasing power and consumers' tastes. At the same time, this growth of the world economy began to create diversified competitive conditions in local markets. Finally, the influence of the Japanese economy has grown bigger. Its influence on the world economy was only 2 per cent of world GDP 20 years ago. But now, it accounts for more than 10 per cent of world GDP. Thus, the responsibility of Japan's economy became heavier than before. This also facilitates globalisation of Japanese companies.

There are several indications that Japanese companies are changing their global strategy. For instance, Matsushita is gradually changing its global strategy, so as to respond to these difficult conditions. The company increased the ratio of outsourcing and also changed product policy. In the case of cassette radios, the Singapore subsidiary imports parts from Matsushita's Malaysian, Taiwanese, and Hong Kong subsidiaries, and manufactures lower-price radios. Then, these lower-price radios are exported to Japan and elsewhere in the world under the Panasonic brand name. The Japanese radio division's role is to produce and sell higher-value-added products which are composed of imported parts from the above countries. The reasons for this move are quite simple. Matsushita's present policy is twofold: one aspect is 'localisation' and the other is 'globalisation'. The company intended to reduce costs by outsourcing, and at the same time, to formulate an integrated product policy on a global basis. Another example is Bandai, a toy maker. The company moved all its plants to Korea, Taiwan, China, Thailand, and Singapore. Bandai HK plays the role of shipping all products. This especially means that Bandai is practising hollowing out of the Japanese toy industry. The aims are to reduce costs and overcome economic friction with the USA and Europe. The role of the headquarters is as an R&D/design center. There are many cases in which companies changed their international or export strategy. The purpose is to respond to changing international conditions.

The problems for these companies are what should the ultimate features of this globalisation be, which direction of globalisation is right in the long run, and how should globalisation be achieved. Many practitioners as well as researchers are seriously seeking the solutions. Therefore, this paper tries to explain these problems and prescribe solutions from within a conceptual framework.

Paradigmatic change of Japanese management

There is much analysis and discussion concerning Japan's success, such as that concerning seniority systems, lifetime employment systems, in-company union systems, and so on. Most of these discussions have focused on the side of Human Resource Management (HRM). Some have focused on the strategic and operational aspects, some on the organisational aspect, and some on the global aspect. However, the environment is changing drastically. There seem, in general, to be four sources of change. One is the increasing thrust of technological innovation. It is usually said that the economy is moving from a 'maturity' phase to a 'dematurity' phase. In this phase, one of the keys to success lie in technological innovation, especially product innovation. Although companies have been very strong in 'process' innovation, the new phase of world competition is shifting to competition in 'product' innovation. Many companies are putting more emphasis on R&D in order to be able to respond to the coming competitive conditions. Second is a shift to a service economy. Japan's present ratio of the labour force in service industries is less than 60 per cent. In the next decade, it is said that it will increase to more than 65 or 70 per cent. This means that from one aspect, domestic plants are going to be transferred abroad and Japan will experience a hollowing out of industries. Third is an increase in the globalisation of the economy. Globalisation implies two things for Japanese companies. One is going abroad; the other is the internationalisation of the domestic market. A good example is the financial market. The Tokyo money market became the world's No. 2 market after Wall Street because of the high value of the Japanese yen. Many foreign financial institutions came into the Tokyo market and began to recruit a Japanese workforce in Tokyo. This movement began to loosen traditional Japanese labour customs. Japanese workers began to start job hopping. Fourth is deregulation. The Japanese government brought about intense deregulation in the telecommunications, transportation, and banking areas. This policy creates opportunities as well as threats for Japanese companies. Opening the markets in previously regulated industries leads to tough competition from other industries and foreign competitors.

These fundamental changes in the environment challenge existing Japanese management, which has worked on the basis of traditional corporations. These changes seemed to start from around the mid 1970s when the Japanese economy began to enter a stage of maturity. The Japanese economy and Japanese companies are gradually seeking a new management style which can fit the coming environment. Several characteristics of new styles of management are emerging in some companies, particularly those which are directly influenced by environmental changes. Recently, even in traditional companies, a new wave of management is appearing. Although the pace of transformation seems slow, fundamental changes are steadily evolving within Japanese companies.

The transformation of Japanese management is described on a conceptual basis in Table 1. The proposed new Japanese management style is mainly directed towards the 'entrepreneurial mode'. The history of Japanese modernization shows that Japan has grown by means of entrepreneurial activities. The new style of management emphasizes the 'revival' of this spirit among Japanese companies so that they will be able to respond to the 'dematurity' phase. The basic features of transformation are as follows: (1) from operation-centred to innovation centred, (2) from a pyramidal hierarchy to a network-type organization, (3) from group to individual-based HRM, and (4) from an incremental approach to innovation to an entrepreneurial approach. Under this new style of management, human resources will assume an ever greater value, and innovativeness and creativity will constitute the core of management. Innovation is the flowering in the real world of new ideas, achieved through the recombination of previously unaccepted ideas. In order to create new ideas, a mixing of 'dissimilars' and a breeding mutation are the most important elements. The present style of management has stressed homogeneity rather than mixing heterogeneous factors. The concept of the new style of management which seeks innovation has several implications for the globalisation of Japanese companies. Although globalisation will be a major task

Table 1   Features of the new style of Japanese management

	Present Style	New Style
Strategic Action	Emphasis on operation	Emphasis on strategy
	Internal accumulated resources	Flexibility (making use of external resources)
	Emphasis on principal line of business	Diversification in related business fields
	Development research	Basic research
	Emphasis on efficiency	Emphasis on innovation
Organisation	Class pyramid	Horizontal division-of-labour network
	Centralisation of authority	Decentralisation of authority
	Large head office	Small head office
	Stable bureaucratic structure	Flexible innovation structure
	Bottom-up type of decision-making	Top-management-led decision-making
	Power base in production division	Power base in R&D division
System, Practices	Lifetime employment	(Retain)
	Seniority system	Meritocracy
	TQC	Partial revision
	Company labour union	(Retain but redefine its value)
	In-house training/ education	(Retain)
	Welfare	(Retain)
Human Resources	Homogeneous personnel	Heterogeneous personnel
	Collectivism	Tolerance for individualism
	Loyalty to company	(Retain)
	Equality	Attach importance to individuality
	Missionary-type leader	Leader of reform
Behavioural Mode	Incremental	Entrepreneurial

Source: Keizai Dōyūkai.

for Japanese companies from now on, they have to build their strategy very carefully.

Looking for an 'innovation-oriented' global strategy

Global strategy can be categorised into three models: (1) scale of economies, (2) scope of economy, and (3) innovation. Of course, there have been several categorisations of global strategy, for instance, Perlmutter (1969) has already identified geocentric, polycentric, and ethnocentric approaches to multinational management. However, his categorisation scheme was the world view of a firm. Our categorisation is primarily based on a global competitive strategy point of view. Some MNCs compete by their cost efficiency, some by their product differentiation, and some by their innovative technology.

Toyota is a typical case of achieving cost efficiency on a global basis. Toyota accomplished the most efficient production system in Japan because Japan must be the most appropriate place for achieving efficiency in the world. The company made global product lines and global marketing systems backed up by its domestic production system. Matsushita also created very cost-efficient global systems in a different sense from Toyota's case. Matsushita intended to utilise the comparative advantages of different countries so as to achieve world-wide cost efficiency. This strategy is typically shared among Japanese companies, and this should be a source of strength in competition. Some companies follow the scope of economy strategy, although they have not been so successful. They belong to the packaged foods or beverage business, such as Ajinomoto or Suntory. There have been very few Japanese companies which followed an innovation strategy. Only some companies, such as Makita, Fanuc, or Disco, which have distinctive technological advantages, could win in global markets. However, many large Japanese companies have never followed this strategy. In summary, it can be said that Japanese MNCs mainly followed the cost-efficiency strategy until recently.

But they began to realise that the past experience of success will not work in the coming global age. Environmental changes are forcing them to reform their strategy as well as their management systems. Although the traditional global strategy and management were primarily directed to facilitate cost efficiency, the main issue for the future will be a more innovation-oriented one. In order to respond to this issue, Japanese MNCs will have to transform their strategy and management.

Conceptually, the cost-efficiency model requires a global hierarchical organisation. MNCs utilise the comparative advantage of different countries to achieve an optimisation of performance on a global basis. Each subsidiary is required to bear its own responsibility. Headquarters has the responsibility to control and integrate the global system. The system is regarded as a precious machine and is designated to process information for resolving problems. This type of organisation is classified as an information-processing model, following H.A. Simon's term.

Although a global hierarchical organisation fits the pursuit of a cost-efficiency strategy, it cannot be suitable for an innovation-generating strategy. Technological innovation shifts the existing competitive edge. A typical example is the watch industry. Japan took over the No. 1 position from Swiss watchmakers by inventing the quartz watch. In many high-tech companies, technological innovation should really be a strategic matter. This thrust becomes prevalent among all companies. Technological innovation literally means corporate strategy. This is also true for globalisation. For instance, Ericcson, NEC, and ITT have competed in innovating telecommunications products on a global basis. This competition brought about technological innovation. Biotechnology is another example. Japanese, European, and American pharmaceutical companies are competing in innovating new agents. Japanese pharmaceutical companies began to open R&D laboratories in foreign countries, whose purpose is to generate innovations. Many other Japanese companies are increasingly beginning to transfer R&D functions abroad. All of these companies realize that they will not survive in the future unless they eventually follow an innovation-oriented global strategy. The thrust is also supported by the nature of the current technology itself. Current technology is originally born global: biotechnology, telecommunications technology, computer technology, and LSI technology are cases in point. This means that if a company follows an innovation strategy, it will lead automatically to a global strategy.

An innovation-oriented global strategy has several characteristics. It is quite dynamic in manoeuvring resources. M&A (mergers and acquisitions) are an example. Japanese globalisation is being speeded up by acquiring companies abroad. Moreover, forming strategic alliances also facilitates globalisation. These strategies tend to save time. If a company intended to develop a new business or technology by itself, it takes more time. Especially, M&A by Japanese companies in the US is becoming popular. Strategic alliances on a world-wide basis are already common in the automobile industry. Recently, pharmaceutical companies have been trying to formulate global strategic alliances, attempting to generate biotech innovation. Since these strategic movements are a new experience for Japanese MNCs, they are learning how to implement this new strategy. In order to manage this

new global strategy, Japanese MNCs have to build a new organisational form, which also has an impact on traditional Japanese management
systems.

Creating a 'Global Dynamic Network'

Japanese global companies are seeking a new organisational form so
as to adapt to the changing environment. The new form is both a cause
and an effect of the current competitive environment; however, companies are seeking an effective way of managing an innovation-oriented
strategy. This is referred to in this paper as a 'Global Dynamic Network'. It should be a unique combination of strategy, structure, and
management processes. The image of a 'Global Dynamic Network'
is depicted in Figure 1.

A 'Global Dynamic Network' has several very distinctive characteristics which differ from the traditional global organisational form.
First, it has a loosely coupled network. Its member units have high
autonomy and look for complete 'localisation'. The requirements of
local markets are different from each other. Moreover, each unit in-

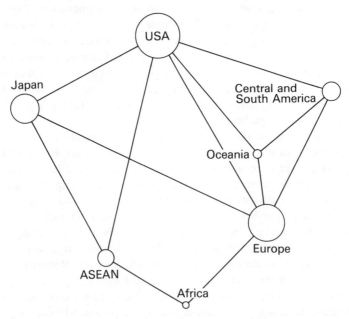

Fig. 1   'Global Dynamic Network'

tends to grow by its own efforts because local markets began to be more heterogeneous as the economy has grown. A corporation, by nature, intends to grow and to keep its autonomy for growth. The greater autonomy each unit has, the looser the relationship among units becomes. Although the traditional hierarchy controls its member units by a tightly coupled relationship and accomplishes a system-wide cost efficiency, it is rather weak in innovations such as new product development, new business creation and generating new technology. A loosely coupled network type of organisation fits the generation of innovations because each unit has autonomy and generates new ideas by itself. Second, its integration mechanisms rely rather on an internal market mechanism than on the headquarters' heavy integration efforts. Transfer pricing, quality, and the performance of a new product which is developed in a local company play a major role in coordinating total activities. Innovation is generated only through this 'invisible' mechanism. Global differentiation and integration are an everlasting problem for MNCs. Although these two concepts are basically antagonistic, the 'Global Dynamic Network' intends to maximise both through a new way of management. Third, a high integration effort is made by sharing information and values. Every member unit understands the value and philosophy of the corporation, and exchanges information and ideas frequently. For example, Matsushita has formal values, called its 'Eight creeds'. Subsidiaries throughout the world hold morning meetings and chant them. Fourth, it facilitates a dynamic synergy among members. Only MNCs can fully utilise the comparative advantages of different countries. In the case of the biotechnology industry, the USA is strong in development, Europe is strong in basic research, and Japan is strong in process technology. MNCs can set up research laboratories in each continent and can make synergies happen. For instance, Honda created a dynamic synergy through developing a new car with the triad co-operation of its Japanese, American, and European engineers, who assembled and developed it jointly. These activities transfer technologies, knowhow, and information/values. Lastly, human resources management will become more flexible. Since localisation and more subtle integration are being promoted, Japanese global companies will be forced to reconsider their traditional HRM systems. Particularly, they have to introduce HRM for expatriates who are extremely scarce in present Japanese companies.

The concept of a 'Global Dynamic Network' is a far more flexible structure than any of the previous forms. It focuses on adapting to a more turbulent environment while maximising its competitive capabilities, and it provides a much more effective use of human resources that otherwise have to be accumulated, allocated, and maintained by a single organisation. In this sense, global learning must be a key for the future of Japanese globalisation. This learning has just started, and Japanese MNCs are at this beginning.

THE INTERNATIONAL ADAPTABILITY OF JAPANESE INTER-FIRM RELATIONS: A ROYAL ROAD TO INNOVATION?

Yoshiya Teramoto
Meiji Gakuin University

Nigel Howard
Nigel Howard Systems

Makoto Kanda
Meiji Gakuin University

Introduction

Japanese managers have so far appeared able to adapt successfully to foreign conditions in the operational spheres of production, distribution, and marketing. They have established successful relationships with foreign firms as well as foreign employees. Some are worried that this success may not continue as more wide-ranging and fundamental operations are transferred abroad. Can R&D and the creation of new businesses be successfully conducted abroad? Can successful relationships with foreign firms be established in these areas? If so, what general advice can be given to Japanese managers?

In order to answer these questions, we will first describe the major characteristics of and new trends in Japanese and European inter-firm relationships. Then we will investigate on a theoretical basis how Japanese management can cooperate in R&D and new business ventures with European partners.

Control mechanisms in Japanese and Western industrial structures

Two different approaches to managing coordination between organisational units are: through the market mechanism and through the hierarchical internalisation of control. The Japanese approach, sometimes called 'intermediate organisation', is to have long-term commitments and mutual dependency among relatively independent firms. The Western approach tends to one extreme or the other: either hierarchical control of units within the firm or unrestrained use of the market mechanism between firms. In Europe, however, in contrast with America, use of the market mechanism tends to be institutionally constrained in ways which may stifle innovation. These broad Japanese/Western and European/American differences provide a framework for the following more detailed comparisons.

Major Japanese-European differences

Japanese inter-organisational relationships in the past have mainly had as their purpose the achievement of efficient operations, i.e., finance, production, and distribution. They have been generally successful, based on the following characteristics, which contrast with European structures.

1. Long-term commitments between firms, particularly within company groups (*kigyō-shūdan*).
2. Complex multi-directional inter-firm relationships, i.e., horizontal and 'diagonal' as well as vertical.
3. Multi-functional inter-firm relations, embracing production, distribution, marketing, finance, etc.
4. Reciprocal mutual dependence and information sharing.
5. Dynamic balancing of stability (assurance of a continuing relationship with mutual help in time of need) and instability (necessity to compete, as when a company contracts with several companies for the same supplies).

The contrast with Europe is indeed striking. To some extent the inter-firm mutual support provided by these Japanese structures is provided in Europe by government intervention. The capability for dynamic adaptation is provided in Europe more by mergers and acquisitions leading to large diversified corporations and by inter-firm 'head-hunting' and mobility of technical personnel. On the other hand, adaptation by the creation of new business ventures and transfer of information between individuals through professional and other associations appears less than in Japan.

Other Japanese/European contrasts are in the motivation and interests of individuals. A Japanese employee tends to be broader in his appreciation of the needs of a particular business, e.g., car manufacturing, where a European tends to specialise in a particular technique applicable to many businesses, e.g., computer programming. This is allied to a relative difference in values: the European specialist tends to have a less commercial and more 'pure' motivation for his scientific or technical interest in a subject.

The 'not invented here' syndrome, whereby new ideas from outside the firm are rejected by specialists inside, is one result of these European attitudes. In general, the contrast between Japan and Europe means that joint efforts in R&D are less likely to be accepted by Europeans than by Japanese.

New trends in Japan and Europe

The above Japanese picture is now altering somewhat. New trends in inter-organisational relationships are becoming based more on the need for innovation and consist more of joint efforts in R&D and the creation of new businesses. The main characteristics of these new trends are:

1. Crossing boundaries of company groups for new commitments.
2. New groupings of small companies for technological development (1).
3. Increased links with university basic research.
4. Science parks attached to universities and major research establishments or established by local interests.
5. Multi-dimensional corporate networking, i.e., one company belonging to various networks for different purposes.
6. Location abroad, increasingly for operational reasons but also foreseen in the future for R&D and new businesses.

With the exception of 1 and 5, these trends are apparent also in Europe, evidence of some convergence. However, the relative unpopularity of joint R&D between European firms may continue.

Innovation and organizational learning: a theoretical perspective

As we have said, the new trends in inter-firm relations derive from the basic need of Japanese companies for innovation. From a theoretical viewpoint, innovation by organizations comes under the category of 'organizational learning' as discussed by Argyris and Schon (2). However, not all innovation is carried out by organisations as such: particularly in the West, change may come through large numbers of people becoming unemployed and starting new enterprises, as with

Table 1   Four types of learning by organizations

	Single-Loop	Double-Loop
Intra-firm	Improvement of operations by internal efforts	Innovation developed within the firm
Inter-firm	Mutual support, e.g., within company groups or help to sub-contractors	Innovation through sharing ideas and cooperative R&D

the growth of new industries in California in the seventies. This, so far, is not the common method in Japan, where creative innovation carried out by organisations themselves is the preferred method.

Argyris and Schon distinguish 'double-loop' from 'single-loop' learning: the former requires changes in perceptions, attitudes, and basic assumptions, rather than the mere selection of a new method to achieve the same end. Combining this with the inter/intra-firm distinction, we have the four types of organizational learning, as illustrated in Table 1.

Looking at the four squares in Table 1, we can say that Japanese economic strength has been largely in the first column, single-loop learning. Innovation (in the second column of the table) has been mostly intrafirm and focused on specific objectives, as in the case of video tape-recorder development. Innovation in the future will need to embrace more exploratory research.

Innovation will also require more inter-firm collaboration, including more joint work with foreign and European companies. This should accompany the globalisation of Japanese industry required by continuing trade surpluses. It will give access to a wider range of ideas, more dynamic and flexible linkages, and time and cost savings through dynamic synergy (3). Hence, companies successful in such collaboration will have a competitive advantage. What factors will lead to Japanese companies being successful in inter-firm innovation, particularly with European partners?

The royal road? the cybernetic games approach

Difficulties Japanese companies may face in succeeding with inter-firm innovation, particularly with foreign partners, include:

– a bias towards the type of 'innovation' which actually consists of continuous improvement of operations;

– a decreasing but still evident gap in business culture between Japanese and foreign firms;
– linked to this, a bias against entering into long-term commitments with foreign firms.

These difficulties may be analysed by using the new 'cybernetic games' approach to organisational learning (4).

This approach sees organisations as networks of expectations and understandings between people. Organisational learning is seen as difficult because it requires these understandings to be re-created and re-negotiated at all levels. Evidently it creates winners and losers; but even apart from this, it upsets established expectations and requires new ones to be created.

Based on this paradigm, the cybernetic-games approach uses various tools to help with the change process, e.g., the CONAN computer program for analysing cooperation and conflict situations (5). Such help takes the form of decision analysis and/or management training.

The approach is evidently even more appropriate applied to inter-firm innovation than to interactions within the firm (6). Here the need to understand the other side's point of view and build agreements on a firm self-reinforcing basis of mutual interest is apparent.

Three scenarios for cooperation

Field work with units of Japanese firms attempting to set up inter-firm R&D in the UK has revealed the following patterns.

– Some success in setting up joint programs with universities and academic institutions; very little success in involving private firms.

– Difficulty in allaying foreigners' potential suspicions that Japanese might 'steal secrets' from research partners and vice versa.

– More generally, an apparent difference in basic assumptions as to the purpose and aims of joint research.

Based on this experience, three CONAN 'scenarios' were set up as in Table 2 (7).

The first scenario, in which Japanese companies contribute funds but contribute no important industrial/commercial 'secrets' of their own, is presented as one which may elicit cooperation from universities and institutions interested in academic research but is unlikely to gain the interest of private firms, except possibly to keep a watch on what is going on while giving the research effort little priority and giving away few 'secrets'.

The second scenario, in which there is an exchange of 'secrets' with

Table 2   Three scenarios for cooperative research with European partners

Japanese company			
fund research	1	1	1
share 'secrets'	0	1	1
share fruits of research	0	0	1
European partner			
share 'secrets'	1	1	1
share fruits of research	0	0	1

no long-term commitment to joint production or other 'sharing of the fruits' of joint research, may interest private firms rather than academic institutions. Interest would depend, however, on perceptions of the relative value of the 'secrets' to be traded, which is by definition hard to judge since they are supposed to be 'secret'! Moreover, collaboration might break down as soon as value had been obtained from 'secrets' imparted. Nevertheless, in certain areas this scenario might be worth considering, in which case its limits, the degree of commitment involved, and the value of information to be traded need to be unambiguously stated beforehand and faithfully implemented afterwards in order to allay suspicion.

The third scenario is the most promising from the viewpoint of fruitful joint R&D. However, it requires the greatest adaptability from Japanese firms, who will need to:

1. Overcome any bias against long-term commitments to foreign firms. The scenario may in fact involve an indefinite commitment of a kind that Japanese managers are familiar with, i.e., the idea of 'sharing the same fate', since with significant innovation it is by definition impossible to forecast how best it might be exploited. The only commitment may be to a genuine 'sharing of the fruits'.

2. In dealing with individuals and groups, understand and allow for the ego involvement and suspicion that may accompany the 'not invented here' syndrome. Western creativity is closely linked to individualism and a sense of the personal ownership of inventions, and Japanese managers may need to give unaccustomedly strong recognition of personal contributions and firm assurance of rewards from them.

3. Avoid the potential danger of enlisting the cooperation of firms that intend to keep a watch on what is happening without themselves contributing much. In order to get meaningful cooperation, given the European tradition of relatively little inter-firm mutual support and information sharing, it may be necessary to make quid pro quos and benefits very clear and contractually binding. Having in this way established a mutually beneficial deal which is fully binding on both sides,

it will be possible to generate goodwill, enthusiasm, and concerted effort. If the nature of the deal is left vague, this will be difficult.

4. The apparent contradiction between point 1—emphasising an indefinite commitment—and point 3—emphasizing the need for clarity —can be resolved in each case by looking at various scenarios of what might happen and making clear each party's intentions.

To sum up: Japanese management must adapt in order to be successful in joint innovation with Western firms. There is no royal road.

Notes

(1) These groups are called Igyōushu Kouryū Group. It is estimated that there were about 1,000 groups in 1986. Organisational characteristics are discussed in our 1984 paper, Y. Teramoto and M. Kanda, 'Network Organization and Technological Innovation: Techno Mixing Groups in Smaller Firms', Working Paper No. 84–01, Institute for Research in Business and Economics, Meiji Gakuin University.

(2) C. Argyris and D. Schon, *Organizational Learning: A Theory of Action Perspective*, Addison-Wesley, 1978.

(3) 'Economy of scope' works strongly here.

(4) The theory of cybernetic games (also called organisational games) is outlined in N. Howard and Y. Teramoto, 'The Really Important Difference Between Japanese and Western Management', *Management International Review*, No. 3,1981.

(5) Details of cybernetic games and CONAN programs are shown in N. Howard, 'Directions for Research in Metagame Analysis (Analysis of Options); Research on Uses for CONAN Program' (Research Note No. 1), N. Howard Systems, 1986, 10 Bloomsfield Rd. Birmingham, UK.

(6) Needless to say that they are interlinked closely.

(7) This would vary according to circumstances. There might, therefore, be a possibility that European companies fund research.

JAPANESE REFERENCES IN FRENCH MANAGEMENT: PATTERN OR PRETEXT?

Martine Bercovici
CNRS—GIP 'Mutations Industrielles'

French managers and models

A great wind of Taylorism spread throughout the world following World War I, but the periodic passion for one foreign model or another as a reflection of current economic problems dates back to post-World War II. Employers discovered the need to look a bit beyond France or Europe as they became sensitive to the international context. At the same time, there was a change in the employers' sociological make-up as management became a profession instead of a heritage. One result of this could be seen in the creation, in 1945, of the CNPF (National Council of French Employers), successor to the CGPF (General Confederation of French Employers) of 1936.

It was necessary after the war to rebuild the economy on a modern basis, and for this the model was the USA. Numerous missions were sent by the government and by private concerns to study productivity. They brought back new ideas, but along with them a feeling of an irreducible heaviness in the field of industrial relations. For example, French engineers visiting American coal mines did not expect to learn very much; they believed the lower production costs were strictly related to geological conditions: superficially layered coal was easy to extract, in contrast to the deep-lying French coal that required numerous deep galleries. Once there, they discovered that a great deal of the cost difference came from the simple system of social relationships, involving small staff and few hierarchical levels, whereas the French mines were run along military lines with strict discipline, many levels of command, and a complex bookkeeping system. To make workers productive, it would have been necessary to make heavy investments in training. But at the time, it seemed impossible to change the strong historical and cultural values in the mining industry without grave risks of destabilisation.

Later, in the 1960s, it was Germany that drew the greatest attention for the rigour of its methods, and there was growing interest in cooperative management. With the social movement of 1968, there was a radical backlash against Taylorism and mass production, new concern about the quality of life and of work and how not to spend a lifetime as an unskilled worker. Employers turned their gaze to Sweden, and experiments began with semi-autonomous production groups in shops. Then, with the crisis of 1973 and others increasingly persistent since then, Japan was discovered as a model. It seemed untroubled by crises and forever improving in the areas of automation, wages, employment, and productivity.

By the late 1970s and early 1980s, employers were filled with admiration for Japan. Missions were sent to try to find explanations for such marvelous performance. A management model for these crises was discovered: mastery of uncertainties, of the short term, broad flexibility at every level, and the famous cooperative spirit with workers' participation in the company's life and productivity management a concern for the entire staff down to the lowest level. Early in the 1980s, Quality Circles were introduced in many factories.

In May 1981, the Socialists came to power bent on extending and institutionalising this modernistic movement. In keeping with one aspect of some claims of the workers' movement, the government's primary tasks in this matter were to actively involve the workers with their work, to recognise ability and know-how, and to vary the work itself. Like a Proudhonian conception of work resuscitated from the past, mixed with socialist and republican values, there was talk of factory 'citizenship' with the proposed Auroux (Labour Minister at the time) laws.

The Auroux report at first frightened the employers. The unions were talking about setting up works councils, and it seemed as if excessive rights were about to be given to the workers, foreshadowing permanent conflict within the firms. The laws that were passed following the report were well received chiefly in large companies that had already led the way in participative management.

The Japanese model

What stands out mainly about the Japanese model is the 'ideal of zero': zero defects, zero returns, zero stock, zero paper, zero delay. A Japanese manager pointed out to me that if one would like to understand something about Japanese management, one should understand that 'zero' was not a goal but a result. In other words, if things were done correctly, if concentrations were right, the result would come of itself. Broadly speaking, he said, Japanese are not concerned with believing, but with doing. This philosophy, involving the preeminence of praxis, is not a priori, in keeping with Western thinking.

A look at Japanese firms by French managers showed them much potential for productivity that has not yet been used in French companies, and that the field of management must broaden its views beyond manageable data and summed-up costs. It needs to encompass the relationship between workers and their firm as a fundamentally economic relationship, that this relationship generates costs even if they cannot be directly assessed. Furthermore, Japan seems to have been able to accomplish, beginning some years ago, something that France has yet to do: obtain flexible production with short runs, a labour force amenable to changing jobs, reduction of stocks, and a minimum of functional services.

French management trends and their relationship to the Japanese pattern

Economic data

In 1973, there began a period of slow economic growth, reflecting a poor relationship in the capital/labour equation, with a general lowering in productivity of nearly 2 per cent between 1975 and 1982. This decrease was due in part to aging equipment, decreased equipment use, and imbalanced capabilities. Faced with this situation, managers set forth the following demands:

a. Reduce labour costs:

– By eliminating some organisational levels. French factories have more hierarchical levels than any other country in Europe.

– By making schedules and work rates more flexible so as to increase the use rate of machines. To this end, a number of important changes are under way in wage relationships and laws.

– By making it possible to function seven days a week, not for technical reasons, but for economic ones, and for women to work at night. This is authorised by the Seguin law, recently voted in by Parliament.

– By appealing to the government for a reduction in social expenses and simplified procedures for mass redundancies.

– By returning to the notion of real work. One of the current trends is for employers to seek to remunerate work in terms of specific items so that wages become a function of the real time of work. This conception, which may be a source of great flexibility, also has a negative side, because it neglects the essential reality that the labour force to be used optimally must be at the factory's disposal and that disposability has a cost.

– By ensuring that salaried workers are competent and mobile both professionally and geographically. This will make wages more of a personalised matter.

b. Make an inventory of productivity potentials so as to manage the 'hidden costs'. At one time, personnel chiefs were former military officers or engineers. Following May 1968, they were recruited from among sociologists and psychologists. Today, they tend to have legal or economic training for the best management of staff. The need has also become apparent for managing firm technologies, research, and know-how. Current strategies are turned towards job redefinition with emphasis on specialisation rather than the diversification of activities.

c. Automation and factory computerising.

Political and cultural data

It is obvious that we are facing a crisis in changing values, and particularly work values. In the face of its economic needs, every company tends to develop its own adaptive modes in the same way that states develop their policies. In this difficult time of slow growth and instability, companies have acquired a socially predominant role and significant influence via the media.

The left-wing government rehabilitated companies by encouraging media breakthroughs. The most positive image in our society is the manager, the contractor, a symbol of dynamic energy, whereas before the Socialist rise to power, they were seen as exploiters by the left-wing movement. Given the economic crisis and the new management practices, the unions' confusion and a decrease in their membership, collective bargaining has gone in new directions. The great 'interprofessional agreements' of the 1970–75 era, where small firms took advantage of larger firms' established rights, have gone by the board. Nowadays, bargaining goes from the national level downwards to the firms. The settings where bargaining occurs are increasingly decentralised in factories, shops, and services, and bargaining is concentrated increasingly on specific problems and conditions of daily life at work. They no longer fall within the scope of the unions' general strategies. Managers can satisfy demands without being shackled by contractual agreements. This trend towards company unionism can be seen throughout Europe, but it has not yet swung to the American or Japanese pattern.

French managerial attitudes vary greatly with respect to this trend. Some would like to keep the unions on the fringe via participative management. Others believe the unions are irreplaceable and that social conflicts are a natural part of normal company life. But even when the latter viewpoint is prevalent, the general tendency as far as social relationships are concerned is to favour the contract and not the law as a social regulator.

In order to overcome rigidities in the Labour Code and to mobilise salaried workers, the CJD (Young Managers' Center), which supported the Auroux laws as soon as they were published, recently proposed the establishment of 'Company councils'. Elected workers (whether union members or not) would negotiate with management about plans, production, management methods, and capital spending. They would have the responsibility for implementing the decisions within the firm. This represents a major departure from the tradition of French social regulation that previously favoured state regulation and collective bargaining with the unions.

There is another important type of disruption affecting company values, and that is the raising of questions about work implementation. This is the result of disappointing investments and poor production rates with repeated setbacks. An awareness dawned of the overly theoretical concept of work defined by the closed circles of research departments or methods divisions that were unable to grasp true work practices and remained ignorant of them. Technical decisions were made and handed down along hierarchical lines regardless of what the shop-floor worker might have had to say about them.

Today, managers are increasingly striving to break such hierarchical patterns and introduce technological changes only after they have been discussed with the people concerned. They come up against the resistance of research departments and supervisors who consider such discussions a waste of time and who also see themselves having doubts cast on their knowledge and authority.

From the workers' side, it was at first thought that such discussions would only lead to a faster pace of production, with no advantages. Now they are perceived as necessary for the efficient working of the firm, and its survival has even become an essential in stirring people into action. After many failures attempting only to redress grievances, the unions are now shyly trying to enter the arena of proposals for improving working conditions.

To overcome resistance, managers often resort to outside consultants, who are flourishing. They tend to recommend 'pertinent methodologies', such as incentives through participation, problem solving, and methods for conducting meetings. But there are still managers who in a pragmatic approach prefer to solve problems as they arise by using the firm's own strengths. Whichever approach may be taken, it is still a fact that participative management has a cost and that it is difficult to measure it. It remains for the means to be brought up to expectations so that at first sight the cost of the means could seem greater than any productivity gains produced.

References to the Japanese pattern

At the beginning of these changes in values, Japan probably served as a model, but it would seem there is now a decline in this because of the radically different culture and the consensus relationship, which has been greatly admired but is not entirely suitable in France. However, the predominant feature of today's changes is a tendency toward a well-developed Western value, the rehabilitation of the individuals within the firm, promoting their creativity and individual personalities. It is an appeal to an individual effort for success, an encouragement to negotiate personally and directly for wages, place of work, work schedules, and conditions and to avoid collective action that can lead nowhere.

Yvon Gattaz (president of the CNPF) said in 1983, 'Salaried workers must be treated as customers, and to "sell" them the firm, one must live up to their expectations and therefore adopt the logic of social marketing'. The Corporate Project ('Projet d'entreprise'), currently very popular, is the equivalent of a consensus. According to Thomas Watson (president of IBM), 'The firm must have beliefs if it is to face the challenges of the changing world; it must be prepared to modify everything in it except its beliefs'.

The Japanese pattern of social relations is not exportable, but Japan remains a model for its results, for opening its companies to social needs to which they are always listening, for know-how in market creation, and for raw materials management, production flow and technical potential. At this level, I think it is useful to make a distinction between personnel management and production management. We more often speak about the Japanese management in general terms.

There is hardly a French firm that has not tried to use *kanban* in at least one of its shops. But I know of no *kanban* experiment in France that was not linked with centralised data on it. Here is material support for one of the most important upheavals of social relations in factories that introduces new forms of cooperation and provides maximum information for the greatest number of people. It breaks up shop corporatism and hierarchic power based on withholding information. Everybody's work becomes easy to verify on any level.

Managers who tend towards maximum flexibility look towards the American performance pattern in Silicon Valley, where there is great individualisation of wages and working hours, a total lack of collective agreements, a corporate culture promoting strong motivation, and a notable scarcity of unions. In contrast, the most important sources of Japanese flexibility cannot be transposed, such as the division of work between large and small firms and the length of working hours. Adjustment of work time in France can be made only to compensate a reduction in working hours.

The US model also has a dark side: excessive labour force flexibility may damage productivity and not be compensated by gains in salary costs; the individualisation of wages may generate a well-paid elite and the demoralisation of others; and if too much flexibility is added the work group may become divided and uncohesive. The kind of flexibility French managers would like to see is an offensive one. By restructuring the firm, they would like to acquire the means to face the future, not only the present. So they now believe they must develop a European (and not only French) management orientation.

A European way

Europe has characteristics of its own. To begin with, it has systems of social protection that are more developed than in other industrialised countries and to which its citizens are strongly attached. For the past ten years, it has seen rigid political alternations generating strategic fluctuations in the relationship between state and industry that have shown a need for finding a coherent means for relating industrial structures to social ones.

In France, political alternations involved a sort of break between industrial life and political life. We can see here a historical change. If managers maintain a 'right-sided heart', a recent poll (IPSOS-Le Monde) shows that the Left does not frighten them any more and that there is a trend of indifference towards the result of the next presidential elections, whereas previously in such a period, politic forces were mobilized in the firms and in media. At a strategic level, the most important date for managers today is 1992, the opening of the Common Market.

Unlike the USA, which counts on flexibility in employment and wages to the detriment of productivity, Europe seems to be tending towards developing a high rate of productivity gains that will lead to a dark side to manage: decreases in real salaries and increases in unemployment. For 'Social Europe' to succeed, labour costs must be controlled and genuine common industrial and common policies must be developed that go beyond the short-term pragmatism of most managers. The development of regional dynamics transcending borders could be a first step.

The relevance of models in the management field

Management is first and foremost a practical art that uses immediate facts. It involves a social group having its own history and culture. Often, it changes faster than any other social group, following its own rules and potentialities that remain regardless of the changes. It may be unstable and so it needs to retain some of its operating forms even if they seem archaic with respect to newer ones.

The crisis has reinforced managerial empiricism and caused it to extend its scope to all areas of company life. At the same time, we have seen a regression of planification, which often turns out to be useless and becomes constraining if it must be referred to when action is to be taken.

The strongest impetus to changes in value comes not from models or abstract systems of reference, but from changes in productive forces and economic data. During my investigation in Japan, I was struck to see, in the same branches of industry and under identical production conditions, the same form of worker groups giving rise to the same relation to work. Relations that were born in production by altering values were described as 'Westernisation', such as trends to individualism, weakening of the giri-ninjō (social obligation and human feelings) relation and the disintegration of life employment in the shukkō (temporary work transfer) system. Similarly, one could find in France the results of 'Japanisation', like a toning down of class ideals within firms, forms of workers' solidarity, and managers gathering around economic plans aiming at the defence of the firm's employment, even if at the expense of some its acquired social benefits.

In the space of five years, one could see changes in company slogans that bordered on the religious or ethical, good or evil, to an ethic of economic success. Take for example this slogan in a personnel office in 1981: 'Loyalty. When you belong to an institution it is normal to defend it. If you want to grumble, condemn and find faults, then quit. Then you can criticise it'. Today, with the development of company newspapers and audio-visual communications, slogans have taken a new form: 'We are a smally among the biggies but are one of the leaders in the field in Europe. We can continue developing only if we improve our cost/price ratio and have a high quality of leadership at all levels in the company. That is the challenge we must face'. More than anything else, such trends spring from the necessities of production relations rather than from the influence of models.

QUALITY CIRCLES AND JOB DESIGN: AN EMPIRICAL EXAMINATION

Oded Shenkar, Ezer Hattem, and Shlomo Globerson
Tel Aviv University

In recent years, Quality Circle programs have become increasingly popular in Western countries. Following the success of such programs in Japan, Quality Circles have been introduced in the USA, Canada, West European countries, and beyond. Today, Quality Circles are used in a large proportion of "Fortune 500" US companies as well as in small- and medium-size firms operating in a variety of manufacturing and service industries.

The impact of Quality Circles on job design was studied for 121 employees in a large industrial organisation in Israel. Data were collected before and after Quality Circles introduction for an experiment group of participants and a control group of non-participants, using the Job Diagnostic Survey (JDS). Participation in Quality Circles was found to have a significant influence on employee autonomy and Motivating Potential Score (MPS); but it had no significant effect on other job characteristics, or on internal work motivation, growth satisfaction, satisfaction with peers and supervision, and absenteeism. Satisfaction with pay has decreased. A significant increase in general satisfaction, however, was noted among those Quality Circle participants with high 'context' satisfaction and those with low growth need.

Despite the munificence of literature on Quality Circles, knowledge of the psychological and organisational impacts of Quality Circle programs is still limited. The majority of Quality Circles' studies are not empirical (1). Most of the empirical studies rarely rely on control group designs with 'before' and 'after' measurements, preventing the testing of causal hypotheses (2).

Another problem typical to studies on Quality Circles is the lack of a comprehensive theoretical framework. Many studies tend to treat Quality Circles as a 'unique' phenomenon, thus making it difficult to

57

compare them to other organisation development practises, such as job enrichment and participatory management (3).

The purpose of this paper is to shed more light on Quality Circle programs by overcoming these two major deficiencies. To anchor the research in a theoretical framework, the present study relies on the well-known Job Characteristics paradigm (4). To enable the examination of causal hypotheses, the study is conducted with the Untreated Control Group Design with Pretest and Posttest (5).

The job characteristics model

Developed by Hackman & Oldham, the Job Characteristics model is now one of the most widely used paradigms in organisational literature (6). The advantages of utilising the model in the present study are (1) reliance on a comprehensive motivational framework covering a broad spectrum of job facets and (2) an ability to treat Quality Circles not as a unique phenomenon, but rather within the context of other alternatives to job redesign.

The Hackman & Oldham model lists five core job characteristics: skill variety, task identity, task significance, autonomy, and feedback. The Motivating Potential Score (MPS) of a given job is determined by a multiplication of its scores on ([skill variety, task identity, and task significance] ÷ 3) by autonomy and feedback. The first three job characteristics determine the experienced meaningfulness of work, and the fourth and the fifth affect the experienced responsibility for the work and the knowledge of the results of the work. Three variables—knowledge and skill, growth-need level, and 'context' satisfaction—act as moderators on the relationship between these psychological states and the outcomes: internal work motivation, growth satisfaction, general satisfaction, and work effectiveness.

To improve outcomes, the Job Characteristics model suggests redesigning jobs by using one of the following strategies: (1) combining tasks to increase skill variety and task identity; (2) creating natural work units to enhance task identity and task significance; (3) establishing client relationships to improve feedback and autonomy; (4) vertical loading to increase worker's autonomy; and (5) the opening of feedback channels.

Quality Circles seem to be consistent with the fourth and the fifth strategies, namely vertical loading of the job through further delegation of authority (7) and the opening of feedback channels through the provision of direct, ongoing feedback on performance (8). Yet, while 'conventional' job redesign strategies alter the entire spectrum of work activities, Quality Circle activities supplement rather than replace existing work tasks.

According to Wood, Quality Circles are likely to have a positive influence over one's job only when a circle's members are allowed to discuss, and eventually implement, job redesign. However, following the social information processing approach, we suggest that the voluntary, explicit, and public decision of employees to participate in Quality Circles meetings generates commitment for continuous participation and eventually an attribution of causality to one's behaviour (9). Thus, individuals may perceive their job differently as a result of participation in Quality Circles, even when there are no material changes in the objective characteristics of their job.

Hypotheses

1. Employees who participate in Quality Circles will experience greater increase in autonomy and feedback than employees who do not participate, but there will be no differences in job variety, task identity, and task significance between the two groups. The Motivating Potential Score (MPS) of Quality Circle participants will increase.
2. Participants in circle activities will report higher general satisfaction, higher growth satisfaction, and higher internal work motivation than non-participants.
3. Participants in circle activities will report greater satisfaction with peers and supervisors than non-participants, but there will be no differences between these two groups in terms of satisfaction with pay and job security.
4. Quality Circle participants with high 'context' satisfaction (satisfaction with pay, peers, supervisor) will report greater increases in general satisfaction, growth satisfaction, and internal work motivation than participants with low 'context' satisfaction.
5. Quality Circle participants with high growth need will report higher increase in general satisfaction, growth satisfaction, and internal work motivation than participants with low growth need.
6. Employees who participate in Quality Circle activities will be absent from work less frequently than those who do not participate.

The survey

The study was conducted between 1986 and 1987 in a large industrial organisation in Israel whose plants are dispersed throughout the country. The organisation had started experimenting with a Quality Circles program in late 1982, launching eight circles in four different plants. The initial success has led to a continuous expansion of the program, which, in mid-1987, encompassed 160 circles and more than 1,500 employees. Most, though not all, Quality Circles include only blue-collar employees.

Data on job characteristics were collected through Job Design Survey (JDS) questionnaires administered in the plants on company time. The original, English-language questionnaires were translated into Hebrew, and translated back to check their accuracy. Data on absenteeism were collected from organisational records.

Eight departments in six different plants were selected randomly from a population of thirty-two departments in which the organisation was planning to open new Quality Circles. The study included all the 160 employees in these departments, with workers who subsequently volunteered to participate in the Quality Circles program forming the experiment group and the rest serving as a control group.

Responses from 157 employees were obtained for the 'before' questionnaire, giving a response rate of about 98 per cent. The very high response rate can be attributed to the endorsement of the study by management. Of these 157, 121 employees also responded to the 'after' questionnaire, giving a response rate of about 77 per cent (out of 157) or about 75 per cent (out of the original population of 160). Twenty employees who filled in the 'before' questionnaires did not complete the 'after' one because the planned Quality Circle in their department did not open. The 16 other employees could not be reached, mainly due to transfers to other departments in the organisation.

The study followed the format of an Untreated Control Group Design with Pretest and Posttest (10). The 'before' questionnaire was administered three months prior to the introduction of Quality Circles. Employees did not have, at that time, any knowledge of the impending introduction of Quality Circles into their department and were not informed—during data collection—of that introduction. The 'after' questionnaires were administered nine months following the introduction.

Table 1 presents the intercorrelational matrices of job characteristics for the 'before' and 'after' measurements. Most correlations are low, supporting the dimensionality of the various job characteristics. Most

Table 1   An intercorrelational matrix of job characteristics

	1	2	3	4	5	6
Skill Variety	–	-.02	.12	.05	-.07	.40
Task Identity	.25	–	.25	.16	-.04	.17
Task Significance	.19	.16	–	-.16	-.11	.33
Autonomy	.09	.22	.06	–	.06	.40
Feedback	.02	.07	.15	.02	–	.20
MPS	.30	.41	.35	.67	.63	–

Note: The upper part of the matrix contains the 'after' correlations, while the lower part contains the 'before' correlations.
MPS = motivating potential score

of the exceptions are correlations involving the MPS score, which is an index composed of the other characteristics.

Table 2 presents the findings on the influence of participation in Quality Circles on job characteristics. The findings partially support Hypothesis 1, as employees participating in Quality Circle programs report significantly higher autonomy following the introduction of Quality Circles, while non-participants report (insignificantly) lower autonomy. In contrast, the increase in reported feedback is only marginally higher for participants than for non-participants.

As hypothesised, there is no significant difference between participants and non-participants regarding skill variety, task identity, and task significance. It is interesting to note, however, that while there is no change at all for either group in skill variety, the perceived task identity of participants increases and that of non-participants decreases, although the difference is not significant.

As hypothesised, the MPS of participants significantly increases, while that of non-participants decreases (insignificantly) following the introduction.

Table 3 points out that participation in Quality Circle activities had no significant impact on general satisfaction, internal work motivation, and growth satisfaction. At the same time, there was a significant decrease in the general satisfaction of those employees who did not participate in the circles' program. Thus, it is possible that those employees were adversely affected (rather than unaffected) by the introduction of Quality Circles.

Table 4 presents the findings pertaining to the impact of participation in Quality Circles on the perceived work environment. In contrast to the hypothesis, satisfaction with supervision and satisfaction with peers did not improve among Quality Circle participants. Furthermore, satisfaction with pay has significantly decreased for that group. One

Table 2 The impact of participatoin in Quality Circles on job characteristics

| | Experiment group (N = 56) | | | | Control group (N = 65) | | | | | |
| | Before | | After | | Before | | After | | | |
	X_1	SD	X_2	SD	X_3	SD	X_4	SD	t^a_{1-2}	t^a_{3-4}
Skill Variety	5.2	0.98	5.2	0.99	4.9	1.23	4.9	1.35	0.16	-0.02
Task Identity	4.9	1.14	5.1	1.17	5.1	1.10	4.8	1.14	0.98	-1.48
Task Significance	5.2	1.16	5.5	1.15	5.3	1.10	5.6	0.99	1.14	1.16
Autonomy	5.3	0.94	5.6	0.79	5.0	1.00	4.8	1.07	1.84*	-1.37
Feedback	5.3	0.95	5.5	0.94	5.3	0.93	5.4	0.87	1.32	0.93
MPS	144.6	54.88	164.6	55.91	137.5	52.31	132.4	45.01	1.91*	-0.59

Notes: 1–7 scale, 7 = highest
^{a}one tail * P < 0.05
MPS = Motivating Potential Score

Table 3 The impact of participation in Quality Circles on general satisfaction, internal work motivation, and growth satisfaction

	Experiment Group (N = 56)				Control Group (N = 65)				t^a_{1-2}	t^a_{3-4}
	Before		After		Before		After			
	X_1	SD	X_2	SD	X_3	SD	X_4	SD		
General satisfaction	5.3	0.88	5.2	0.97	5.4	1.00	4.9	1.13	0.57	-2.67**
Internal Work motivation	5.6	0.62	5.5	0.86	5.5	0.59	5.6	0.67	0.7	-0.90
Growth satisfaction	5.3	0.93	5.4	0.86	5.1	1.14	4.9	1.27	0.59	0.61

Notes: ^{a}one tail ** $P < 0.01$

Table 4 The impact of participation in Quality Circles on 'context' satisfaction

| | Experiment Group ($N = 56$) | | | | Control Group ($N = 65$) | | | | t^a_{1-2} | t^a_{3-4} |
| | Before | | After | | Before | | After | | | |
	X_1	SD	X_2	SD	X_3	SD	X_4	SD		
Satisfaction with pay	4.3	1.53	3.7	1.75	3.9	1.80	3.7	1.81	-1.93*	-0.32
Satisfaction with peers	5.5	0.92	5.6	0.85	5.2	1.23	5.3	1.06	0.60	0.50
Satisfaction with supervision	5.6	0.91	5.6	0.99	5.5	0.99	5.4	1.14	0	0.53

Notes: ^{a}one tail * P < 0.05

possible explanation for this finding is that participants perceived they had to be rewarded for Quality Circle activities.

Influence of moderating variables

Examining the impact of participation in Quality Circles on general satisfaction, growth satisfaction, and internal work motivation, when satisfaction with pay is a moderating variable, we found that among Quality Circle participants who are satisfied with their pay, Quality Circle participation contributed significantly to higher general satisfaction. Increase in general satisfaction among participants not satisfied with their pay was marginal and insignificant. No significant impact on internal work motivation and on growth satisfaction has been found for either group (11).

Also, respondents who are more satisfied with their peers show a significant increase in their general satisfaction following participation in Quality Circles, while participants who are less satisfied with their peers show a marginal, insignificant increase in internal work satisfaction and in growth satisfaction. Those participants who are satisfied with their supervisors show a significant increase in general satisfaction, while other relationships are not significant (12).

The role of growth need as a variable mediating the relationship between Quality Circles participation and satisfaction and motivation is presented in Table 5. In contrast to the original hypothesis, the findings show that an increase in general satisfaction occurs among those Quality Circle participants whose growth need is lower. This may be explained, perhaps, in terms of Quality Circles fulfilling lower-order growth needs.

Impact on absenteeism

One of the main criticisms of the Job Characteristics model has been the possible bias generated by the concomitant reliance on employee perceptions for both independent (job characteristics) and dependent (satisfaction and motivation) variables (13). To partially compensate for that, we used one of the most popular objective correlates of employee satisfaction, namely, absenteeism (14). Following Chadwick-Jones, Nicholson and Brown, we differentiated between 'voluntary' absenteeism (employee-controlled) and non-voluntary absenteeism (such as the result of sickness or accident) (15). Table 6 presents the differences in absenteeism between the employees who participated in

Table 5   The impact of growth need on satisfaction and motivation of participants in Quality Circles

| | High growth need ($N = 28$) | | | | Low growth need ($N = 28$) | | | | t^a_{1-2} | t^a_{3-4} |
| | Before | | After | | Before | | After | | | |
	X_1	SD	X_2	SD	X_3	SD	X_4	SD		
General satisfaction	4.5	0.50	4.7	0.67	4.3	0.43	4.5	0.40	0.99	2.28*
Internal work motivation	5.3	0.47	5.4	0.46	5.4	0.63	5.2	0.62	0.86	-1.54
Growth satisfaction	5.4	0.93	5.7	0.77	5.2	0.95	5.2	0.90	1.06	-0.35

Notes: ^{a}one tail   * $P < 0.05$

Table 6 The impact of Quality Circles participation on absenteeism

| | Experiment group ($N = 56$) | | | | Control group ($N = 65$) | | | | | |
| | Before | | After | | Before | | After | | | |
	X_1	SD	X_2	SD	X_3	SD	X_4	SD	t^a_{1-2}	t^a_{3-4}
Total absenteeism	607.3	26.29	616.2	24.40	556.2	30.20	571.5	35.30	0.24	0.32
Employee-controlled absenteeism	237.6	18.72	233.1	20.24	250.5	22.98	268.1	33.1	-0.16	0.43

Note: ^{a} one tail

Quality Circles and those who did not. It is apparent that although voluntary absenteeism declined for the experiment group, the decrease has not been significant.

Discussion

The significant impact found for Quality Circle participation on employee MPS scores provides empirical support for the assumption that Quality Circles are basically a job enrichment technique (16). This implies that Quality Circles can enrich jobs despite the absence of actual job redesign, thus allowing job enrichment in circumstances where job redesign is not technologically or economically feasible.

An interesting finding is that general satisfaction increases significantly for Quality Circle participants with low growth need, while the increase for participants with high growth need is insignificant. This finding is inconsistent with Hackman & Oldham's model, which expects individuals with high growth need to respond more positively to work enrichment, while those with low growth needs are expected not to value such enrichment or even to feel threatened by it. A possible explanation is that because Quality Circles do not involve actual job redesign, employees with low growth needs can value the enrichment without feeling threatened and thus respond more favourably to the change.

The present findings also highlight an important methodological issue. The employees who did not participate in Quality Circle activities were not, in fact, an untreated group. Rather, one might speculate that these employees could have been negatively affected by the introduction of Quality Circles because of their exclusion from an important group activity. Although most of them have chosen to do so, some might have wanted to join when the circles already filled up or perhaps decided in retrospect that they would like to join. Thus, an accurate assessment of Quality Circle programs in the future must take into account a possible negative impact on non-participants.

The present findings are consistent with those of Rafaeli, who found Quality Circles producing positive changes in the job characteristics of participants (17), but not with Marks and Mohrman and Novelli, who have not found such impact (18). There are several possible explanations for the discrepant findings.

1. The use of different indices: the Marks et al. and the Mohrman and Novelli studies did not use the JDS model. Indeed, Mohrman and Novelli found a significant increase for feedback, a variable which is also included in the JDS.

2. Differing perceptions among employees in the various studies as to whether Quality Circles constitute an integral part of their jobs. The source of such differences may be the attitude of senior management towards the program, the nature of the training preceding the introduction of the Quality Circle program, or the trust among circle members (19).

3. Different timings of the 'after' data collection: nine months in the present study, ten months in the Mohrman and Ledford study and twenty months in the Marks et al. study. Thus, it seems that the later the measurement, the less significant the results. This may be explained by the 'life cycle' proposition of Lawler and Mohrman, according to which after the novelty of the Quality Circle program gradually wears off, the number of new ideas diminishes, and cynicism and 'program burnout' develop (20).

4. The extent to which suggestions made by Quality Circles were indeed implemented or at least perceived as having received serious consideration. The positive record of implementation in the organization we studied was probably an important factor affecting employee attitudes towards the circles.

Notes

(1) For one of the exceptions, see M.L. Marks, P.H. Mirvis, E.J. Hackett, and J.F. Grady, Jr., 'Employee Participation in a Quality Circle Program: Impact on Quality of Work Life, Productivity and Absenteeism', *Journal of Applied Psychology*, Vol. 71, No. 1, 1986, pp. 61–69.
(2) D.T. Campbell and J.C. Stanley, *Experimental and Quasi-experimental Designs for Research*, Rand McNally, Chicago, 1963.
(3) R.P. Steel, A.J. Mento, B.L. Dilla, and N.K. Ovalle, 'Factors Influencing the Success and Failure of Two Quality Circle Programs', *Journal of Management*, Vol. 11, No. 1, 1985, pp. 99–119.
(4) J.R. Hackman and G.R. Oldham, *Work Redesign*, Addison-Wesley, Reading, Mass., 1980; see also J.R. Hackman and E.E. Lawler, 'Employee Reactions to Job Characteristics', *Journal of Applied Psychology*, Vol. 55, 1971, pp. 259–86; A.N. Turner and P.R. Lawrence, *Industrial Jobs and the Worker*, Harvard University Press, Cambridg,e Mass. 1965.
(5) Campbell and Stanley, *op. cit.*
(6) On the use of the Hackman and Oldham model in the organizational literature, see W.H. Glick, G.D. Jenkins, Jr., and,N. Gupta, 'Method versus Substance: How Strong Are Underlying Relationships Between Job Characteristics and Attitudinal Outcomes?', *Academy of Management Journal*, Vol. 29, No. 3, 1986, pp. 441–64.
(7) R. Barra, *Putting Quality Circles to Work*, McGraw-Hill, New York, 1983; N. Hatvany and V. Pucik, 'Japanese Management Practices and Productivity', *Organizational Dynamics*, Spring 1981; A Rafaeli, 'Quality Circles and Employee Attitudes', *Personnel Psychology*, 1985; P.C. Thompson, *Quality Circles: How to Make Them Work in America*, Amacom, New York, 1982.

70 SHENKAR ET AL.

(8) I. Nonaka and J.K. Johansson, 'Japanese Management: What about the "Hard" Skills?', *Academy of Management Review*, Vol. 10, No. 2, 1985, pp. 181–91; R. Wood, F. Hull, and K. Azumi, 'Evaluating Quality Circles: The American Application', *California Management Review*, Vol. 26, No. 1, 1983; E. Yager, 'Quality Circle: A Tool for the '80s', *Training and Development Journal*, Aug. 1980.

(9) G.R. Salancik and J. Pfeffer, 'A Social Information Processing Approach to Job Attitudes and Task Design, *Administrative Science Quarterly*, Vol. 23, June 1978, pp. 224–53; J. Thomas and R. Griffin, 'The Social Information Processing Modeling of Task Design: A Review of the Literature', *Academy of Management Review*, Vol. 8, No. 4; 1983, pp. 672–82.

(10) Campbell and Stanley, *op. cit.*

(11) Detailed data are not presented in order to save space, but can be obtained from the authors.

(12) Detailed data are not presented in order to save space, but can be obtained from the authors.

(13) C.A. O'Reilly and D.F. Caldwell, 'Information Influence as a Determinant of Perceived Task Characteristics and Job Satisfaction', *Journal of Applied Psychology*, Vol. 64, No. 2, 1979, pp. 157–65.

(14) K. Davis and J.W. Newstrom, *Human Behavior at Work: Organizational Behavior*, McGraw-Hill, New York, 1985.

(15) J.K. Chadwick-Jones, N. Nicholson, and C. Brown, *The Social Psychology of Absenteeism*, Praeger, New York, 1982.

(16) F.M. Gryna, *Quality Circles: A Team Approach to Problem Solving*, Amacom, New York, 1981; E.G. Yager, 'The Quality Control Circle Explosion', *Training and Development Journal*, April 1981.

(17) E.g., Rafaeli, *ibid.*

(18) Marks et al., *op. cit.*; S.A. Mohrman and L. Novelli, Jr., 'The Design and Use of Effective Employee Participation Groups: Implications for Human Resource Management', *Human Resource Management*, Vol. 24, No. 4, Winter 1985, pp. 413–28.

(19) R.W. Napier and M.K. Gershenfeld, *Groups: Theory and Experience*, Houghton Mifflin, Boston, 1973; M. Shaw, *Group Dynamics: The Psychology of Small Group Behavior*, New York, McGraw-Hill, 1976.

(20) E.E. Lawler, III and S.A. Mohrman, 'Quality Circles after the Fad', *Harvard Business Review*, Jan.-Feb. 1985, pp. 65–71.

Appendix 1:
Demographic characteristics of respondents

	% in Sample	% in Experiment Group	% in Control Group
	N = 121	N = 56	N = 65
Sex			
Male	93	100	88
Female	7	0	12
Age			
20 and under	0	0	0
20–29	26	25	26
30–39	46	50	43
40–49	23	21	25

50–59	5	4	6
60 and over	0	0	0
Marital status			
Single	11	7	14
Married, no children	7	2	11
Married with children	81	89	74
Divorced/widowed	1	2	1
Education			
Elementary	7	9	5
Vocational/High School (partial)	29	27	31
Vocational (full)	28	27	29
High School (full)	18	14	21
Academic (partial)	11	12	11
Academic (full)	7	11	3
Seniority			
Less than 1 year	5	5	4
1–3 years	14	10	17
4–5 years	4	4	3
6–10 years	31	36	28
10 years and over	46	45	48

Appendix 2:
Distribution of response by departmental affiliation

Domain	No. of employees in sample	No. of respondents 'before'	No. of employees 'after'	
			Experiment group	Control group
Maintenance & product improvement	16	16	9	7
Maintenance & product improvement	20	18	7	11
Production	18	18	7	4[a]
Electronics	25	25	7	13
Electronics	23	23	8	14
Electronics	20	19	10	7
R & D	18	18	8	9
Technical	20	20	0[b]	0[b]
	160	157	56	65

Notes: [a]Organisational change
[b]Quality Circle not opened

Appendix 3: Reliability of indices

	Reliability coefficient	
	Before	After
Job characteristics		
Skill variety	0.69	0.77
Task identity	0.51	0.59
Task significance	0.59	0.58
Autonomy	0.60	0.63
Job feedback	0.38	0.58
Critical psychological states		
Experienced meaningfulness of work	0.59	0.57
Experienced responsibility for work	0.82	0.72
Knowledge of results	0.60	0.48
Work Environment		
Satisfaction with job security	0.20[a]	0.45
Satisfaction with pay	0.75	0.78
Satisfaction with peers	0.65	0.57
Satisfaction with supervision	0.66	0.76
Satisfaction and Motivation		
General satisfaction	0.84	0.84
Internal work motivation	0.52	0.58
Growth satisfaction	0.79	0.85

Note: [a]omitted

THE CONCEPT OF HOLIDAY IN DIFFERENT PARTS OF THE WORLD

Takashi Takeshita
Sanyo Electric Co. Ltd.

Introduction

With the current trends of the curtailment of working hours from 40
to 35 hours a week, European workers have attained a 38-hour working
week. In Japan, actual working hours, which already approximate to
40 hours in large corporations, are gradually taking over from the
conventional 48 hours, though legal provision of a 40-hour working
week still has a long way to go. The purpose of this research is to compare and contrast, first, the concept of holiday (non-working days,
such as days off and weekends) held by the peoples of the world, and
second, the ways they spend their holidays under various working
conditions. The research was conducted among male and female employees of strictly a 5-day week, Japanese multinational electric makers
in 15 countries in 5 continents, and from the end of 1982 to the summer of 1986. The total number of questionnaires returned was 2,360.
(See Appendices 1 and 2 for the questionnaire and countries and
companies surveyed.) At the time of research, the working hours in
the companies surveyed ranged from 37.5 to 41.5 hours a week.

Purpose of holidays

During the primitive age, when human beings alternately worked and
took a rest, the purpose of a holiday or a rest was probably to restore
enough energy for the coming work day. Whether the same concept of those days has been passed down and whether a holiday still
serves the same purpose in contemporary society are points discussed
in the following question. Question 'A4: Your weekly day(s) off is/are
a time in which to store up energy for the coming work week' has

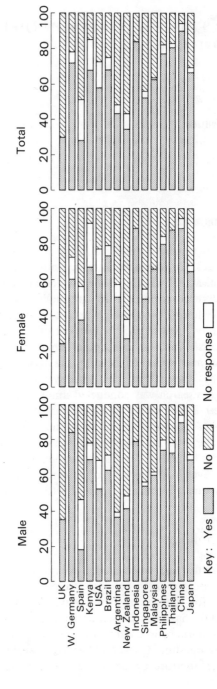

Fig. 1   Your weekly day(s) off is/are a time in which to store up energy for your coming work week

produced controversial replies, as shown in Figure 1. A significant result can be obtained when replies are classified into country groups and not into age or sex groups, not only for this question, but also for the rest of the questions. The results indicate that a difference in sex or age hardly yields a difference in the concept of holiday; rather it is the worker's resident country that forms the distinctive concept of holiday.

Sets of replies from each country showed a clearly distinguishable distribution, with Spain and China at opposite ends. Those who replied yes to the question 'Your weekly day(s) off is/are a time in which to store up energy for the coming work week' totaled 27 per cent of all the replies from Spain, whereas they totaled 89 per cent of all the replies from China. In addition to China, Indonesia, and Thailand, for which yes exceeded 80 per cent, 72 per cent and 66 per cent for Germany and Japan are also noteworthy.

In order to further clarify the concept of holiday, the results of the previous question were then investigated in relation to question 'C1. For you, work is the most important activity in your life', as in Figure 2, which checks the concept of work. The results of the two questions are perfectly correlated. Those who replied yes to this question total 8 per cent of all the replies from Spain and 95 per cent from Indonesia, with all other countries scattered between the two. By closely studying these figures, it can be concluded that many workers in Indonesia, Thailand, China, and the Philippines regard weekly day(s) off, i.e., Saturdays and Sundays, as a time in which to store up energy for the coming working week, and thus they lead their lives based on the concept that 'work is the most important activity in one's life'. On

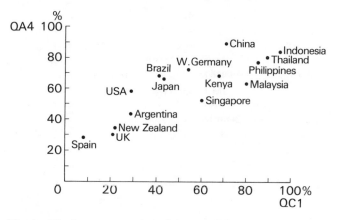

Fig. 2   The importance of work in your life

the contrary, more workers in Spain and England than in any other country regard 'weekly day(s) off as a time in which to store up energy for the coming working week' as meaningless and consequently do not lead their lives based on this concept.

The research has proven that the basic or perhaps primitive concept of holiday, that is, that a holiday is to restore enough energy for the coming working day, still exists in some countries today. On the other hand, there are many countries at the present time whose workers do not believe this. Other countries whose workers support neither side spread themselves evenly between the two extreme concepts.

Holiday for religious activities

Religion has a long history of placing restrictions on holiday activities in certain societies or countries. Some religions even force their followers to perform rites at certain hours of the working day. Whether the concept of religion still remains in the holiday behaviour patterns of present-day workers is investigated in this section.

Replies to question 'A3: Your weekly day(s) off is/are a time to go to church, synagogue, temple, etc., to pray and serve' reflect the characteristics of the concept in each country. The two countries at both ends of the graph are the Philippines, with over 90 per cent of workers going to church on Sundays, and England, with no such workers. The other countries spread themselves evenly between the two. The correlation graph (Fig. 3) between yes to question A3 and no to question C2 ('For you, work has a meaning greater than even religious

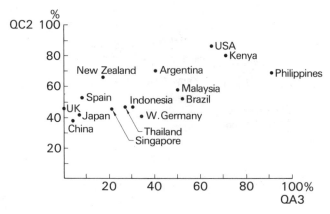

Fig. 3   Religious activities and holidays

activities') shows that the countries with workers who go to church on Sundays match the countries with those who consider religious activities more important than work.

However, the importance of religion does not necessarily depend on the concept of holiday as a time to store up energy for the coming working week or on the concept that work is the most important activity in your life. Thus, religious activities are not affected by the concept of work nowadays; instead, they are affected by the ways of spending holidays. Still, it is difficult to state exactly the relationship between holiday and religious concepts.

Holiday as personal time

Life may be viewed as either self- or group-oriented. A person is said to be leading a self-oriented life if he/she places more importance on his/her own activities or behaviour patterns and sets much value on individuality, whereas a person is said to be leading a group-oriented life if the group to which he/she belongs takes precedence over anything else in determining his/her activities. The ways to spend a holiday also tend to be either self- or group-oriented. Let us take a look at question 'B1: Your yearly vacation is a time to enjoy your personal life', as in Figure 4. One hundred per cent of the replies were yes in the USA and Spain; so were nearly 100 per cent of the replies from England, New Zealand, Germany, and Singapore. In contrast, a high percentage replied no in Indonesia and China, which means that the yearly vacation has a purpose other than just to enjoy one's personal life. Fifty per cent of the replies were yes and the other half no in Japan and Brazil. The concept of holiday as personal time, therefore, also shows diversity among different countries, as did the results of the previous questions.

However, yes to 'a time to enjoy your personal life' does not necessarily mean spending the holiday entirely for oneself. Some still consider it personal time when holidays are spent with other people. Therefore, yes is broadly interpreted as self-oriented, placing more value on individuality than no, which includes such group-oriented countries as China and Indonesia.

Let us further investigate the concept that 'holiday is a time to enjoy one's personal life' in relation with seven other items in the questionnaire (Fig. 5). Similar curves can be drawn for the countries that belong to the same culture, and the contrast between cultures becomes more definite when the countries are classified into four cultural groups:

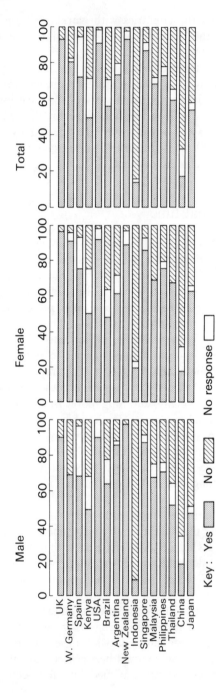

Fig. 4 Your yearly vacation is a time to enjoy your personal life

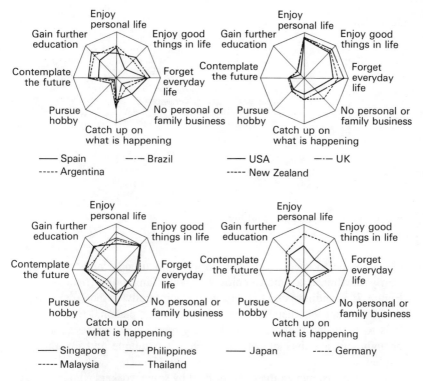

Fig. 5 Concepts of holidays by cultural and regional groups

Anglo-Saxon, Latin, Southeast Asian, Japanese, and German. Japan and Germany form a separate group, though they are not of the same culture.

Holiday with your family

In modern society, most families are composed of one or two generations, the so-called nuclear family, and the family composed of three or more generations has become very rare. The workers in this survey also belong to the former type of family and include single persons who probably assumed themselves to be nuclear families as they filled out the questionnaire. Almost all the workers, regardless of what country they are from, marked yes to questions 'A2: Your weekly day(s) off

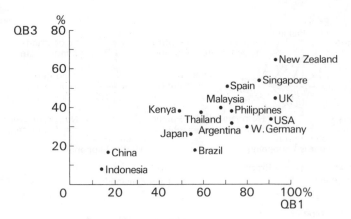

Fig. 6 Enjoyment of personal life

is/are a time to spend with your family and friends' and 'B2: Your yearly vacation is a time to enjoy with your family and friends', as in Figure 7. Spending your holiday with your family is therefore a universal concept whether holiday is thought of as personal time or not. It is to be noted that this was the only question in the research that brought out a universal concept, which is a unique and exceptional tendency.

The inconsistency in the concept held by some workers who said that holiday is both personal time and time to be spent with the family was clarified by the replies to question 'B3: Your yearly vacation is a time to take care of personal or family business', as in Figure 6. The replies from Spain and England were mostly no, while those from China and Indonesia were mostly yes. The workers who regard holiday as both personal and for the family do not take care of family business, but the workers who do not regard holiday as personal time do take care of family business.

A correlation graph of 'personal' on the X-axis and 'family' on the Y-axis visualizes this interesting concept, as in Figure 6. Those who strictly regard holiday as personal wish to spend their holiday free from family business. For workers in England, New Zealand, Singapore, and the USA, especially, a holiday should be unrestricted. However, the workers in so-called socialist countries, such as Indonesia and China, have a tendency to think that a holiday keeps one occupied, and workers in Japan and Germany position themselves apart from the other countries, which indicates their uniqueness. To conclude,

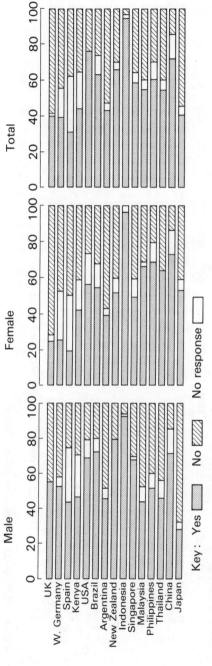

Fig. 7   Work is a source of pleasure

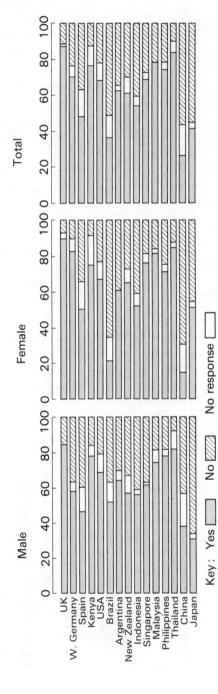

Fig. 8   Work is the only way to make a living

there exist two concepts: the concept that a holiday is not only free from work. but also free in the sense of being unrestricted, and the contrary concept.

Leisure

Work has two corresponding concepts, leisure and holiday. This section investigates, first, leisure as an activity of holiday and, second, the conceptual relationship between leisure and work. Question 'C6: For you, work is a source of pleasure' (see Fig. 7) is supported unexpectedly by those who said that 'work is the most important activity in your life' or 'your weekly day(s) off is/are a time in which to store up energy for the coming work week'. At a glance, it seems self-contradictory, but question 'C5: Work is the only way to make a living' (see Fig. 8) denies it. To explain, those who do not regard work as a source of pleasure place less value on work and simply categorise work as a way to make a living, and are therefore able to distinguish clearly between leisure and work in their concept.

The relationship between leisure and holiday has stronger than that of leisure and work because it is greatly influenced by existing economic conditions. A correlation graph (see Fig. 9) between questions 'B5: Your yearly vacation is a time to travel' and 'B9: Your yearly vacation is a time to eat, drink, and be merry' reflects the GNP per capita of the respective countries.

It can be concluded that the conceptual differences among those countries in regard to the relationship between leisure and work is due to the factor of cultural maturity in addition to economic conditions. On the other hand, it can be said that such factors as economic conditions create the conceptual differences among those countries in regard to the relationship between leisure and holiday.

Conclusion

This research has shown that the concept of holiday differs from country to country. This finding will be quite useful to those who deal with international management, and further insight into it will help solve some management problems. For instance, it has been reported that productivity on Monday in countries composed of self-oriented workers goes down. The effort to raise productivity by using criteria that worked in non-self-oriented countries would be in vain. It is almost a natural

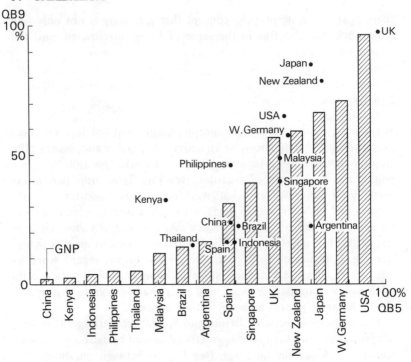

Fig. 9   Concepts of holidays in correlation with GNP

and inevitable phenomenon created by the cultural, historical, and economic circumstances of these countries. In such cases, it works better to think in terms of the weekly and not the daily cycle, and instead of trying to raise productivity on Monday, maintain the same pace but increase productivity on Wednesday or Thursday.

In addition to the concept of holiday, its counterpart, working hours, is far more important. It is quite obvious that holiday activities are more fully enjoyed by workers in Europe, where working hours are relatively short, than in any other part of the world. At this point, the focus of comparative management returns to the curtailment of working hours. In contrast to the most industrialised countries in the world, where a 38-hour working week is standard, a 4-day, 32-hour working week now seems to be the next goal. After the current goal of a 35-hour working week is attained, nobody can predict what will come next. It is very interesting to imagine what corporation management would be like if a 20-hour working week (4 hours a day), as practised by the Kalahari San of Africa, who still maintain a primitive life-style, were adopted in modern society.

Unlike British, Spanish, German, and other European workers, Japanese workers welcome working overtime or even on holidays because they simply regard it as a way to increase their income. This tendency, together with the concept of holiday and work found in this research, supports the image of the overworked Japanese. Therefore, it is true that the realization of a 20-hour working week would have different outcomes in Japan and Europe.

Lastly, we need to enlarge our scope of comparison onto a global base and at the same time to recognise the differences in consideration of the most effective method of international management.

Appendix 1: Questionnaire used in this research project

Please answer the following questions from your own personal viewpoint. Please do not reply 'in general' or 'what most people do'.

Male	Female	Age	
A. Your weekly day(s) off is/are			
1. a time in which to take it easy.		Yes	No
2. a time to spend with your family and friends.		Yes	No
3. a time to go to church, synagogue, temple, etc., to pray and serve.		Yes	No
4. a time in which to store up energy for the coming work week.		Yes	No
B. Your yearly vacation is			
1. a time to enjoy your personal life.		Yes	No
2. a time to enjoy with family and friends.		Yes	No
3. a time to take care of personal or family business.		Yes	No
4. a time to enjoy the 'good things in life'.		Yes	No
5. a time to travel.		Yes	No
6. a time to get away from it all (to forget everyday life).		Yes	No
7. a time to catch up on what is happening— news, sports, entertainment, music, etc.		Yes	No
8. a time to seriously pursue a hobby.		Yes	No
9. a time to 'eat, drink, and be merry'.		Yes	No
10. a time to contemplate the future.		Yes	No
11. a time to get involved and get in touch with what is happening around you.		Yes	No
12. a time to gain further education.		Yes	No
C. For you, work			
1. is the most important activity in your life.		Yes	No
2. has a meaning greater than even religious activities.		Yes	No
3. is totally meaningless.		Yes	No
4. is only a means.		Yes	No
5. is the only way to make a living.		Yes	No
6. is a source of pleasure.		Yes	No
7. is secondary to other activities.		Yes	No
8. keeps you occupied.		Yes	No
9. is necessary for a full life.		Yes	No

Appendix 2: Countries and companies used for this research

Country	Company	Working hours/ week 1983-86	Literary rate (%) 1980	TV diffusion rate (%) 1984	GNP per capita($) 1982
UK	Sanyo Industries (UK) Ltd.	40.00	99	33.8	8,465
West Germany	Fisher Industries Deutschland GmbH	40.00	99	34.9	10,672
Spain	Eurotron S.A.	40.00	87	25.9	4,707
Kenya	Sanyo ARMCO (Kenya) Limited	40.45	47	0.4	390
USA	Sanyo Manufacturing Corporation	40.00	99	77.9	14,600
	Sanyo Electric Inc.	40.00			
Brazil	Sanyo da Amazonia S.A.	41.30	78	12.6	2,240
	Industria Electronica Sanyo do Brasil Ltda.	41.30			
Argentina	Sanelco S.A.	41.30	93	17.6	2,520
New Zealand	Autocrat Sanyo Holdings (N.Z.) Ltd.	37.30	99	29.8	8,927
Indonesia	P.T. Sanyo Industries Indonesia	40.00	62	3.0	580
Singapore	Sanyo Industries (Singapore) Pte., Ltd.	41.30	83	16.6	5,910
Malaysia	Sanyo Industries (Malaysia) Bhd.	41.30	60	7.8	1,833
Philippines	Sanyo (Philippines) Inc.	41.30	75	2.1	796
Thailand	Sanyo Universal Electric Co., Ltd.	41.30	86	1.7	793
People's Republic of China	Sanyo Electric (Shekou) Ltd.	40.00	69	2.7	310
Japan	Tokyo Sanyo Electric Co., Ltd.	40.00	99	25.9	10,080

Sources: *The World Yearbook* (Kyodo Press), *UN Statistical Yearbook.*

INSTITUTIONALISATION IN BANKING IN MEIJI JAPAN: THE CASE OF THE CORPORATION

H.C. Maat
Erasmus University

Introduction

The relation between Japan and the Western countries concerning the transferability of Japanese management methods to the West has been studied extensively during the past few decades. However, some hundred years ago this flow of information concerning the organisation of economic life had an opposite direction: Japan, trying to become 'equal' to the Western powers, 'imported' many Western institutions in order to modernise its economy. This article will deal with this process: attention will be focused on the role of entrepreneurship in banking during the Meiji era (1868–1912).

What is entrepreneurship? In order to answer this question, a lot of theories have been developed: however, they will not be treated at this time. For our purpose, it is much more interesting to see how the entrepreneur is depicted in the literature on Japanese economic history (1). We can do so with the help of a scheme developed by the economist I.M. Kirzner.

Kirzner states that entrepreneurial activity can be studied on four different levels (2):

1. 'Standard economic theory'. This term refers to the classical micro-economic theory. On this level, we do not have to bother about entrepreneurs, for they simply do not exist in this concept.
2. 'Transcendency of maximisation'. This is, in fact, an extension of the 'standard theory'. Attention is focused on special qualities of entrepreneurs (social and educational background, character, etc.) in order to create an image of them. In this way, the Japanese entrepreneur has been described at length: a perfect example is the famous book *The Origins of Entrepreneurship in Meiji Japan,* by J. Hirschmeier (3).

3. 'Equilibrium-disturbing entrepreneurial decisions'. Here we do not focus on the determinants of decision making by entrepreneurs (as on levels 1 and 2), but on the market consequences of these decisions. We do not look at what factors make the entrepreneurs do what they do, but at the results of their actions. On this level, their actions are considered to be equilibrium disturbing: the economy is assumed to be in equilibrium, and the entrepreneurial action creates a shock. The theoretical concept of J.A. Schumpeter ('innovation', 'creative destruction') belongs to this level.

4. 'Equilibrium-creating entrepreneurial decision'. On this level, attention is also focused on market consequences of entrepreneurial decisions, but now these decisions are considered to be equilibrium creating: an innovative shock is necessary to take the economy to a new equilibrium. However, this equilibrium is not permanent: the innovative shock bears in itself the seeds for a new disturbance.

The debate concerning 'equilibrium disturbing' and 'equilibrium creating' is too theoretical and too lengthy to be dealt with here: we will therefore confine ourselves to the 'shock' itself, irrespective of the theoretical consequences for the economy as a whole.

The statement underlying the argument of this paper is that the 'traditional view' on entrepreneurship in Meiji Japan rests on studies belonging to the second level. However, if level 3 is chosen as a starting point of analysis, entrepreneurship in the Meiji era will be put in a different light. We can take, for example, the concept of 'innovation' as defined by J.A. Schumpeter. As is well known, Schumpeter distinguished five different forms of innovation (4):

1. A new product or a new quality
2. A new method of production
3. A new final market
4. A new market of raw materials
5. A new form of organisation.

'Entrepreneurial activity' can thus partly be defined as 'the creation of new forms of organisation': everyone creating a new form of organisation is an entrepreneur. In this article, 'new' means 'non-Japanese', and 'non-Japanese' means everything which is (or was) not originally rooted in Japanese society. A form of organisation fitting the definition just mentioned (i.e., an organisation which was 'new' to the Japanese) is the 'corporation'. This is a very broad term, including all organisations which can exist independent of natural persons or groups of natural persons. Examples: joint ventures and the jointstock company (5).

The corporation was transferred from the West to Japan, a transfer which will be studied here. In this article, it will be argued that the concept of the corporation was not adopted in Japan 100 per cent: particularly, the philosophy behind it was interpreted in a somewhat different way. At first, the corporation was 'imported' in an attempt to establish a form of organisation which would make possible the pooling of capital for large investments, but the private sector merely used the corporation in order to achieve other more 'defensive' goals, such as avoidance of bankruptcy and the obtaining of governmental favours. This adjustment to Japanese circumstances is not so much dure to cultural and social differences between Japan and the West, but merely a result of the unstable conditions in Japan after the Meiji Restoration.

It can thus be concluded that we get another view on entrepreneurship in the Meiji era by defining the 'entrepreneur' more broadly than has been done in the past. Now the entrepreneur can be anyone, irrespective of background, as long as he fits the definition, i.e., he has to be someone who creates a new form of organisation. This reduces the value of the 'traditional' view in which the samurai play the most important role in the development of Japan's modern economy. In fact, almost all persons appearing in this article who can be called an 'entrepreneur' in the sense just mentioned were of common origin and did not belong to the samurai class.

This argument will be applied to banking in the Meiji era because banking was the first sector in the Japanese economy in which Western forms of organisation were successfully introduced (6). This introduction took place in two phases (7). At first, the government took the initiative and established 'exchange companies', or *kawase kaisha,* and shortly afterwards it established the first bank in Japan (Dai-Ichi Ginkō). These governmental actions will be studied in more detail in the second part of this article. However, private business took over very soon. This process will be outlined in the third part in the light of the experiences of the Mitsui Bank, the first private bank in Japan.

The initiative from the center: the Kawase Kaisha and Dai-Ichi Ginkō

After the Meiji Restoration, the economy was still a 'backward' economy in comparison to the Western economies: a lot of work needed to be done in order to change it into a modern economy. Initially, this task was largely undertaken by the government, attempting to create a sound financial system. Government interest in the domestic transplantation and adaptation of advanced Western financial institutions was highly developed from the beginning of the Restoration, but the government had little knowledge concerning these institutions. This was especially reflected in the first attempt to set up modern banks: the establishment of the *kawase kaisha* (8).

The government was looking for the appropriate Western banking system in order to accumulate mercantile capital for industrialisation and in order to provide for orderly development of the currency system, which would solve the problem of inconvertible government currency circulation (9). Therefore, it established the Trade Bureau (Tsūshōshi) in February 1869. The goals of this bureau were quite ambitious (10):

1. To assure stable prices and the flow of goods,
2. To organise money-exchange operations,
3. To maintain the flow and stability of relative prices of gold and silver,
4. To promote exports and imports at posts open to foreign traffic and to guide international transactions,
5. to establish *shōsha*.

To accomplish these ends, the bureau established eight *kawase kaisha* in such port cities as Tokyo, Yokohama, and Osaka. Literally, the name *kawase kaisha* means bills or exchange companies, but the actual translation soon became bank. The *kawase kaisha* were authorised to issue their own notes, and capital was supplied by wealthy merchants, rich farmers, money exchangers, and the government (11).

However, all *kawase kaisha* failed, except the one in Yokohama (this one later became a national bank). There were various reasons for this failure (12). Government control was strong, which made the merchants unwilling to cooperate. Many times, the government used its power to force loans for risky businesses like international trade, tea-growing, and the purchasing of cocoons. Because of reluctance on the part of the merchants, the government had to supply almost half of the capital for the *kawase kaisha*. Apart from the government's control, an administrative reorganisation of the Trade Bureau and the unstable conditions of the first years after the Meiji Restoration did not contribute much to the development of the *kawase kaisha*.

Notwithstanding the fact that the *kawase kaisha* were a failure, the attempt to establish them had at least one good side: seeing the government's failures, merchant families like Mitsui, Ono, and Shimada asked for permission to establish their own banks. Mitsui, for example, took an active part in setting up and operating a *kawase kaisha*. It was Mitsui's first attempt at conducting modern banking affairs, and, according to the Mitsui Bank itself, 'much was learned in Mitsui about modern banking and the system of stock companies from the experience' (13).

The *kawase kaisha* failed, but the government did not give up its attempts to establish a Western banking system. Essentially, two models were available: the American National Banking system, according to which every bank had the right to issue its own bank notes, and the British system with its private banks, according to which only a central bank was entitled to issue bank notes (14).

Itō Hirobumi, an officer in the Ministry of Finance and later Minister of Industry, was an advocate of the American system. He proposed the issuance of bonds for the redemption of the government's notes. These bonds should constitute the collateral for the issuance of bank notes with which the inconvertible paper could be taken up. Others, however, argued that a national banking system would be unable to solve the problem of paper money and would only add another kind of inconvertible paper currency. According to this group, the solution to Japan's financial problems was to establish a conversion system by the foundation of a gold bank, i.e., the establishment of a banking system according to the British model (15).

This controversy caused a clash of opinions within the government. The advocates of the British system seemed to prevail at first, but in the end a national banking system was established. However, the system finally agreed upon was merely a compromise between the two opposing parties, rather than a 'pure' system. The advocates of the national banking system decided to accept the convertibility into specie, whereas the defenders of the gold bank dropped their opposition to the proposal of sufficient gold holdings to back up the bank note issues by government bonds.

This compromise is clearly reflected in the National Banking Act of 1872 (16). The newly established national banks were required to hold 60 per cent of their capital in government bonds yielding 6 per cent: the banks could issue an equivalent amount of bank notes. The remaining 40 per cent was to be held in specie to provide a reserve for the redemption of bank notes, which were convertible into gold upon request. Under this law, four national banks were established, the most important one being the first: Dai-Ichi Ginkō.

It has already been said that some rich merchants wanted to establish their own banks after the failure of the *kawase kaisha*. However, the government refused to give permission because it wanted a bank which would be a model for a national bank and which would eventually smoothly handle the collection of land taxes in money. Moreover, it wanted to recall nonconvertible notes from the financial markets and establish a system of negotiable notes as quickly as possible (17). According to many government officials, these goals could only be reached by the establishment of a bank with enormous funds and a national network of branches.

The strongest advocate of this view was, without a doubt, Shibusawa Eiichi, who was at that time assistant to Inoue Kaoru, a high officer of the Ministry of Finance (18). He convinced his boss that a joint venture between the two richest merchant houses (Mitsui and Ono), thus taking advantage of merchant capital, was the best way to form a bank which was able to carry out the the tasks mentioned before. Inoue agreed, and the houses of Mitsui and Ono were 'invited' to establish a bank together. Ono accepted, but Mitsui had to be pressed before giving in: the government threatened to withdraw its funds from Mitsui's vaults, in which case Mitsui would not longer be a financial agent of the government (19).

Dai-Ichi Ginkō opened business on 20 June 1873. It was organized as a joint enterprise: the houses of Mitsui and Ono each held 10,000 shares with a total value of ¥2m. The remaining 10,000 shares with a value of ¥440,000 were for public subscription, the first of its kind in Japan. The bank had several responsibilities. Apart from the issuing of negotiable notes and the recalling of bullion, it was supposed to handle public funds. In this way, the government tried to replace the merchant houses as fiscal agents, but this worked out somewhat differently (20).

The problem of leadership, caused by the equal distribution of shares between Mitsui and Ono, was solved by the introduction of a rotating directorship with Shibusawa Eiichi acting as a 'supervisor' (21). In order to be able to carry out this function properly, he resigned as Deputy Minister of Finance (22). However, this situation would not last long. The government got into financial trouble more and more, and this had its effect on the merchant houses which were, despite Dai-Ichi, still acting as financial agents. The rules concerning the amount of collateral to be held by merchant houses became gradually more severe.

The climax was reached in 1874 when the government suddenly announced that the amount of liquid collateral to be held by the merchant houses should be equal to the value of government deposits held by these houses (23). The houses of Ono and Shimada went bankrupt, but Mitsui, having been informed beforehand, escaped this fate (24).

Now, being freed from Ono, Mitsui tried to 'take over' Dai-Ichi in order to make it its own bank, but Shibusawa Eiichi succeeded in keeping the bank out of Mitsui's hands. Gradually, Shibusawa made Dai-Ichi more and more his own organ, especially after having been elected president in 1875 (25). However, throughout the period 1876–85 Mitsui still held 50 per cent of the shares of Dai-Ichi, and all bank officers (except Shibusawa) were Mitsui appointees (26).

In spite of this setback, Mitsui did not give up its idea of establishing its own bank, and it was soon helped by new opportunities. The government was not satisfied with the Banking Act of 1872: only four banks were established, and apart from Dai-Ichi they did not function well. This was, of course, partly due to the ignorance of Western banking, but still more important was the fact that the public mistrusted the bank notes. It changed them for specie, and in this way, the banks had great difficulties in keeping the notes circulating. Moreover, the 6 per cent yield on government bonds was far below the short-term market rates of interest, which were rated 10 to 15 per cent (27).

Therefore, the Banking Act was amended in August 1876. The national banks were allowed to hold 80 per cent of their capital in government bonds, while the remaining 20 per cent could be held in government paper currency rather than in specie. The national banks could issue bank notes of up to 80 per cent of their paid-in capital, and the notes were convertible only into inconvertible government notes. This amendment meant an enormous profit incentive, and during the period 1877–79, about 150 national banks were established until the government halted the stream because its goals had been achieved (28). The Banking Act of 1876 finally made possible the development of a modern banking system, and the form of the corporation spread rapidly in the banking business. Dai-Ichi (and especially its president Shibusawa Eiichi) encouraged this development, thus gaining a special position in the system (29). Soon the time came for a new step towards a mature banking system: the change from government-regulated banking to private banking.

Private business takes over: the case of Mitsui

Various stages of development can be distinguished in the history of the Mitsui Bank (30):
1. Money Exchange House (1683–1867)
2. Bank Inception Period (1867–76)
3. Société Anonyme Period (1876–93)
4. The Partnership Period (1893–1909)
5. The Joint-Stock Company Period (1909–   )

In this section, attention will be focused on the second and third periods.

Ever since the days of the *kawase kaisha*, Mitsui wanted to establish its own bank. Around 1871, Minomura Rizaemon, who handled Mitsui's business at that time, had managed to persuade influential people in the Ministry of Finance to let Mitsui establish its own bank and be responsible for issuing convertible notes (31). Very soon, preparations began: a new building was erected in Western style (the Mitsuigumi House) and became the attraction of Tokyo. Furthermore, the position of Ōmotokata (main headquarters of Mitsui) within Mitsui was strengthened and moved from Kyoto to Tokyo (32).

In July 1871, a formal application for establishing a modern bank was sent to the Ministry of Finance. In part, it said (33):

We members of Mitsui family have become convinced of the desirability of establishing modern banks in Tokyo and other open ports, and of engaging in the banking business in the most sound and trustworthy way, modelled after the tried methods obtaining in Europe and America, thereby to facilitate the financial transactions of the country. We pray that the Government grant us the privilege of issuing convertible notes and beg to submit herewith the plan of the proposed bank and the method of issuing notes for stated amount.

Permission to establish the bank was given in August 1871, but it was soon withdrawn because the government changed in favour of a national banking system, as has been described before: Mitsui was forced to cooperate together with Ono in Dai-Ichi.

However, Mitsui did not give up. In February 1872, five young members of the family plus two assistants were sent to the USA to study banking. Their ages varied between 16 and 23, and most of them had studied Western culture at schools in Kyoto. They studied English in New York before they underwent on-the-job training in local and city banks (34).

In July 1875, a new application was sent to the Ministry of Finance. It was Minomura's goal to obtain financial sanction and permission to use the title *ginkō* for the new bank and to adopt a limited liability system that would protect Mitsui from meeting the same fate Ono had befallen the previous year, i.e., bankruptcy (35). Because there was no law in Japan which made this possible, the petition asked for permission to establish a non-national bank and for guidelines (36): 'Though we are ignorant and uninformed and not confident that we ourselves can formulate perfect rules, yet we dare to present for your esteemed consideration . . . our drafts of bank rules and other documents in the hope that you will instruct and enlighten us' (37).

The application was granted in March 1876, shortly before the introduction of the new Banking Act of 1876, and reflected the change in government policy: the national banking system had turned out to be a failure and something new was needed.

However, there were certain restrictions. The government wanted the shareholders to be fully responsible, whereas Mitsui wanted limited liability. Furthermore, the government wanted 25 per cent of the reserves to be deposits (20 per cent government securities and 15 per cent in cash), while Mitsui did not want to go beyond 20 per cent. Finally, Mitsui accepted, and the Mitsui Bank started business on 1 July 1876 (38).

The Mitsui Bank was organised in the form of a Société Anonyme with unlimited liability (39). The starting capital of ¥2m was divided in 20,000 shares: 10,000 held by Ōmotokata, 5,000 held by the nine (shortly afterwards, eleven) Mitsui families, and the remaining 5,000 held by employees. Together, there were 383 shareholders. In August 1876, a contract was signed between Ōmotokata, the Mitsui families, and the Mitsui Bank: Ōmotokata would borrow money from the Mitsui Bank, using real estate it owned as collateral, and it would use the borrowed money for capitalizing the bank. Furthermore, Ōmotokata would manage its own shares as well as those held in the Mitsui family name. In this way, Ōmotokata was positioned between the Mitsui family and the Mitsui Bank, thus effectively blocking any arbitrary behaviour by family members regarding the bank's affairs (40).

The Mitsui Bank was the first private bank to use the word *ginkō*: before, only the national banks were allowed to do so. The word *ginkō* is said to have been taken from an English-Chinese dictionary, published in Hong Kong but in use in Japan (41). The new term had a strongly favourable connotation indicating privileged status and power. After Mitsui, other private banks were given permission to use the word *ginkō* (42).

As stated before, the adoption of the form of the Societe Anonyme stemmed partly from the desire to avert risks in uncertain times. This becomes clear when we examine a statement made by Minomura Rizaemon, in the capacity of Director-General of the Mitsuigumi, on the opening of the Mitsui Bank (43):

Many are the commercial houses known for their great wealth from the days of Tokugawa Shogunate which have become of late painfully reduced in circumstances or have even gone out of business altogether. This lamentable fate has overtaken them because they have erred in their aims or blundered in their policy. In view of the warnings they afford we must not remain idle. The way to avoid the false steps they have taken is to form a company. Companies are of various kinds, but the best is the Société Anonyme, in which the names of members do not appear, but it is named after the business it undertakes to conduct. Its policy and system are decided by majority votes and are carried out openly, thus ensuring justice and fairness. Moreover, the Articles of Association and Regulations are all subject to the approval of the Government and must be strictly observed, leaving no room for deviation. Herein lies the excellence of such company formation. In adopting this superior method of running our business, we meet the requirements of the times.

This uncertainty is also reflected in the fact that Minomura was worried about whether Mitsui would be able to continue its handling of public funds: only after the promise that this would continue (at least temporarily) did Minomura set about to establish the Mitsui Bank (44).

Soon after the establishment of the bank, a series of misfortunes occurred. The Matsukata Deflation of the 1880s caused an economic recession, and when the Bank of Japan was established in 1882, the Mitsui Bank had to return all its public funds to this bank (45). This was a severe setback for Mitsui (46). In 1885, the same year in which the Bank of Japan issued its first negotiable notes, the decision was made to turn the national banks into private banks. Now Mitsui had to face more competitors for private deposits (47).

The solution to all these problems was clear: the Mitsui Bank should try to become a regular bank, more independent of the handling of public funds. Several internal measures were taken, but they were not very successful, so the Mitsui Bank was not ready for the recession which hit Japan in 1890 (48). One of the main problems was that the old clerks, who had remained from the pre-Restoration period, tried to gain favour with officials and high institutions by granting loans in spite of insufficient security. This pattern of lending, which resembled the pattern of daimyo lending of the Tokugawa days, nearly made the bank collapse when the government called its deposits from the banks in order to solve its financial problems (49).

However, help was on its way. Inoue Kaoru negotiated a loan to the Mitsui Bank from the Bank of Japan. Moreover, he 'supplied' Mitsui with a new reformer: Nakamigawa Hikojiro (1854–1901) (50).

Nakamigawa introduced a plan to reform the whole of Mitsui, and he carried it out very vigourously. He collected bad loans and established rules clarifying the conditions and procedures for granting new ones. The old clerks were dismissed and replaced by young managers, most of them from Keiō college (51). Nakamigawa also sold Mitsui's shares in Shibusawa's Dai-Ichi Ginkō (52).

The most important reform was the transformation of the Mitsui Bank into an unlimited partnership by buying up all the shares held by non-Mitsui shareholders and by limiting the number of partners to five members of the Mitsui family (53). The new name became Gōmei Kaisha Mitsui Ginkō (Partnership Mitsui Bank) (54). One of the reasons to do so was the introduction of the Commercial Code of 1890 (which took effect in July 1893), a law meant to unify the banking system. According to this law, private banks and quasi-banks had to change into 'ordinary' banks or lose their banking status.

Another reason to adopt the form of the unlimited partnership was that it would not hurt the family overall in case of failure: the willingness to accept unlimited liability would help Mitsui to retain the public trust it enjoyed. Also, an unlimited partnership would mean fewer requirements for public disclosure of business operations (55).

One more step was necessary in order to reach maturity in banking: the Mitsui Bank had to become a joint-stock company with limited liability. Once again, bank personnel were sent to the USA and Europe to study banking, and in November 1906, Hayakawa Senkichirō, at that time Executive Director, proposed to make the Mitsui Bank a joint-stock institution, which should use its funds for investment and financing (56). However, because of an economic crisis (1906–7), these plans were not effectuated.

After the crisis, representatives of the Mitsui Bank were again sent to the USA and Europe and their mission resulted in two reports, of which the one written by Masuda Takashi was the most important one. In both reports, it was proposed to reorganise Mitsui (including the bank) into a joint-stock company with limited liability, controlled by one unlimited partnership (Mitsui Gōmei), which should hold all shares of the bank (57).

In October 1909, the Mitsui Bank became a joint-stock company. The paid-up capital was ¥20m, divided into 200,000 shares, of which 38,000 were held by Mitsui family heads and the rest by other Mitsuis or their trusted associates (58). The circle was closed: Mitsui had transformed itself from a government-dependent financial agent into an independent modern private bank.

Conclusion

In this paper, it was shown how the corporation, defined as a form of organisation which can exist independent of (groups of) natural persons, was introduced in Japan, how it was used, and how it was adjusted to specific needs by the various groups in the society. It was brought by a group of pioneers like, for example, Shibusawa Eiichi, and it was first introduced in banking in order to develop the sound financial base needed to create a modern economy. The government took the initiative and established the *kawase kaisha* and Dai-Ichi: later, private business took over. This tends to support the 'traditional view' according to which the government played an active role during the early Meiji days and the merchants a passive one. However, reality was more complicated.

It is true that the government established the *kawase kaisha* and that the merchants were not very willing to cooperate, but this seems to be more due to the lack of control the merchants had over their own capital than to their risk-aversity. In fact, the merchants were willing to build up a financial system, but the government just did not approve of the kind of system they had in mind. The previous part showed that Mitsui wanted to establish its own bank, but that the government favoured a national banking system and forced Mitsui to participate in Dai-Ichi.

Nevertheless, the *kawase kaisha* were very useful in giving the merchants the opportunity to learn modern banking techniques. They would have learned them anyway (Mitsui, for example, was already sending its employees abroad at a very early stage), but because of this initiative of the government, things were certainly accelerated.

The same argument goes, more or less, for the national banking system: it contributed much to the development of Japanese banking, but its creation is not a result of a passive attitude on the part of the merchants (59). Mitsui wanted to establish its own bank, but the government wanted a national banking system in which there was no place for a private bank. Only after the national banking system proved to be malfunctioning were private banks given permission to start business. Gradually, government-regulated banks disappeared and private banking developed, but the case of Mitsui shows that the road to maturity was long.

It can be concluded that there was no real contrast between the government and the private sector in terms of 'active' and 'passive': both were active in a process of searching for the best way to deal with each other, a process in which the government had the upper hand at first in terms of power to make rules.

How should all this be viewed in the light of entrepreneurship? As stated in the introduction, the traditional view rests upon studies with a strong sociological background: attention is focused on special qualities which distinguish the entrepreneur from the rest of the people. In this view, the concept of the entrepreneur is strongly connected with the samurai class.

However, looking at the market consequences of entrepreneurial decisions, we get another view. In this paper, the entrepreneurial act was defined as the introduction of the corporation (a non-Japanese form of organisation) into the economy, in accordance with the definition of Schumpeter. According to this definition, anyone can be an entrepreneur, regardless of background. The government and the private sector have been acting, in this sense, in a kind of interaction: it is difficult to separate their behaviour. Both can be called entrepreneurs without reference to social background, etc., which reduces the value of the 'entrepreneur = samurai' theory.

A second point stated in the introduction is that the form of the corporation was not adopted 100 per cent. Particularly, the philosophy behind it (enlargement of capital) was interpreted in a different way. On the government's side, pooling of capital was the main goal. For example, Shibusawa Eiichi tried continuously to combine the capital of private sources in order to create large units for carrying out large investments. He was the architect of the combining of the capital of Mitsui and Ono in Dai-Ichi, and he was also a driving force behind the Commercial Code of 1890, aiming at pooling the capital available in the economy. On the other hand, Mitsui, for example, introduced the corporation clearly in order to avoid bankruptcy in uncertain times: they were more interested in protecting their own (family) capital and not in enlarging it by attracting sources from outside. This can be called a 'conservative' policy, but the introduction of the corporation was nevertheless a great innovation considering the circumstances in Japan at that time. In any case, it was not a 'passive' policy.

In this paper, an overview is presented of the introduction of the form of the corporation in Japanese banking during the Meiji era. Of course, this overview is all but perfect: only the most important facts are given, and only three cases (the *kawase kaisha*, Dai-Ichi Ginkō, and the Mitsui Bank) are studied. Many questions remain: who exactly were the people behind the introduction of the corporation in Japan, what was their philosophy, and what was it in Western forms of organisation that struck them? Also, more case studies should be performed in order to obtain a better picture of the spread of the corporation through banking and other industries.

Another topic to be studied is the Japanese interpretation of the corporation. The fact that, notwithstanding public subscription, most shares of large companies were owned by a small group of rich families has been studied at length, but attention is usually focused on the zaibatsu during the 1920s. Much less attention is given to the development of this phenomenon during the early stage of Japanese industrialisation, i.e., the Meiji era.

Notwithstanding this imperfect presentation, the conclusion seems justified that the Japanese corporation was not just a copy of the Western model and that relations within Japanese banking in the Meiji era were far more complicated than suggested by the traditional view with its stress on the role of the samurai.

Notes

(1) For an elaborate discussion, see, for example, H.W. de Jong, '*Markteconomie, ondernemerschap en economische theorie*', unpublished paper, Amsterdam, 1987, pp. 3–9.

(2) J. Ronen (ed.), *Entrepreneurship*, Lexington Books, Lexington, Mass., 1982, pp. 284–88.

(3) For a formulation of this traditional view, see also K. Yamamura, *A Study of Samurai Income and Entrepreneurship: Quantitative Analyses of Economic and Social Aspects of the Samurai in Tokugawa and Meiji Japan*, Harvard University Press, Cambridge, Mass., 1974, pp. 137–43.

(4) See, for example, H.W. de Jong, *Dynamische markettheorie*, Stenfert Kroese, Leiden/Antwerpen, 1981, pp. 56–57.

(5) For an elaborate discussion, see *ibid.*, pp. 89–100.

(6) R. Cameron (ed.), *Banking in the Early Stages of Industrialization: A Study in Comparative Economic History*, Oxford University Press, London/New York/ Toronto, 1967, pp. 259–60. See also T. Nakamura, *Economic Growth in Prewar Japan*, Yale University Press, New Haven/London, 1983, pp. 60–61.

(7) Cameron (ed.), *op. cit.*, p. 277.

(8) *Ibid.*, p. 249.

(9) *Ibid.*, p. 250.

(10) This section draws heavily on Yamamura, *op. cit.*, pp. 163–64.

(11) T.F.M. Adams, *A Financial History of Modern Japan*, Research, Tokyo, 1964, p. 9.

(12) Yamamura, *op. cit.*, p. 225.

(13) Mitsui Ginkō, *The Mitsui Bank: A History of the First 100 Years*, The Mitsui Bank Ltd., Tokyo, 1976, pp. 34–35.

(14) Cameron (ed.), *op. cit.*, p. 250.

(15) Adams, *op. cit.*, p. 9.

(16) See, for example, Cameron (ed.), *op. cit.*, p. 255.

(17) Mitsui Gōmei Kaisha, *The Mitsui Bank: A Brief History*, The Mitsui Bank Ltd., Tokyo, 1926, p. 42.

(18) J.G. Roberts, *Mitsui: Three Centuries of Japanese Business*, Weatherhill, New York/Tokyo, 1973, p. 98. Shibusawa Eiichi (1840–1931), perhaps the most

outstanding entrepreneur of Japanese modern history, was born the son of a
rich farmer in Musashi province. He entered the service of the Tokugawa family and gained the confidence of the last shogun. He accompanied the shogun's
younger brother as his financial manager to the World Exhibition in Paris in
1867. Here Shibusawa became acquainted with Western ideas concerning banking, business, and policy. After his return to Japan (1869), he founded the first
partnership trading company in Shizuoka (the hometown of the then retreated
Tokugawa family), but he soon left the firm to look after itself in order to become an officer of the Ministry of Finance of the new government. However,
he resigned in 1873 to become general superintendent of Dai-Ichi Ginkō. Being
elected president of this bank in 1875, he made it the 'base' from which he
established, coordinated, and directed many of the newly emerging business
and industrial enterprises during the Meiji era and after (J. Hirschmeier, *The
Origins of Entrepreneurship in Meiji Japan*, Harvard University Press, Cambridge, Mass., 1964).
(19) Mitsui Ginkō, *op. cit.*, p. 43, and Yamamura, *op. cit.*, p. 226n17. It is interesting
to note that the Mitsui Jubilee Commemoration of 1926 talks about the Mitsuigumi being 'persuaded to agree to the Government's scheme' (p. 25), whereas in *The Mitsui Bank: A History of the First 100 Years* (1976) it is stated that
the Mitsui leaders 'acceded' after having been 'threatened' by the government
'to abolish Mitsui's position as a fiscal agent unless it complied' (p. 43).
(20) Mitsui Ginko, *op. cit.*, p. 43, and Mitsui Gōmei Kaisha, *op. cit.*, p. 27. See
also, Roberts, *op. cit.*, p. 99, and Cameron (ed.), *op. cit.*, p. 256.
(21) Roberts, *op. cit.*, p. 99.
(22) Cameron (ed.), *op. cit.*, p. 257. However, Shibusawa's resignation also seems
to stem partly from his will to avoid being blamed for the nation's financial
difficulties, which grew stronger and stronger.
(23) *Ibid.*, p. 256.
(24) Mitsui Ginkō, *op. cit.*, p. 44.
(25) *Ibid.* The older works (for example, Mitsui Gomei Kaisha, *op. cit.*) do not
mention this attempt.
(26) Hirschmeier, *op. cit.*, p. 168, and Cameron (ed.), *op. cit.*, p. 256. See also Yamamura, *op. cit.*, p. 168, and R.W. Goldsmith, *The Financial Development of Japan
1860–1977*, Yale University Press, New Haven/London, 1983, p. 25.
(27) Cameron (ed.), *op. cit.*, p. 255, and G.C. Allen, *A Short Economic History of
Modern Japan*, Macmillan, London, 1981, pp. 45–46. For an excellent overview on this subject, see Yamamura, *op. cit.*, p. 226n20.
(28) Cameron (ed.), *op. cit.*, p. 257. See also Hirschmeier, *op. cit.*, p. 166.
(29) Shibusawa Eiichi helped local banks to overcome set-up difficulties by helping
them to deal with the government in case of problems and by printing and dis-
tributing instruction booklets on banking (Hirschmeier, *op. cit.*, p. 60).
(30) Mitsui Gōmei Kaisha, *op. cit.*, Table of Contents.
(31) Minomura Rizaemon (1821–77), born as the son of a *rōnin* in Kyushu, went
to Kyoto at the age of 14 and after having traveled widely throughout the country, he finally settled in Edo at the age of 19 to become a merchant's apprentice.
His extraordinary abilities brought him into the Mitsui combine and eventually
to the position of Deputy President of the Mitsui Bank. Notwithstanding his
sudden death in 1877, his influence on the process of creating the Mitsui
Bank was a decisive one (Hirschmeier, *op. cit.*).
(32) Mitsui Ginkō, *op. cit.*, pp. 36–37.
(33) Mitsui Gōmei Kaisha, *op. cit.*, p. 21.
(34) Mitsui Ginkō, *op. cit.*, p. 41.
(35) Roberts, *op. cit.*, p. 106.
(36) Mitsui Gōmei Kaisha, *op. cit.*, pp. 31–32.
(37) Roberts, *op. cit.*, p. 106.

(38) Mitsui Ginkō, *op. cit.*, p. 46.

(39) Mitsui Gōmei Kaisha, *op. cit.*, p. 34.

(40) Mitsui Ginkō, *op. cit.*, p. 48, and Roberts, p. 107.

(41) Adams, *op. cit.*, p. 9. Fukuzawa Yukichi, who translated this dictionary into Japanese, first translated 'bank' as *ginza*, but later it became *ginkō*. In fact, between 1868 and 1871, both *ginza* and *kaisha* were used to mean bank, until *ginkō* finally gained the upper hand.

(42) Cameron (ed.), *op. cit.*, p. 261.

(43) Mitsui Gōmei Kaisha, *op. cit.*, pp. 34–36.

(44) Mitsui Ginkō, *op. cit.*, pp. 48–49. Minomura Rizaemon sent a petition to the Ministry of Finance:

> If the government should change its current practise and withdraw the money deposited with us, we shall find it very difficult to keep going. . . . If such a situation should arise, our company's distress aside, the flow of private capital would be obstructed and financial operations paralyzed. Considering this, we urge you to continue to allow us, for the coming few years at least, to handle official money of government ministries and agencies and not to change that policy.

> To this plea, Ōkuma, Minister of Finance, replied, 'Your request will be granted, and you will be entrusted with official money without fail'. (Roberts, *op. cit.*, p. 107).

(45) Cameron (ed.), *op. cit.*, pp. 251–52.

(46) Mitsui Ginkō, *op. cit.*, p. 52.

(47) *Ibid.*, pp. 52–53.

(48) *Ibid.*, p. 54.

(49) Hirschmeier, *op. cit.*, p. 219.

(50) Nakamigawa Hikojirō (1854–1901), a nephew of Fukuzawa Yukichi, studied at Keiō college and spent three years in England, where he had a successful career as a teacher and newspaper editor. Having been appointed Deputy President, Nakamigawa set himself to the enormous task of reforming Mitsui. In the case of the Mitsui Bank, he was notorious for his ruthless policy towards dubious debtors. He even refused to grant a loan to a statesman and collected a loan from the powerful Buddhist Higashi Honganji Temple in Kyoto, something which was 'not done' in those days. Although his policy proved to be a blessing for Mitsui in later years, he made many enemies both inside and outside Mitsui. Nakamigawa died young at the age of 47. (Hirschmeier, *op. cit.*).

(51) Mitsui Gōmei Kaisha, *op. cit.*, p. 62 and Roberts, *op. cit.*, p. 140.

(52) Roberts, *op. cit.*, p. 140.

(53) Mitsui Gōmei Kaisha, *op. cit.*, p. 46.

(54) Mitsui Hachiroye, Mitsui Gennosuke, Mitsui Takayasu, Mitsui Hachirōjirō, and Mitsui Morinosuke. In November 1898, six new partners were added (Mitsui Genyemon, Mitsui Fukutarō, Mitsui Yōnosuke, Mitsui Saburōsuke, Mitsui Takenosuke, and Mitsui Tokuyemon), thus enlarging Mitsui Bank's capital from ¥2m to ¥5m.

(55) Mitsui Ginkō, *op. cit.*, p. 62, and Cameron (ed.), *op. cit.*, p. 264.

(56) Mitsui Ginkō, *op. cit.*, p. 65.

(57) *Ibid.*, pp. 74–75.

(58) Roberts, *op. cit.*, p. 171.

(59) Cameron (ed.), *op. cit.*, pp. 259–60. According to Hugh Patrick, the contributions of the national banking system were the following:

1. It provided the first sustained successful experience in modern banking techniques.
2. It made modern banking a highly respectable and prestigious occupation.

3. It popularized important Western business institutions, especially the corporate form of business organization.
4. It introduced the first modern bookkeeping system in Japan, including depreciation accounting.

Part II
Japanese Management Overseas

KAO CORPORATION'S DIRECT INVESTMENT AND ADAPTATION IN EUROPE

Akira Kudō
University of Tokyo

Introduction

In this paper, I wish to examine the motives and strategies of Kao Corporation Limited in its entry into Europe and discuss the problems of adaptation which may be encountered in this process. Kao was one of the first soap manufacturers in Japan. It has a history of almost one hundred years and is a leader in marketing and advertising. Moreover, it has been a keen investor in research and plant equipment in the areas of oil and fat, surface, and polymer sciences and has proceeded with a rapid diversification to cover the production of detergents, cosmetics, paper diapers, toners, floppy disks, etc. The change of the official company name in 1985 from 'Kao Soap Company' to the present 'Kao Corporation' is, incidentally, one sign of this strong diversification drive.

My primary reason for examining the case of Kao was the strong impression made, while I was engaged in completing the company's centennial history, by the marked development in international activities recently set against the general managerial development of the company. Another reason was the easy facility to information sources. But these were not my sole reasons. The entry of Japanese chemical firms into European markets is less apparent than that of electric appliance or car manufacturers. Consequently, chemical firms are not yet at the centre of the trade conflict, and problems in adaptation have not yet become evident. However, since Kao actually represents the case of a firm which is making an entry on the strength of its managerial as well as its technological superiority, it is likely that the adaptation problems discussed below will prove to be even more significant. Kao, in this sense, provides interesting material as a case study of

107

localisation and of the adaptation attempts of Japanese firms in Europe.

Why Europe? the development of overseas activities

From the periphery to the centre and diversification

Already before the Second World War, Kao had set up manufacturing centres throughout East and Southeast Asia. However, these were lost with the Japanese defeat and bear no direct relation to present development. The new starting point after the war dates from 1955 with the resumption of exports of household products to Southeast Asian markets. Direct investment began in 1961 when joint venture enterprises were begun in Thailand and Taiwan. During the sixties, joint ventures were successfully created throughout the Southeast Asian area. Development policy in the sixties centred on domestic products (personal care products, household products, hygiene products, cosmetics) and chemical products (fatty and specialty chemicals) and on the creation of these joint ventures in Asia.

Only towards the end of the sixties did Europe finally enter the company view. First, in 1968 a liaison office was opened in Brussels for exporting and marketing chemical products and for the collection of sales and technical data. At the same time, the British chemical corporation Bibby Chemicals, Ltd., was acquired and polyurethane production started. Further, in 1970 a joint venture in Spain was started and manufacture of the chemical product amine began. However, of these activities only the production of amine in Spain was continued; the Brussels office was closed in 1972 and the British subsidiary was sold off to ICI in the same year. In 1979, another joint venture was begun in Spain to manufacture a surfactant. We can sum up these developments in Europe in the seventies as being a failure in Northern Europe, while only the stronghold gained south of the Pyrenees remained.

Finally, in the eighties Kao established a firm stronghold in Northern Europe. In 1979, Kao, in collaboration with the West German company Beiersdorf AG., acquired Guhl, manufacturer of such hair care products as shampoo, rinse, and hair dye. However, this subsidiary was formally in Beiersdorf's 100 per cent ownership until 1986, when a 50–50 division of rights with Kao was formalised. Sales of the subsidiary increased steadily after acquisition, and it estabished a leading position in sales of shampoo to the commercial hairdressing network. It established its own subsidiaries in Holland, Austria, and Switzerland.

The strong yen after the G5 Conference of September 1985 created a very favourable context. Developments proceeded rapidly. In 1986, Kao took a 60 per cent capital participation in a toner manufacturer and established a 100-per-cent-owned floppy disk sales subsidiary in West Germany, and in Dusseldorf, a sales subsidiary for cosmetics was set up. Also, sales of cosmetics in Europe began from June 1987, and at the same time localisation of research and development began with the establishment of a research laboratory for cosmetics and hair-care products in Berlin. This had the double aim of the accumulation of technical and sales know-how and of using the appeal to Japanese consumers of the brand image of products sold in Europe.

A similar pattern of development was evident in North America. In Canada, a 70 per cent capital participation was taken in a floppy disk manufacturer; in the USA, a research institute was established in Los Angeles. The sales of cosmetics began, and in the summer of 1987, the American manufacturer of surfactants, High Point Chemical Corporation, was acquired.

The developing pattern of Kao's overseas activities, with regional development in Southeast Asia in the sixties, expanding to Europe around the seventies, followed by a period of stagnation from the seventies to the mid-eighties, after which activities moved to North-western Europe and North America, shows an overall movement from the periphery to the centre of the world economy. Investment activities in the first half of the sixties to the early seventies and in the early eighties roughly match the overall pattern of direct investment by Japanese firms. Moreover, the sequence of regional development is also typical of Japanese firms.

One of the characteristic traits of Kao's developing overseas activities at present is diversification. Apart from soap products, dating back to the pre-war years, Kao, starting from a line of household (detergents, etc.) and chemical products, has recently diversified to include cosmetics, hair-care products, and information-storage media. This is clearly related to the regional expansion of its international activities. However, it is especially interesting that the hypothesis of product cycles à la Vernon does not seem to be applicable in this case (1). As can be seen from the basic chronology outlined above, both multinationalisation and diversification were proceeding simultaneously. In any case, any time lag between domestic and international developments in diversification would seem to have been much smaller than Vernon postulates. In the field of cosmetics, floppy disks, and toners,

Kao has not saturated the domestic market to the extent of creating an oligopolic system. While establishing its domestic position in the fields of household and chemical products and information storage media, it is simultaneously following a similar programme in each of the three main areas of its overseas activities: Asia, Western Europe, and North America.

Summing up, the overseas activities of Kao can be characterised as showing a movement from the periphery to the centre in geographical terms and towards diversification in terms of product lines.

Idealism in strategy of diversification and multinationalisation

The central strategy behind the overseas activities outlined above was an idealistically motivated multinationalisation. This was the result of a strong desire to do business somehow or other in Europe and North America. In September 1982, a very critical moment in hindsight, President Maruta stated that 'our real aim . . . is, in one way or another, to become an international company'. Of course, considering the future competition with international companies like Procter and Gamble or Unilever, it was not possible for Kao to content itself with the Asian market. Moreover, particularly in the fields of cosmetics and hair-care products, the Euro-American market is the trend-setting market from the consumer's viewpoint, and the market size and scale of management resources make it very attractive. There is no doubt, then, that significant incentives existed for entry into the Euro-American market.

Further, a factor making entry possible was Kao's early establishment of its own independent technical base in the field of surfactants. Its technical standard was so high that a joint venture undertaken in Japan in the immediate post-war period could be summed up as 'not up to expectation in terms of production technology'. Kao, therefore, quickly set its aim on direct overseas investment while introducing new technology. Incidentally, Kao's first partner in a joint venture, Atlas Chemicals, an American surfactant manufacturer, was a mentor for Kao's overseas development activities, providing know-how on capital participation, take-overs, and the marketing of specialty chemicals, as well as being an invaluable information source and liaison with world markets.

However, when considering Kao's strategies of multinationalisation, diversification, or vertical integration, it is the constant presence of this idealistic managerial philosophy that is most striking. It is impossible to separate this managerial philosophy from the person of President Maruta, who combines an un-Japanese thoroughness in his technical rationalism with personal charisma and who epitomises the strategic style of management. President Maruta, who has exercised forceful leadership since 1971, has been the major driving force behind both Kao's multinationalisation and diversification policies.

In accordance with this idealistic strategy of multinationalisation in the late sixties and early seventies, Kao entered the Euro-American market, but then withdrew, not having found a suitable product to sell. In the seventies, when its overseas activities were stagnant, a series of trial-and-error attempts at co-operation, licensing, take-overs, joint ventures, etc., took place in northwestern Europe and North America. To explain the failure of these attempts would require a wide-ranging examination, including the advent of the international money and the oil crises. However, it is clear that Kao's multinational policy was not reluctant (2). Rather, during the seventies it could be said that the desire to enter foreign markets was unmatched by a sufficient ability to realise that desire. With the eighties, this desire became even stronger, and thanks to the favourable climate created by the strong yen, this desire was rapidly realised.

Incidentally, the trial-and-error attempts mentioned above influenced the parent company's structure. In July 1982, that is, after the launching of the Sofina cosmetic line, the Main Office for Overseas Activities was disbanded, and separate offices for the European American, and Pacific sectors were created. In 1983, with the exception of the American Office, these area offices were elevated to division status and were put under the direct supervision of the company vice-presidents. At about the same time, branch offices were opened in Dusseldorf, New York, and Singapore. Since then, structural reforms have taken place almost annually, and the employment of local managers in Dusseldorf and Paris was tried out. At present, the main division for each particular product is in charge of its own overseas activities so that company organisation is a matrix of 'sales field × sales region'. Further, in Germany and America regional headquarters are being set up. Given the tardy reform of Kao's Main Office structure, it would seem appropriate to see the eighties as the beginning of Kao's full-scale move towards the centre of the world economy.

In this sense, we can say without exaggeration that the policy of multinationalisation preceded product diversification and developed as technical and capital resources accumulated.

Adaptation and localisation

Now let us turn to a brief examination of the questions of adaptation and localisation. Applying to companies the concept of adaptation in its original biological sense, we might say that those will survive which are capable of adapting to their environment. However, following this line of thought we reach the conclusion that adaptability to surroundings equates with a firm's competitiveness. But the recent question of a firm's international adaptability cannot adequately be accounted for by its international competitiveness alone. Put simply, such an account underestimates the conflict involved.

Conflicts can be classified into those originating within a firm, that is, arising from the firm's internal decision-making process, and those arising between a firm and its external environment, for example, with other firms, the local society, and governments. Of course, these two categories are closely related, as in the case of an internal conflict about labour conditions which is taken to a labour tribunal. However, a firm's efforts to adapt to the environment are generally more effective in the internal rather than the external sphere. In internal affairs, its leeway for an active response is relatively greater, whereas with external conflict, it tends to be more passive. In psychological terms, the resistance to adjustment is greater in the latter case. Further, adaptation to external conditions tends to be more decisive. Put rather extremely, while it is possible for a firm having internal conflicts to continue its regular achievements, its continued existence becomes impossible if it is ordered by a government to leave the country.

Consequently, when discussing adaptation, I take this to include relations between the parent company and its local subsidiaries, and not only in the sense of a firm's internal problems.

Now let us examine localisation. The three main alternatives for international development open to a firm—export, licensing, and direct investment—entail in that order an increasing necessity for localisation. Aspects of localisation include ownership and management localisation, production technology, research and development, and labour relations. With direct investment, these issues become more likely to arise and require greater consideration.

Even if localisation has taken place, this does not mean that adaptation is immediately possible. Localisation does not equal adaptation. The solution to the problem of adaptation would be much simpler if this were the case. But any attempt to examine adaptation leaving out a consideration of localisation would be extremely narrow. It is fair to say that most Japanese firms making direct investment abroad test out the possibility of international adaptation through localisation. Kao is no exception to this general pattern.

When localising, Japanese firms see the European environment as more problematic than other areas because differing approaches elicit a greater variety of response. Of course, this impression is partly due to the small size of the Japanese entry, but also to the strength of Europe's socio-economic structure and cultural traditions. The existence of the Common Market is another influence. Gilpin's neo-mercantilist model more adequately accounts for the economic relations of Japan and the Common Market than either Vernon's liberalist model or Hymer's dependency model (3). Japan's direct investment in the Common Market, even if unintentionally, is inevitably influenced by the motive of Euro-Japanese co-operation in industrial technology. For this reason, more so than in other regions, such as North America or Southeast Asia, the question of international adaptability is more pressing than that of international competitiveness.

Kao's localisation attempts

Now let us examine the four main aspects of Kao's localisation policy in Europe: ownership, management control, technology, and labour relations.

Localisation of ownership

Kao, having judged it impossible to localise the quality control of household products with a policy of exportation and making it a principle of company policy not to license out key chemical products or technology, decided in its international activities on a strong commitment to direct investment. For direct investment, Kao chose total ownership instead of joint ventures, whether through a new investment or by acquisition (between these two methods there was no systematic preference). The joint venture enterprise in Spain, established in 1970, later came under total ownership, and the joint venture set up in 1979 was in actual fact totally owned by Kao.

One reason for this policy was the awareness from previous experience that joint-venture ownership limits the functioning of decision making in questions of profit use, plant and equipment investment, and sales. This was stated as follows: 'Effectiveness is lost while discussions take place between joint venture partners having differing managerial cultures. An equal division of ownership would mean that we could only realise half our ideas. So we decided to continue with our chosen policy of 100 per cent ownership, which is what management à la Kao entails'.

Further, while it had been previously felt that managerial resources, such as technology, experience, human resources, and capital, had been insufficient, it was judged that these were now sufficient. Another regional factor was the fact that whereas in Asia total control had been virtually impossible for legal reasons, this was quite possible in Europe.

Localisation of managerial control

Although it is difficult to characterise the Kao management style simply, any outline would include the principles of rapid decision making, prominence given to research and development, a marketing philosophy that whatever quality improvements might be made, no changes are made to brand names, prices, or packaging, and finally the principle of in-house information sharing.

As long as these aspects are seen as essential to Kao's managerial style, attempts to localise the managerial function will meet considerable difficulties. Whereas localisation entails a large transfer of authority to local managers, it is unlikely that they would put into practice the managerial style outlined above. Rather, localisation of this aspect would probably have to be postponed until management of the local subsidiaries had reached a level of smooth running practice.

Localisation of technology

Kao had already gained experience in localising research and development facilities and production technology with the amine plant in Barcelona and with the production of surfactants. In these cases, research centres for production technology were set up in the plants, and a desire to localise was strongly present from the start. At present, the Barcelona plant supervisor is Spanish, and of the 30 to 40-strong research team, only one Japanese is stationed in the research and development division and one is employed in production technology. Further, since Barcelona is pursuing product development in line with the needs of the European market, this contributes to sales experience. It is the policy of Kao's Head Office that development of the Spanish venture be done with the Spanish system constantly in mind and that capital and technology transfer from the parent company take place only when necessary.

The localisation of research and development was a particular aim in the establishment of the research laboratory for perfumes and cosmetics set up in West Berlin in 1987. Its main aim was local research and development of products suited to local market particularities arising from conditions of climate or consumer habits. Actually, some 12 different types of products have been developed, and furthermore, a phase-two plan has been set up, including the establishment of further research centres in Dusseldorf and Paris.

In the case of West Berlin, the research staff is divided into two groups; each group consists of one Japanese researcher, one German researcher having a doctorate, two to three German laboratory assistants, and a number of German secretarial staff. As the venture is of recent date, it is on a small scale with the localisation of research staff still in its development stage. For reasons of seniority and experience, the team leaders are, in fact, Japanese. As occasion demands, extra researchers are dispatched from Japan, and regular research results are available to the research institute in Tokyo through on-line information sharing. The Head Office in Tokyo centralises authority over such administrative aspects as the setting of research targets, decisions on research planning policy, allocation of resources, and use of research results.

Localisation of labour relations

Localisation of labour relations is generally inevitable, and this is particularly so in Europe because of the strict legal limitations in operation. In Kao's case, local production is confined to Spain, where no significant problems have arisen to date because of the small scale of operations.

Conclusion

In summing up the above examination, I think we may make the following hypotheses.

If direct investment is taken to be based on some superior aspect possessed by a firm, we may suppose this superiority to be either technical or managerial. When direct investment takes place on the strength of technical superiority, one would suppose that localisation of technology would present the biggest obstacle. Where managerial superiority is the basis, then the localisation of ownership and management are the biggest problems. This is because where technical superiority is the basis of investment, it is difficult for the investor to decide on the localisation of production technology and research facilities, since these will ultimately undermine the parent company's special superiority, and where investment is based on managerial superiority, the parent company is reluctant to localise ownership and management.

An examination of Japanese firms to date will show the majority as being examples of direct investment based on technological superiority, whereas only a small number belong to the latter type of investment on the basis of managerial superiority. Kao to date has in general proceeded with direct investment on the strength of its technological superiority in either production technology or marketing. This has been true in both Southeast Asia and in Spain. However, the pattern of foreign activities from the eighties can be seen as an attempt to change to an entry strategy based on managerial superiority. This is a clear manifestation of the drive to realise the Kao style of management with its central principle of 100 per cent ownership. This is a strategic rather than an incremental style of management, inseparable from the forceful leadership practised by the company's president, Mr. Maruta.

At present, the company's local production is confined to the periphery of Europe, and it will require time to evaluate the results of the research laboratory in Berlin. However, Kao's desire to expand its local production in Europe is very strong.

Given this change in emphasis from its technological to its managerial superiority, Kao will be faced with the question of how it can adapt to the firmly rooted European managerial environment, resistant as this tends to be to efforts of Japanese firms to effect change. Kao seems to have embarked on a pioneering course which will take it off from the beaten track, down a little travelled path of uncertain issues.

Notes

In the course of preparing this paper, several interviews took place with Mr. Ikuo Nakamura, in charge of overseas activities in the presidential office of Kao. However, the author alone is responsible for compiling the present paper and for any mistakes that may have been made herein. The author gives his warmest thanks for the invaluable assistance received from Mr. Nakamura, Mr. Toshikazu Nomura, Head of the Editing Office for Company History, and to Ms. Masumi Mori, researcher at the Institute for the Business History of Japan.

(1) Cf. Raymond Vernon, *Sovereignty at Bay*, New York, 1971.

(2) It can be a counter-evidence to Trevor's thesis developed in Malcolm Trevor, *Japan's Reluctant Multinationals*, London, 1983.
(3) Robert Gilpin, *U.S. Power and the Multinational Corporation: The Political Economy of Foreign Direct Investment*, New York, 1975; Vernon, *op. cit.*; Stephen Hymer, *The International Operations of National Firms: A Study of Direct Foreign Investment*, Cambridge, Mass., 1976.

APPLICATION-ADAPTATION PROBLEMS IN JAPANESE AUTOMOBILE AND ELECTRONICS PLANTS IN THE USA

Hiroshi Itagaki
Saitama University

Introduction

Japanese manufacturing companies operating in the USA confront two types of problems: problems in application and in adaptation. To what extent can Japanese companies transplant their own production system? To what extent do they have to adapt to the American business envirionment? This paper examines these two problems by basing itself on the data collected from a 1986 field study conducted by a joint Japan-US research team and the subsequent discussions held by the group (1).

Fourteen companies from three industries were targets in our case studies: five automobile firms (from A to E), two of which were parts and components manufacturers (D and E); six home electronics appliance and components companies (from F to K), mainly colour TV and microwave oven manufacturers; and three semiconductor firms (from L to N) (see Table 1). Data and information were collected through both interviews with Japanese and American managers at these companies and plant tours with company personnel.

Major manufacturing firms have led Japan's rapid export growth, causing trade friction, and have now embarked on local production in advanced industrialised countries, especially in the USA. The competitive advantages of Japanese manufacturing firms have a great deal to do with the 'Japanese production system'. This system is characterised by a flexible operation of different parts of the organisation and a unique method of skill formation, which is sustained by a sense of participation at various operational levels, from shop-floor to engineering and marketing divisions.

The system is also based on the existence of a great number of vendors and sub-contractors, who provide leading manufacturers with

Table 1 Japanese-owned plants targeted as case studies

	Location	No. of Employees (1986)	Date of Plant Opening	Mode of Entry	Main Products
Automobile					
Company A	Tennessee	3,200	June, 1983	Startup	Small pickup trucks, passenger cars
Company B	Ohio	3,900	Nov., 1982	Startup	Passenger cars, motorcycles
Company C	California	2,500	Dec., 1984	Acquisition	Passenger cars
Company D	Tennessee	422	Feb., 1984	Startup	Air conditioners for automotive vehicles
Company E	Tennessee	131	July, 1985	Startup	Instruments for automotive vehicles
Home Electronics					
Company F	Illinois	1,340	May, 1975	Acquisition	Colour TVs, microwave ovens
Company G	Arkansas	1,550	Jan., 1977	Acquisition	Colour TVs, microwave ovens
Company H	Tennessee	847	Oct., 1979	Startup	Colour TVs, microwave ovens
Company I	Tennessee	650	Aug., 1978	Startup	Colour TVs, microwave ovens
Company J	California	570	Jan., 1979	Startup	Colour TVs
Company K	Tennessee	216	Nov., 1979	Startup	Transformers for microwave ovens
Semiconductor					
Company L	California	620	June, 1984	Startup	IC memory chips
Company M	California	200	April, 1980	Acquisition	IC memory chips
Company N	California	330	May, 1981	Startup	IC memory chips

parts and components of high quality at reasonable prices and with accurate delivery times. Trade between leading manufacturing firms and parts suppliers is often characterised by long-term and mutually evolving relationships based on technological ties rather than arm's length trade. The system has resulted in a high quality and low cost of products which meet the needs of foreign markets as well as the domestic market (2).

There is no doubt that such a production system has been created in an environment of high economic growth that has enabled corporations to maintain the so-called lifetime employment system (*shūshin koyōsei*) and the Japanese-style seniority system (*nenkō joretsusei*). These systems in turn lead to a sense of participation among the employees and the accumulation of the specific skills of those companies. Of course, many firms have developed the structure in a conscious manner and sometimes by trial and error. We may also say, however, that such a system is sustained by the fact that Japan is a relatively homogeneous and group-oriented society. These are the reasons why most Japanese manufacturing companies have engaged in export-oriented behaviour rather than one of local production in the industrialised countries that have accounted for the major portion of Japan's foreign market.

If Japanese firms fail to transplant the whole intra- and inter-company system developed in the home country into different business and cultural environments, it could result in a deterioration in quality and efficiency. Such anxieties have made Japanese companies to be very hesitant about undertaking overseas production until recently. Now, however, whether Japanese corporations like it or not, trade friction and the rapid appreciation of the yen have compelled them to embark on local production.

Working hypothesis and methodology

Our working hypothesis is that Japanese manufacturing firms inevitably face a difficult situation regarding application and adaptation in the management of their foreign production plants. In order to maintain their competitive advantages, they should apply and transplant the production system created in the home country to the greatest extent possible. However, such practices can result in serious friction in the American environment where different social and business customs exist. Japanese firms have had to and will have to adapt to the local environment to reduce this friction.

We have identified six groups of key items to analyse the extent to which Japanese companies can apply their own production systems, especially at the shop-floor level, and the extent to which they must adapt to American business society.

Group I is 'Job Organisation and Its Operation and Administration', which includes issues concerning job classification, wages, training, job rotation, promotion, and supervisors. This group is related to the core human factors of the Japanese production system. It includes the skill formation of multi-skilled operators as well as supervisors and maintenance people. Skill formation results from on-the-job training and planned job rotation. Such employees can support flexible operations. If a Japanese subsidiary in the USA has complex job classifications and rigid demarcations, it is hard to introduce the skill formation system and flexible practices developed in Japan.

Group II, 'Production Control', concerns process technology, quality control, and maintenance. In many Japanese companies, the experiences and ideas of shop-floor employees are fed back into engineering divisions, resulting in improvements in machinery and equipment, and sometimes affect the choice of equipment itself. Skilled operators on the shop floor take part in maintenance and quality control, and their know-how is accumulated in the companies to create a distinctive production control system. The practices mentioned in Group I enable the formation of this kind of production control system.

Group III, 'Sense of Participation', consists of such items as employment security, small group activities, uniforms, and open-style offices. Also, socialising within companies includes such activities as summer picnics and Christmas parties. Meetings of various kinds are another activity encouraging a sense of participation. Group III is related to the devices and ideas for fostering a cooperative atmosphere and mutual understanding that facilitate the transfer of practices developed in the home country.

We consider these three groups the application groups, that is, as factors used to evaluate the extent of application of the Japanese production system. The application groups consist of various items that are closely related to the competitive advantages of Japanese companies: to what extent their plants in the USA can transplant such practices will have a strong bearing on their competitiveness. We evaluate the extent by a five-point evaluation method. If a company gets five points with respect to some item, it means that an affiliate has introduced almost the same practices as in the Japanese plants. We must say, however, that such an evaluation method is tentative and operationally convenient. A method should be devised to evaluate the extent of both application and adaptation for each group, but this was not possible because of time limitations and the number of researchers.

Groups IV to VI relate to the extent of adaptation in our tentative methodology. The adaptation groups are composed of those items that will be favourably regarded by American society if Japanese firms adopt such practices. Or, at the very least, their adoption will mean that Japanese plants can avoid trouble with the community and local employees. Such adaptation-oriented policies may impair the efficiency of Japanese plants to a greater or lesser degree by decreasing the extent of application of the Japanese production system. According to circumstances, however, those practices can enable plants to transfer the core of the production system more smoothly by reducing friction with the local environment.

Group IV is 'Labour Relations', issues concerning the homogeneity of employees, turnover ratios, and labour unions. This group measures the willingness and intention of Japanese firms to accept the American business environment. Group V is 'Procurement of Parts and Components', namely, issues concerning local content ratios and the character of vendors. Group VI is 'Relationship between Parent and Subsidiary Companies', which concerns the proportion of expatriates, allocation of decision making between parent and subsidiary, and distribution of responsibility among Japanese and American managers. If an affiliate gets five points, that company has adapted to the American environment entirely or accepted local practices.

Overall analysis

Figure 1 shows the distribution of the firms chosen for our case study according to their average application and adaptation ratings. Generally speaking, there is a trade-off relationship between the degree of application and adaptation of each firm: that is, the higher the rating of application of a company, the lower the extent of adaptation, and vice versa. However, we should also take note of some firms whose ratings of both application and adaptation are relatively high (A, C, H, K, and J).

Furthermore, the distinctive features of each industry are clear. On the average, the automobile industry has the highest application rating of the three industries, and, moreover, in the application groups the difference between automobile companies is small. But automobile firms differ from one another in their degree of adaptation. On the

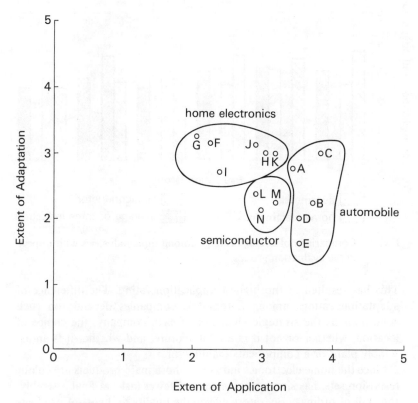

Fig. 1   Distribution of Japanese-owned firms in terms of the application and
adaptation ratings

contrary, the home electronics industry has the highest adaptation
rating on average, and the difference between the firms is insignificant,
while the degree of application in this industry is low on average but
varies considerably depending on the company. Semiconductor companies do not differ from one another in either application or adaptation ratings. The semiconductor industry appears to be located
between the automobile and home electronics industries regarding
the degree of application; on the other hand, its adaptation rating is
the lowest among the three industries (See Fig. 2).

Comparatively speaking, automobile companies have endeavored
to introduce Japanese practices of work organisation and skill formation because this industry is characterised by a complicated manufacturing process involving a great number of parts and components.

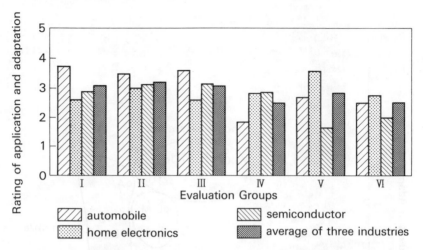

Fig. 2   Comparison of average ratings among three industries with respect
to the evaluation groups

This has resulted in the highest application rating. The difference of
adaptation ratings among automobile companies depends on such
conditions as the strategic character of each company, the choice of
location, whether or not it is a joint venture, and whether it is an assembly plant or a components manufacturer.

Since the home electronics industry, whose main products are colour
television sets, has simpler processes and fewer tasks at final assembly,
the skill of ordinary operators affects the quality and cost of products
to a lesser extent than in the automobile industry. Consequently, home
electronics companies lack an impelling incentive to introduce Japanese
practices that can invite trouble with local employees. However, management policies vary between companies that are willing to transfer
practices, including the method of skill formation of key personnel,
and those that have engaged in local production by the acquisition of
existing plants. Such a difference leads to a wider gap in the extent
of application. The above-mentioned conditions and the fact that the
home electronics industry started operations in America earlier than
the two other industries have resulted in a higher adaptation rating.

Japanese semiconductor plants in the USA rely crucially on their
parent companies for process technology as well as product technology,
and the scale of these US plants is rather small. Moreover, the quality
and cost of chips depend on the method of installing, operating, and
maintaining machinery and equipment rather than on the skill of
ordinary operators. These factors have resulted in the lowest adaptation

rating, and the reason why the extent of application of semiconductors exceeds that of the home electronics industry lies in the fact that no semiconductor firm has especially low ratings for application, unlike the home electronics industry.

Discussions of evaluation groups

Group I. Job organisation and its operation and administration. All the automobile firms have drastically simplified job classifications to a few jobs, whereas the number of job classifications in American corporations sometimes approaches one hundred. Thus, each automobile plant endeavors to train multi-skilled operators and to foster key personnel, such as supervisors, within the company by rather extended job rotation and by emphasizing the team concept. All the firms also sent hundreds of employees to Japan for training at the start of local production.

Since the basic wage rates correspond to simplified job classifications, the structure of wages takes an extremely flat and peculiar form, in which the wage rates of all workers reach the maximum level 18 months after entering the companies. Though these companies make attempts to modify the wage system structure through bonuses or encouragement of multi-skilled operators, crucial problems arise on the treatment of longer-serving workers in the future. Therefore, we can consider that such a peculiar wage system is just a tentative one designed to destroy the established work organisation in the USA.

Most of the home electronics and semiconductor companies do not have the simplified job classifications that can give rise to problems with the local employees. One of the most important reasons why complicated job classifications (which seem almost ridiculous from the Japanese viewpoint) prevail in many American companies is that workers and labour unions have backed rigid demarcations to protect their rights and to exclude the arbitrary power of foremen in the course of establishing New Deal-type of industrial relations. In fact, Company G, which has the most complicated job classification system consisting of 20 jobs in a colour TV plant, inherited from the former company, faced a serious strike when the management attempted to simplify it.

Since, as mentioned above, the skill of ordinary workers does not affect the cost and quality of products so much, many Japanese firms were hesitant to introduce practices which could result in dissatisfaction among local employees, especially in the earlier stages of manufacturing direct investment in the USA. During that period, most Japanese colour TV companies embarked on local production. Therefore, the extent of job rotation and formation of multi-skilled operators has been considerably limited.

Although both colour TV and semiconductor plants have occasionally sent core personnel and engineers to Japan, unlike automobile companies they have not adopted the practice of training a great number of employees in home plants. Even if there is no need for electronics plants to train all the workers as earnestly as in the automobile industry, it is crucial to foster core personnel in the work organisation within the plant in order to operate efficiently according to their own methods. Although many plants are eager to do so, in some cases ordinary employees are not responsive to a system that promotes them to more responsible positions, as supervisors, for example. In other cases, employees who have acquired highly developed skills often quit the firm to seek promotion in another company. Of course, there are cases like Company J where a president (Japanese) insisted that this system had worked well. It seems, however, that this was not the dominant opinion among Japanese expatriates in US plants. This poses the interesting question of whether a company can improve on the prevailing practices in a local business environment within the firm.

Group II. Production control. Manufacturing affiliates have introduced process technology and control systems basically as developed in Japan. There are some cases in which automobile companies, including both assembly firms and component manufacturers, first built and operated the equipment in Japanese plants and then shipped it to the USA and rebuilt it in US plants in order to ensure its correct functioning. Japanese firms, however, have often modified their equipment to some extent, even in cases where the machinery itself is procured from Japan. One colour TV manufacturer (Company J), in particular, was willing to localise the machinery and equipment, and American engineers planned the layout of the plant to be suitable for local employees under the direction of the Japanese president who had a background in engineering.

Semiconductor plants rely almost entirely on technology as well as equipment developed by the parent companies because of the ease with which they can analyse the causes of unusual problems.

We can say that all the Japanese subsidiaries have introduced Japanese-style production control systems insofar as they have emphasised quality control and maintenance in order to prevent defective products. They have, however, run up against a serious contradiction in that the greater the dependence on 'external' technology for the local plants —namely, technology from Japan—the harder it is to enforce the workplace-oriented method of quality control and maintenance, one of the crucial characteristics of the Japanese production system.

In relation to this point, Japanese affiliates have problems with how to motivate American engineers. The process engineering staff in the Japanese production system plays an important part in improving product quality and efficiency, although their status is lower than that of product engineers in the USA.

Group III. A sense of participation. Japanese affiliates have introduced various devices to encourage a sense of participation, to foster a cooperative atmosphere, and to facilitate mutual understanding as groundwork for transplanting Japanese-style work organisation and administration. Figure 3 demonstrates the strong correlation between Groups III and I ('Job Organisation and Its Operation and Administration'), in terms of both companies and industries.

The so-called lifetime employment system has played an important role in sustaining skill formation within companies as well as in encouraging a sense of participation among employees in Japan. However, five affiliates operating in the USA have already laid off employees. These companies consist of four home electronics companies (F, G, I, and K) and one semiconductor plant (M). Although eight affiliates, including all the automobile companies, two home electronics firms (H and J), and one semiconductor plant (N) informed their employees that they intended to avoid lay-offs as far as possible, the employment security in Japanese affiliates in America has different implications from that of firms in Japan.

Most companies have some kind of small group activities, such as Quality Control Circles and suggestion systems. While the ratio of employees involved in such programs varies from 100 per cent (namely, mandatory) to some 10 per cent, the substantial purpose of the activities lies in increasing a sense of participation and in facilitating communications between managers and workers rather than in improving product quality and productivity at the present phase. Meetings of various levels also play similar roles.

Group IV. Labour relations. As mentioned before, evaluation was made of the extent of adaptation to the American business environment by using Groups IV to VI. The companies that had higher adaptation ratings consisted of those which were on the West Coast, where ethnic backgrounds are diverse and turnover ratio higher, and those

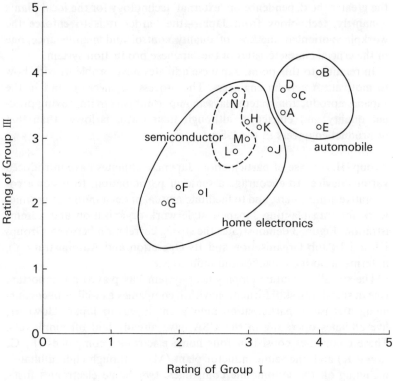

Rating of Group I

Fig. 3   Correlation between Group I and Group III

whose employees are organised by labour unions. All the automobile companies except for Company C were non-union and chose locations where the ethnic background of residents was homogeneous and/or their mobility was lower. By contrast, four electronics plants (J, L, M, and N), including three semiconductor firms, were located on the West Coast and three home electronics companies were unionised.

Group V. Procurement of parts and components. Local content differs by industry and in the automobile industry accounts for approximately 50 per cent of the total value of finished cars. Local content in colour TV sets varies from 50 to 70 per cent, depending on the sort of product and company, whereas in semiconductors local content is extremely limited. Key components procured directly or indirectly from Japan constitute one of the crucial factors in securing the product quality of all affiliates' plants.

Some Japanese managers complained about the quality and delivery of parts and components procured from local manufacturers. It seems very difficult for Japanese plants to establish a long-term and mutually evolving relationship based on technological ties with parts suppliers as in Japan. Even if a company can establish a mutual technological relationship, it is easily destroyed by the resignation of personnel in responsible positions.

From now on, however, Japanese firms must face the urgent problem of how to develop international logistics involving North America, Mexico, and Southeast Asian countries, taking cost and quality into consideration. Some companies have already developed local and international networks of component production. Company A has procured engines from its Mexican affiliate and has plans to establish an engine plant in the USA. Company B also has an engine factory near the assembly plant. Company J acquired a picture tube plant from a leading American firm in Canada, and Company I set up a picture tube plant as a joint venture with another leading US electronics manufacturer. Company F, which seems to have developed the most extended international logistics among Japanese companies, procures picture tubes from both its parent plant in Japan and a US electronics firm, cabinets from local suppliers, tuners from a Malaysian affiliate, speakers from a Taiwanese affiliate, and the chassis from a Mexican co-plant—which in turn receives the key components from Japan.

Group VI. Relationship between parent and subsidiary companies. No significant difference between automobile assembly plants and home electronics firms were found with respect to the localisation of managers and decision making, except for the rate of Japanese expatriates, which varies from 0.4 to 4.6 per cent. However, one automobile (A) and one electronics (F) company have American presidents, and another colour TV plant (G) is a joint venture between a Japanese electronics enterprise and a leading American retail merchandiser. Also, one automobile plant (C) is a joint venture between leading Japanese and American automobile firms. The extent of adaptation of automobile component and semiconductor plants is lower because of the small size of the operation and technological dependence on parent companies.

Conclusion

We can divide Japanese manufacturing affiliates operating in the USA into three groups. The first group consists of several automobile companies (B, D, and E), and it has a higher application rating and lower adaptation rating. These companies seem to attain efficient production now, but may face problems in dealing with friction and tension among employees caused by an application-oriented management.

The second group consists of several automobile and electronics companies (A, C, H, and J) that have higher ratings for both application and adaptation. These firms seem to be able to introduce some aspects of the Japanese production system smoothly, owing to the deliberate localisation of management resources. In the event that they can transplant the rational core of the Japanese production system modified for a different business environment—separated from its Japanese cultural soil—we can be optimistic about the transferability of Japanese-style management. In any case, these companies pose the interesting and critical question of whether such adaptation-oriented practices result in sacrificing the application aspect or rather in sustaining it.

Third is the group of the companies including a few electronics plants (F and G) that are evaluated as low in application and high in adaptation. The competitive advantages of this group rely on their networks of international production or established distribution channels as well as the technology of the parent companies and the reliability of key components from Japan.

To our regret, we could not collect enough data to examine to what extent the application- and adaptation-oriented practices influence a plant's performance with respect to labour efficiency (productivity) and product quality. Almost all the managers of Japanese affiliates stated that besides productivity, the product quality of US plants was nearly the same as that in Japan. However, we should take into account the limited size of local production which enables managers to implement various practices, which in turn lead to good performance. Furthermore, the affiliates attach great importance to product quality, even if it means sacrificing productivity to some extent.

From now on, however, each plant will be required to become a profit center to a greater or lesser degree in consequence of the expansion of manufacturing units and the extension of individual operations. Under such cirumstances, if the affiliates fail to operate their production systems, including industrial relations, in accordance with local conditions, more fundamental cultural friction can result. Balancing the relationship between application and adaptation will increasingly become a crucial problem for Japanese subsidiaries.

We can also say, however, that the experiences gained from local production in quite different business situations will become valuable managerial resources for Japanese companies' headquarters. In the future, Japanese multinational enterprises may be staffed with a generation 'foreign' to Japanese-style management. This new generation, bred in a rapidly changing environment, may have a different sense of values and behave in a different way from its predecessors.

Notes

(1) In September 1986, the Japanese Multinational Research Enterprise Group, headed by Professor Tetsuo Abo at the Institute of Social Science, University of Tokyo, conducted a field study on Japanese automobile and electronics companies operating in the USA. This group is a Japan-US joint research team, and the field study was carried out by five of the group members, including two US-based scholars, Abo, and myself. This project was given a grant-in-aid by the Toyota Foundation.

For a more detailed discussion, see Abo Tetsuo, ed., *Nihon Kigyō no Amerika Genchi Seisan: Jidōsha to Denki; Nihonteki Keiei no 'Tekiyō' to 'Tekiō'* (Local production of Japanese enterprises: Automobiles and electronics; 'Application' and 'adaptation' of Japanese-style management), Tōyō Keizai Shinpōsha, 1988.

(2) For a discussion on the Japanese production system, see, for example, Monden Yasuhiro, *Toyota Production System: Practical Approach to Production Management*, Industrial Engineering and Management Press, 1983; Urabe Kuniyoshi, *Nihonteki Keiei wa Shinka Suru* (Japanese-style management is evolving), Chūō Keizaisha, 1984.

A COMPARATIVE STUDY OF INTERNATIONAL SUBCONTRACTING SYSTEMS: THE AUTOMOTIVE PARTS INDUSTRIES OF THE USA, THE UK, FRANCE, AND JAPAN

Masayoshi Ikeda
Chūō University

Introduction

As a result of Japan's trade surplus, which has continued to increase over the past several years, the serious trade frictions between Japan and its major trading partners, the US and European countries, has worsened. The trade surplus has prompted the sharp appreciation of the yen, causing the country's major export industries, such as the automobile and electrical appliance industries, to shift their production bases overseas.

Recently, there has been increased debate on the 'Japanese-style management' which forms the basis of the international competitiveness of Japanese companies. However, the majority of the export items which are rapidly increasing in volume are such items as electrical goods and automobiles, which come from machine assembly industries. Therefore, when we turn our attention to the fact that such machine assembly industries are supported by a wide range of medium and small subcontracting companies, there is some doubt as to whether the competitiveness achieved by Japan's exporting industries is simply a matter of the management of the large companies.

It is not just the productivity and management systems of large companies which produce fully assembled products which sustain the export competitiveness of Japan's assembly industries. Rather, it can be attributed to the productivity of the component manufacturers and subcontractors which support these companies, namely, the production sub-system, and it is the existence of this sub-system which has formed the strong base of the international competitiveness of Japan's assembly industries. Using the automobile industry as an example, this paper will illustrate the characteristics of the structure of the production sub-systems common to Japan's assembly industries.

Automobile production systems: Japan, the USA, and Europe

As has been shown by statistical data available up until now, the ratio of dependence on outside production by manufacturers of fully assembled products in the Japanese automobile industry is markedly higher than that of their counterparts in the USA and European countries. For example, the dependence ratio for subcontracting production for Toyota, Nissan, and other Japanese automobile producers is around the 75 per cent level, whereas in the USA and in Europe it is only 50 per cent at most.

The Japanese automobile industry does not have a high ratio of dependence on subcontracting in terms of quantity alone. The parts manufacturers and subcontractors which are used are organized into a vertical tier-shaped system, and the production system which has been made in this way features an exceedingly high level of efficiency in terms of quality as well. Figure 1 shows the differences in production structures between the automobile manufacturing industries in Japan and the USA. In the case of Japan, a vertical pyramid-shaped structure is formed with the fully assembled automobile manufacturers at the top and the first-, second-, and third-tier subcontracting companies placed beneath them in descending order. Whereas the production system adopted by the first-tier subcontractors involves the supply of unit parts, such as engine parts, electrical parts, and car-body parts, to the auto producers, the second- and third-tier subcontractors placed below either supply parts required for the manufacture of unit parts or engage in the machining process or partial assembly. However, over the past ten years the first-tier subcontractors have diversified their operations so that they have now become specialist parts manufacturers, thus making it more appropriate to call them first tier parts manufacturers.

The further the distance between the auto producers at the top and the second and third tier companies below, the smaller the size of operations and the lower the technical level of production of the lower tiers. However, as in the case of the first subcontractors, the second and third subcontracting companies are also organised into cooperative associations which have direct links with the parent companies which form the nucleus of the associations. Through this organisation the stratified structure becomes wider the nearer it gets to the bottom. And the lower down this tier-shaped structure, the greater the extent to which the parent companies function as a cushion. The whole of this deep cushion-like structure is utilized to the maximum in order

Structure for Company A in Japan   Structure for Company B in US

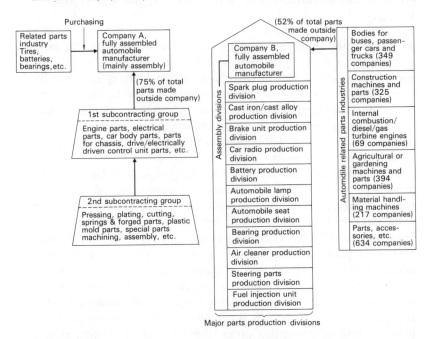

Major parts production divisions

Fig. 1   Comparison of automobile manufacture structures

Source: "Report on the Roles Played by Small and Medium Enterprises in Production Specialization" by the Small and Medium Enterprise Agency commissioned in January 1980 by the Small and Medium Enterprise Research Center.

Notes: 1. Subcontracting rate (1978)

$$= \frac{\text{purchasing costs} + \text{subcontracting (incl. processing) costs}}{\text{total production costs}} \times 100$$

2. Among the first subcontracting enterprises, the parent enterprise is not necessarily one company.

to strengthen the international competitiveness of the auto producers at the top of the pyramid.

But in comparison with the above, as shown in Figure 1, automobile producers in the USA have a strong tendency to produce parts in-house by having separate assembly divisions. At the same time, they purchase a large number of parts from component manufacturers and subcontractors. Taking the example of the largest American auto producer, General Motors, and looking at the company as a whole, we find that in the area of parts and services there are as many as 10,024 suppliers and subcontractors which sell directly to GM. A breakdown reveals that there are, for example, 700 companies which supply a truck assembly plant which has a GM division, and there are some 1,600 suppliers which work for the Orion plant where Cadillacs and Buicks are assembled. Also, as of 1986, France's Renault Corporation had dealings with some 1,400 parts manufacturers and subcontracting companies. In contrast to this, in 1965 West Germany's Daimler-Benz had dealings with as many as 10,084 subcontractors.

The structural pattern for American and European auto manufacturers is one in which a very large number of subcontractors are used despite the low ratio of dependence on outside production. In contrast to this is the Japanese pattern where automobile manufacturers are highly dependent on subcontracting, but use only a few subcontracting companies. In the case of Japan, because the subcontracting companies are placed vertically in separate tiers, the auto producers at the top only directly manage the highest level first subcontractors, and they have the advantage of being able to control through them the subcontracting companies placed at all the levels below. This is quite different from the situation in the USA and Europe where the subcontractors are not organized in any fashion and the auto producers must deal directly with all the parts manufacturers and subcontractors whose services they require. Also, the situation is such that they have no influence whatsoever over the subcontractors with whom they do not deal directly.

But just why has it been possible for the Japanese auto-producing companies to form this sort of vertical subcontracting structure? To proceed directly to answer this question, it is due to the existence of sub-assembly contracting companies unique to Japan which fulfil the role of bonding the links in the subcontracting tiers. In Japan, unlike in other countries, it is common practice for the operations of subcontractors to be aimed exclusively at one parent company. Because of this, the manufacturers of finished products have the production lines which they themselves look after center on the final assembly process, thus making it possible to reduce the percentage of in-house production to an extremely low level. Also, because the sub-assembly process is an extremely labor-intensive process, the producers of finished products leave the process up to assembly subcontractors, whereby they conserve labour and make it possible to make extensive use of the low wages of subcontracting companies.

Below, specific examples shall be used to examine the differences between the sub-assembly processes within the production systems in Japan and Europe. They will also illustrate the special characteristics of Japan's sub-assembly subcontracting companies.

A comparison of the production systems

The distinguishing features of the Japanese subcontracting system will be shown by way of the following comparison of the production systems for the automotive electrical parts industries in Japan, France, the UK, and West Germany.

Case study I: a French electrical parts manufacturer

In 1977, the automotive electrical parts manufacture Company P joined the VALEO group, which is led by the Renault Corporation, and today its operations have been reorganised and its scale of production reduced. In 1977, the company produced alternators (generators), starters, wiper motors, ignition coils, and distributors and carried a workforce of 6,000. But today, production is restricted to alternators and starters, and the number of employees has been reduced to 3,600.

During this period, the proportion of turnover represented by in-house production dropped from 60 to 50 per cent, while the ratio of dependence on outside production increased from 10 to 50 per cent. (It is assumed, however, that outside production includes the cost of materials.) A more detailed look at this change in production shows that in-house production for the machining process has been reduced considerably. In-house production for the casting and plastic processes has been halted altogether, and it has been taken over by outside production. However, the *bobinage* process and the final assembly process are undertaken in-house, as before.

Figure 2 provides a detailed diagram of the components of the alternator which are produced outside. As the illustration shows, in France outside production takes place for the machining and casting processes, but sub-assembly processes, such as the *bobinage* and the rotor assembly processes, are basically carried out through in-house production. In the case of the *bobinage* for the rotor, which is the most labor-intensive process, although technological advances have led to the development of a semi-automated winding machine which has raised productivity considerably, in the factory there were quite a number of female workers who each operate two semi-automated machines.

Case study II: a British electrical parts manufacturer

The British Company L is part of a huge automotive parts manufacturing group and is involved in the production of electrical parts, instruments, and lighting lamps. Since the oil crisis, Company L has let go a large number of workers so that its workforce, which once stood at 20,000, has been significantly reduced and today stands at 7,300. The number of workers employed at the plants manufacturing alternators and starters is 1,700, with 600 workers engaged in alternator and starter production. The alternators and starters which are produced in the plant are basically produced in-house, with the ratio for outside production standing between the 15–20 per cent mark. (This, however, excludes the cost of materials purchased by the plant. If the cost of purchasing materials were to be included, outside production would rise to around the 40 per cent level.) It is of particular interest that in this case the ratio of in-house production is higher than that of the French company.

For instance, the ratio of in-house production for the armature, which is the most labor-intensive part of the alternator, is between 80–85 per cent, and the *bobinage* process, which is the main sub-assembly process, is carried out entirely within the plant by female assembly workers. Also, the machining for shafts is carried out by using a large NC (numerically controlled) lathe. Consequently, the processes which are left up to outside companies are those for very small parts, such as small screws and cast and plastic parts. (The outside companies include some which are affiliated with Company L.)

However, in Company L there are seven different types of starters which are divided further into some 300 different varieties. The average production lot is 300 units, showing a move towards wide-variety, small-lot production. Because of this, the time required for set-up becomes lost time. However, management is well aware of the fact that by adopting a production system for complete in-house manufacture a decrease in efficiency is unavoidable, and it is planning to set the ratio for in-house and outside production at 50:50 in the future. Work has apparently already begun on the reorganization of its subcontracting companies.

Case study III: an American electrical parts manufacturer

D.R. Plant is a division of GM, America's largest automobile manufacturer, and as such it is different from the independent type of automotive parts manufacturers which have been looked at so far. During the first half of the 1970s its factories were concentrated in Indiana, but today they have been dispersed so that they are found in Georgia and Mexico. Also, as a result of the introduction of new technology, the company's workforce has been reduced to 9,000. Today, there are

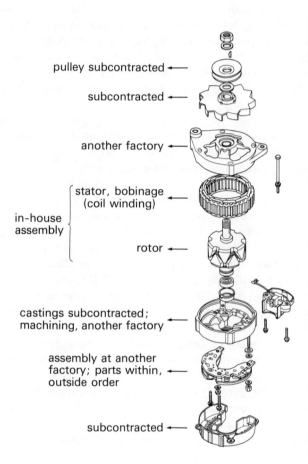

pulley subcontracted

subcontracted

another factory

stator, bobinage
(coil winding)

in-house
assembly

rotor

castings subcontracted;
machining, another factory

assembly at another
factory; parts within,
outside order

subcontracted

Fig. 2   Division of in-house and outside production at alternators at P Company of France

12 plants in Indiana, and out of this number, 7 are involved in manu-facturing.

Let us now take a look at the situation in Plant 11 (produces alter-nators and vacuum actuators), which has been included in the current survey. At the plant, 900 employees are employed on an hourly wage basis, and 80 are paid annual salaries. The plant produces the latest types of machinery, and there are two production lines. One line pro-duces 9,000 units per day, with the daily total output of alternators being between 17,000 to 18,000 units.

An examination of the ratios of outside and in-house production for the alternators shows that among the 47 parts, only 5 very small parts, such as slippings, bearing retainers, and battery terminals, are produced outside. Of course, the sub-assembly processes, such as the *bobinage* process, are carried out entirely within the plant. Although it is said that outside production makes up 50 per cent of the costs, as this in-cludes all of the materials which are used within the plant, this figure would be no more than 10–15 per cent if these material costs were ex-cluded.

Parts are purchased from 16 companies, the majority of which are situated less than 250 miles away from the plant. Although the size of the workforces of these companies varies considerably, the average size is between 150 and 250 employees. There are 6 to 8 companies which supply such materials as copper, steel, and plastic. Although as a general rule the parts are manufactured in accordance with specifica-tions which have been provided, the battery terminator has been produced through joint development.

Case study IV: a Japanese electrical parts manufacturer

Company Z is a typical Japanese general electrical machinery and appliance manufacturer. Its five plants have a combined workforce of just less than 5,000, and they produce electrical parts for automo-biles, such as alternators, starters, carburettors, air conditioners, and electronic parts. By comparison with the French, British, and American electrical parts plants already examined, the five plants are noticeable for their high ratio of dependence on outside production.

Plant S and the group of subcontracting companies which are closely linked to it in respect to production belong to a cooperative association, the total membership of which is approximately 70 companies. Among this number there are about ten large subcontractors which manufac-ture the same finished products as the parent company. These products include alternators, starters, and carburettors. Companies which pro-

duce finished products under the brand of the other company are referred to as Original Equipment Manufacturing companies. The parent
company has provided much in the way of guidance in regard to technology and management in order for these companies to reach a level
where they were able to undertake OEM. An example of the efforts
made by the parent company is the formation of a study group in the
1960s which has continued to meet regularly once a month.

A look at the division of production in regard to finished product
production between the parent company and the large subcontracting
companies shows that the parent company looks after mass-produced
products and newly developed products, and the subcontracting companies produce one third of the total output for alternators and starters. At the same time, because the subcontractors undertake a wide
range of processing and assembling, such as the processes for cast and
forged parts, plastic parts, shafts, and also armature assembly and rotor
winding, the ratio of dependence on outside production is very much
higher here than it is in the case of the electrical parts manufacturers
in Europe and the USA. For example, if, as in the case of the American
and British examples, the costs of purchasing materials were also included, the dependence ratio would be in the order of somewhere between 70–80 per cent.

As we have already seen, the European and American electrical parts
manufacturers are unable to have sub-assembly processes, such as
coil winding, performed outside and so undertake the processes in-
house. This is in contrast to the case of Company Z and Plant S, which
have had such processes undertaken by subcontracting companies
beginning not long after the end of the Second World War. Moreover,
since about 1965 these subcontractors engaged in the winding process
have gradually received assembly know-how from the parent plant
and, while it is large-variety small-lot production, have become fully
engaged in the production of finished products.

Table 1 provides an outline of the activities of some Japanese subcontracting companies which are involved in the production of finished
products in this way. As is shown in the table, Companies A, B, and
C have no capital relationship whatsoever with the parent plant.
However, all three companies are tied exclusively to the parent company S Plant on which they are 100 per cent dependent, and it might
be even more appropriate to call them branch plants.

Although most of the parts required for assembly are supplied to
the plants by the parent plant, products which are not mass produced
and those which are made through sub-assembly processes, such as
armatures, stator cores, and the winding of rotors, are undertaken in-

Table 1   Subcontracting enterprises assembling finished products in three Japanese companies

	Company A	Company B	Company C
Finished products	Starters	Alternators	Alternators
Capital relationship	None	None	None
Ratio of dependence of sales to S Plant of Z company	100%	100%	100%
Employees (head office factory)	75 (50 men, 25 women)	140 (70 men, 70 women)	150 (70 men, 80 women)
Daily production of finished products (est.)	900/day	2,000/day	1,500/day
Sources of parts supply	Armatures: Mass-produced products supplied by parent factory Not mass-produced 4 models, in-house assembly 200/day Shafts, commutators, etc. Supplied by parent factory	Welding of stator cores: Mass produced products, in-house assembly Not mass-produced products, piecework assembly Winding of rotors: in-house assembly Aluminum diecast, rotor core, etc.: Supplied by parent factory	Welding of stator cores: Mass-produced products, in-house assembly Not mass-produced products, piecework assembly Winding of rotors: in-house assembly Aluminum diecast, rotor core, etc.: Supplied by parent factory
Secondary subcontracting enterprises	Assembly and machining of field coils: 16 enterprises, of which 70 jobs done as piecework and 30 sub-subcontracted as piecework	Assembly of stator core windings: 6 enterprises, piecework; Machining done by 1 enterprise	Forming and finishing of stator core windings: 10 enterprises, piecework; Machining done by 1 enterprise

Table 1 (contd)

	Company A	Company B	Company C
Production lot of finished products	3 starter assembly lines: 1. 8 models/ line, 3–4 job changes/day 2. 26 models/ line, 4–5 job changes/day 3. line assembly not by division of labour but manually by 2 men, 3 models/ day	2 alternator assembly lines: 75 alternator models, of which 15–20 models of comparatively large lots	2 alternator assembly lines: 10 alternator models, 4 job changes/line/ day. Average production lot, 300–2,000 month

house. Also, through this sub-assembly process some of the second tier, subcontracting companies (on the basis that Company Z's S Plant is a first-tier subcontractor for an automobile manufacturer) have in creased their homework activities. In other words, these second tier companies (sub-assembly subcontractors) form the links between the first and third tiers, illustrating the complexity of the Japanese stratified structure.

Summary of the case studies

A comparative study of the differences in production systems in Japan, Europe, and the USA has been presented above using the example of the manufacture of electrical parts. From what we have seen, in the USA and Europe there appears to be no sub-assembly subcontracting companies involved in the electrical parts sector. However, as a few examples are to be found in the area of electrical home appliances and a few automobile parts industries, these have been used as a basis for a comparison of the characteristics of Japanese and European sub-assembly subcontracting companies as shown in Table 2.

As can be seen from this table, in Europe the producers of finished products undertake the main parts of the assembly processes, and a small amount of supplementary work is given to sub-assembly subcontractors outside. In sharp contrast to this sort of production system is the Japanese production system, where the producers of finished

Table 2 Japanese and European sub-assembling subcontractors

	Europe	Japan
Number of subcontractors	Few	A large number, in multi-tiered structure
Works commissioned	Mostly over 10 customers (diversified)	Mostly a single, specific customer (exclusive)
Transactions		
Price	Relatively high	Relatively low
Quality	High defect ratio	Defect ratio of 1% or less
Delivery	Irregular	In most cases, daily
Technical transfer	Rare	Frequent
Adaptability to small-lot production of many different items	Little	Great (shift from sub-assembly towards assembly of finished goods under OEM contracts becoming more evident)

products undertake only the final stages of assembly and depend upon subcontracting companies for the bulk of the sub-assembly processes.

What is more, in Europe and the USA there is a very clear line of demarcation for the division of labour between finished product manufacturers and subcontractors. This also contrasts with the situation in Japan where there is a fair degree of flexibility between the two and the subcontracting companies absorb production know-how from the parent company, expand their production lines progressively and become a mini parent company. In particular, the period of slow growth, which was caused by the oil crisis and the ensuing production trend towards variety small-lot production, was accompanied by a marked increase in the growth of subcontracting companies.

Here I would like to take a look at the changes in the management structure of these subcontractors which were able to expand their production lines. But it should be added that as no appropriate examples were to be found in the area of automotive parts, the example which has been chosen here is that of a company involved in the manufacture of electronic machinery for industrial use.

Figure 3 shows the production processes and the change in production items for M Electric (which has a workforce of 180 employees) which is a subcontracting company for F Electric, which produces electronic machinery and equipment for industrial use. The illustration shows that in 1966, in response to a request from its parent company, M Electric changed the bulk of its production to the unit assembly of

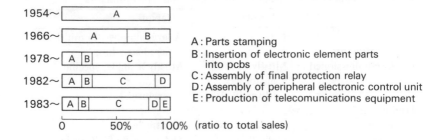

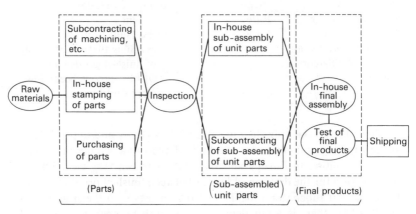

Fig. 3   Chronological changes of main products and the production process of M Electric

printed circuit boards. As a result, a change took place in the composition of its workforce so that the former concentration on skilled male workers was replaced mainly by unskilled female workers, causing a significant change in productivity.

Since the latter half of the 1970s, the parent company, F Electric, has expanded its scope of production from heavy electrical machinery to light electrical machinery. This shift to wide-variety small-lot production has been accompanied by a growing trend towards having some of the production processes for finished products entrusted to sub-assembly subcontracting companies. As part of these moves, M Electric has been successively expanding its scope of production since 1978 to include the manufacture of relays, electronic control peripheral machinery, and communications machinery. During this period, not only was M Electric provided with extensive assembly know-how for these finished products by F Electric, but also the necessary testing and trial machinery and equipment for this was either lent to M Electric by F Electric or was developed jointly by the two companies. The production management for this was also accumulated under the direction of the parent company.

As can be seen in Figure 3, as a result of M Electric's changeover from assembling parts to assembling finished products, the structure of the production processes have become much more complicated. In particular, M Electric's use of outside production expanded from its former use of machining process subcontractors to include subcontractors to undertake the assembly of unit parts, raising the number of its subcontracting companies to 40. As it is quite conceivable that the assembly processing subcontractors which M Electric uses themselves use subcontracting companies for the machining process, this has probably resulted in the tier-like structure of the subcontracting companies having become even more complex. In this way, since the mid 1970s the Japanese system of the division of labour among subcontracting companies has become more complex along with the trend towards variety small-lot production and the shortening of the production cycle. Also, the increased complexity of the subcontracting division of labour system has contributed to the increased international competitiveness of Japanese industries today.

Conclusion

Let us now look at whether it is possible for the Japanese type of subcontracting system, which can be seen as unique when viewed from an international perspective, to be transferred to the USA and European countries in the future. As the trade frictions between Japan and Europe and the USA worsens, there is increasing interest on the part of the Europeans and Americans in the Japanese style of management for the automobile and electrical appliance industries, the bases of which are formed by the Japanese subcontracting system. From this arises the question of whether it is possible to transfer the Japanese system, which constitutes an important part of its style of management, to Europe and the USA. This interest does not come simply from just the European and American sides, but Japanese companies which are involved in the automobile, colour television, and VTR industries overseas have also been displaying a keen interest in this system.

But what conditions are required for the transfer of the Japanese subcontracting system to Europe and the USA? As has already been illustrated, Japanese sub-assembly subcontracting companies have been able to expand their production in response to requests from the parent company because the second- and third-tier subcontractors produce exclusively for the parent company, and, while the production processes are conducted outside, they work as one in synchronisation as exemplified by the processes which are interlinked with the parent company. In order to make this high degree of exclusivity possible, the parent companies also consider their own functions in the branching out of production, provide the subcontracting companies with their manufacturing know-how, and also provide management skills to make linked and synchronised production possible.

From the perspective of the subcontracting companies, because the parent company provides them with a function in its expanded production and gives them long-term orders, they adapt their production processes to the parent company's specifications, and they are able to arrange their plant and equipment so that it also meets the needs of the parent company as much as possible. One example of this sort of equipment, which can be said to be unique to Japan, is the simple round-shaped belt conveyor which has become most common among Japanese subcontracting companies, but which is not to be found anywhere in Europe or the USA. Such moves to specialise in this way are not simply restricted to machinery and equipment as the short-time delivery, or *kanban*, system has also been widely adopted.

Because the assembly subcontracting companies are strengthening their function of serving as separate production branches for the parent company in this way, the parent company is able to transfer all its production and management know-how to the subcontracting companies at intermittent periods. What is more, even if changes occur in production, it does not mean that the subcontracting companies will be discarded. Instead, they will be used in a different area of production in line with the parent company's continued policy of long-term relationship.

If a similar situation to the above were to be planned, even if there were some sub-assembly subcontractors in Europe and the USA, it is clear that it would be of a completely different type from the Japanese situation. If attempts were made in Europe and the US to use subcontractors as in Japan, it would be necessary for the parent company to take positive steps to foster subcontracting companies which would specialise in production for them. This by no means is easy to achieve, all the more since cultural differences also come into play here.

However, when the American automobile industry was surveyed last spring, it was found that GM, Ford, and Chrysler had started to change over to outside production from their former systems of mainly in-house production. In particular, a staff member of GM's purchasing division stressed that they were 'in the process of making a tier structure', thus illustrating that the automobile producers are reorganising and selecting with emphasis on parts manufacturers which are strong in the area of development. In other words, the American supplier subcontracting system is fast approaching the Japanese-style system.

Also of most interest was that since the beginning of the 1970s, a division of GM, Packard Electric, which had been manufacturing wire harnesses in-house, has been setting up its own integrated suppliers. This has resulted in a dramatic increase in the company's workforce, from 200 employees in the early 1970s to 7,000 in 1987. On top of this, Packard Electric has introduced the just-in-time system for its specialist sub-assembly subcontractors and is strengthening the linkage in production.

In addition to this, a number of Japanese companies which have established operations in the USA and Europe have adopted the policy of fostering subcontracting companies by lending machinery and equipment and providing technical know-how to a selected number of their subcontractors. If those on the subcontracting side come to realize that by strengthening their links with the parent company it is possible to increase their profitability, a move in the direction of exclusive production is not necessarily out of the question.

In all events, because this is a problem which involves social structural and cultural differences, it cannot be solved easily. However, there is no doubt that from now on in the American automobile industry in particular, there will be an even greater trend towards the Japanese-style use of outside production.

A PROPOSAL FOR TRANSFERRING A JAPANESE MANAGEMENT SYSTEM OVERSEAS: APPLYING THE INFORMATION-SHARING SYSTEM APPROACH IN THE UK

Masaru Sakuma
Kanagawa University

Introduction

This study intends principally to identify common factors in the Japanese management system and to establish a theory of management system that can be applied to both Japanese management and foreign management overseas. The study of how such a system can be transferred to management in other countries has become an increasingly important issue, considering the scale of Japanese interna tional investment and the development of Japanese multinational management.

The Information-Sharing System (ISS) approach is one example of a multiple strategy adopted at one time or another, depending on the nature of the organization, its technology, its people, and its goals and priorities. It is an approach inherent to Japanese management practices. The ISS includes sharing of information concerning daily tasks and operations; managerial information, including profit and loss conditions; and a share in the authority to conduct business. It is information the management shares with its rank and file to define company goals and the benefits the workers can gain therefrom.

ISS cannot function only by itself; instead, it functions when it is implemented within the framework of human resource management (HRM). The ISS approach can function effectively to help develop employees' potential in a systematic as well as a long-term manner; as a result, group cohesiveness and cooperation would be fostered rather than conflicts brought on by the system of trade unionism.

The purpose of the ISS approach is to encourage employees to remain within an organisation over a long period of time. To this end, the ISS approach is intended to create positive attitudes, values, and, as a result, performance levels in the workplace. The objective is to develop a climate of trust in an organisation, and the notion of team spirit should be pervasive within any organisation which has implemented this approach.

The concept of ISS is to lead and motivate employees so that all group members share the consequence of group performance. In other words, peer pressure is on an individual to contribute efficiently to group performance, and such pressure becomes an important mechanism of control.

Framework of the ISS approach

A model of the Japanese management system based on (i) fairly universal elements suitable for human resource management and (ii) the concept of Information Sharing System will be explored. Its framework is illustrated in Figure 1. The ISS approach will be effective in highlighting the full relationship between the human resource management practices observed in Japan and positive work outcomes, such as commitment and productivity. Also, interconnection between the human resource management practices and the significant organizational outcomes will be clarified. In addition, the integration of policy and strategies which are implemented by ISS instruments will be reviewed.

Pucik and Hatvany (1983) explain that positive employee commitment in organizations, which emanate from a complex set of behavioural patterns, refer in a limited manner to a specific culture. Such commitment as well as integrated management practices, particularly information-sharing policy and strategies, promote the achievement of corporate objectives, that is, the managerial infrastructure.

A study of a Japanese multinational in the UK

The experimental research on the applicability of the hypothesis (ISS approach) to Japanese multinational management in the UK was carried out in 1985, 1986, and 1987. Five companies which have been manufacturing colour televisions for the past two to six years were selected as case studies (Table 1). We sought to examine (1) whether any aspects of ISS are implemented in daily operations; (2) reasons they have introduced such aspects and the development process; (3) any difficulties they have had and how they have overcome

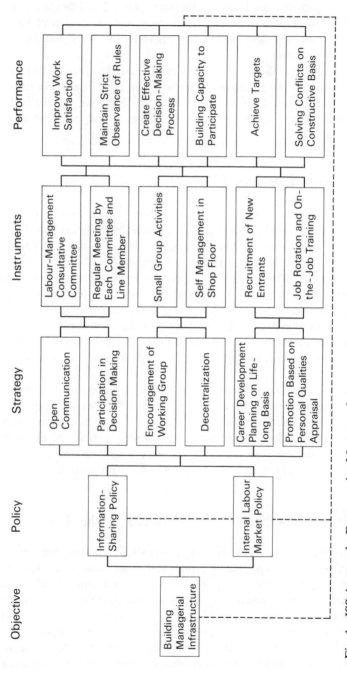

Fig. 1 ISS Approach: Framework of Japanese human resource management

Source: Developed from Pucik, V. and Hatvany, N. (1983) with suggestions also from Prof. K. Thurley, London School of Economics, and Prof. R. Cole, University of Michigan.

Table 1   General information of the five companies in the UK

	Company				
	A	B	C	D	E
Establishment	1981	1982	1976	1979	1984
Managing Director	English	Japanese	Japanese	Japanese	Japanese
Employees	450	300	620	500	780
(1984 total)					
Non-manual	80	50	185	50	240
Manual	370	250	435	450	540
CTV	310	200	400	300	540
VTR	60	50	35	150	–
Annual Production					
Units of CTVs	145,000	125,000	160,000	62,000	360,000
(1983)					
Trade Union	EETPU	EETPU	GMBATU	non-union	EETPU
Union	100%	98%	100%		60%
Membership	(closed	(open	(closed	n.a.	(open
	shop)	shop)	shop)		shop)

Notes: EETPU: Electrical Electronic Telecommunication and Plumbing Union
GMBATU: General Municipal & Boilermakers' & Allied Trade Union
CTV: Color television
VTR: Video tape-recorder

them; and (4) any other measures except aspects of ISS they think they need, and the reasons.

Methodology

(1) To select five Japanese companies operating in the UK that have had a long and rich experience (successful or unsuccessful cases) of management in the UK, and the common factors that Japanese management overseas faces in such difficulties that they have had.
(2) To gather secondary data concerning these in the UK.
(3) To visit their factories in the UK and to interview management staff, both Japanese and local.
(4) To visit their headquarters to elucidate the characteristics of their strategy of international operations particularly, of Human Resources Management for both their own staff and for local employees.

Survey results

Questionnaires were prepared to survey various aspects of the five companies: worker behaviour; the existence and regularity of meetings; initiative and responsibilities; recruiting, job rotation, and training. Evaluation scores were given, with four for the highest performance and one for the lowest. Thus, the maximum total score in the six categories surveyed was 24. (See Appendices 1 and 2 for complete survey and scores obtained.)

Those Japanese companies which have operated more than five years have already established their own systems and implemented ISS instruments. Small group activities and motivating employees' initiative and responsibilities in the workplace will require a longer time than expected to implement, since the local employees are not familiar with them. As a result, it will take time to upgrade the score of these ISS instruments. Regular meetings by each committee and line member as well as policy meetings are regularly held. This means that regular meetings are implemented to improve communication between management and employees, and meetings are recognized as being crucial for the proper functioning of the information-sharing system. As far as Co. E is concerned, it has improved its ISS score from 14 to 19 within one year. As far as Co. A is concerned, the turnover ratio and absenteeism of non-manual workers has declined. In the case of Co. A, the president is local, and employees can work towards the goal of being promoted to this position. The manual workers of all five companies have improved the scores of absenteeism and turnover ratio (Tables 2 and 3).

These ISS instruments are held on a daily operational basis. The findings that were obtained from the five Japanese companies in the UK seem to show rather limited practices; however, those figures

Table 2   ISS score and turnover ratio

	ISS score		Non-manual workers (%)		Manual workers (%)	
	1984	1987	1984	1987	1984	1987
Co. A	21	21	9	4	18	15
Co. B	19	20	8	9	18	17
Co. C	17	18	10	13	22	20
Co. D	14	16	10	15	19	20
Co. E (1985)	13	17	18	10	24	18

Table 3   ISS score and absenteeism

	ISS Score		Non-Manual workers (%)		Manual workers (%)	
	1984	1987	1984	1987	1984	1987
Co. A	21	21	0.70	0.50	4.00	3.10
Co. B	19	20	0.75	1.00	2.72	3.00
Co. C	17	18	2.20	1.80	5.10	4.50
Co. D	14	16	4.10	3.50	4.80	3.80
Co. E	13	17	6.00	4.00	8.00	5.00

illustrate the framework of our further study by which the ISS Approach will be applied to over thirty Japanese companies in other countries, including the USA.

Application of the ISS approach

The business environment towards Japanese ventures overseas is becoming more hostile as the recent trade conflicts between Japan and other major industrial countries worsen. One of the strategies that Japanese management has to adopt in order to overcome such conflicts is to develop international operations, particularly to increase direct investment in overseas markets. Facility in communications in English makes the UK one of the most important countries for their international management.

One practical business strategy which may be used to overcome the hostile business environment is to use local resources extensively, particularly human resources, in overseas plants. The UK workers are appreciated for better communications than those in countries where English is not spoken. The crucial variable for establishing such international business strategies center around the selection of management style and policy towards labour unions, and the application of the ISS approach may prove quite effective in these two areas.

Selection of management style

Open-style management. One of the first steps that needs to be taken to improve manager-subordinate relations in an organization is to foster open communications among all levels of employees. The term 'open communications' as used in this paper is based upon many of the principles advanced in Likert's theory of management (System 4 theory). This ISS strategy can be a practical method that management may use to implement many of Likert's ideas in the daily operations of an organization.

No lay-off policy. To help create an atmosphere of trust among the employees of an organisation, management, when hiring, should look upon each new employee as a long-term commitment. Although not required by law, Japanese management is culturally very concerned about employment continuity, which means a lifetime job commitment to an employee on the part of the firm. Employment maintenance is crucial to the effective development of the ISS Approach.

No Japanese company overseas, including the five companies surveyed, has ever made a lifetime employment commitment in written form to its employees. However, they have made such commitments as a 'no lay-off policy' (Sakuma 1984) in the hope of creating a stable environment in which (i) a group of employees will work over a long period of time, thereby fostering loyalty to the company; (ii) the employees (and their unions) will not fear technical innovations; and (iii) since employees could be spending a large part of their working life with the same organization, their long-term objectives (career development programmes) will support the goals of the company.

Employee participation. Management's responsibility towards employees cannot be spoken of without addressing the subject of an employee's right to participate in important decisions affecting his or her welfare, present and future (Robinson 1984). A change in the traditional relationship between employee and employer is obviously occurring worldwide as dissatisfaction with the traditional forms of hierarchical corporate control mounts. Labour is demanding a larger role in decision making, at both the job and the enterprise level (Cole 1979, Robinson 1984). This pressure arises out of an increasing awareness on the part of individuals of their humanity. The need for autonomy and self-fulfillment is now part of the world industrial culture (Cole 1985).

Management's response to this increased awareness has taken many forms, from flexible work hours (flextime), group-assigned tasks, group assembly operations, workers' councils, co-determination (labour participation at the board level), and employee ownership to profit sharing. In the process, the prerogatives and roles of both managers and workers are redefined, and the socio-economic disparity between managers and workers is narrowed (Robinson 1984). A systematic approach to establish such participation policies is provided by the ISS Model.

Aspects of the ISS approach management style. The management style advanced by the ISS approach will include a degree of employee participation in making major decisions that affect the organization. In brief:

- Superiors make decisions, but give fairly complete explanations of those decisions to gain the support of subordinates (supportive).
- Superiors make decisions after consulting with subordinates (consultative).
- Decisions are made jointly by superiors and subordinates but must be articulated by the superior to his boss (participative).

Participation requires time. The greater the pressure of time, the less the degree of participation is likely to be (Robinson 1984). It has been observed that the relatively high degree of participative decision making in Japan, for instance, arises at least in part from the tendency of the Japanese to demand great detail prior to a decision.

Degree of formality of communication: Very little can be written about national differences in respect to the degree to which informal channels of communication are open from subordinates to superiors. Some differences may be apparent, in part a function of status-consciousness within a society and the degree to which voluntary, private associations are present. Regardless of these matters, if a subordinate wishes to speak with someone above his superior, it is right to do so, and an interview will be scheduled within a certain period.

Policy towards labour unions

The role of a union varies for country to country. Unions also differ from one country to the next in regard to their degree of political involvement. One generalisation that one can make is that the weaker the union, the more likely it is to turn to external sources of support, typically to a religious or political organization (Robinson 1984).

As far as Japanese management overseas is concerned, it should limit its policies and responsibilities essentially to those related directly to the job at hand. It will then be in a better position to negotiate with trade unions on strictly economic issues. The broader range of subjects in negotiations, the more likely the negotiation will take on a political tinge.

It is a safe assumption that sooner or later, regardless of its environment, a company will be faced with the problem of dealing with a local labour organization. Under most circumstances, it would appear to be in the best interest of management to deal with unions that are strong locally, essentially non-political, and representative of the workers. The problem lies in how to encourage whatever unions there are to develop in these directions.

It is appreciated that bargaining with local unions rather than national unions may so strengthen local labour as to make it virtually independent of national control. If a union is organized on a craft basis and is represented locally by means of a shop steward system (which may mean one shop steward per shop regardless of the mix of unions represented in that shop), then management can find a power center not controlled by any union (Robinson 1984).

Fox argues that 'the skills and arts of promoting conflict-free co-operation and commitment are crucial for the survival of constantly changing dynamic societies' (Fox 1974, p. 241). The ISS approach is one such skill which can be used to promote cooperation between labour and management in a changing dynamic organization.

Single-union agreements. Japanese management overseas must be patient when trying to find one local union to represent its workforce. As the cases of the five companies in the UK indicate, a single-union agreement is essential for management, particularly Japanese management, to develop overseas. One further case is that of Toshiba which spent many years looking until finally concluding a single-union contract with the EETPU (Electrical Electronic Telecommunication and Plumbing Union). Hitachi was finally able to solve labour conflicts by concluding the same type of contract with the EETPU.

As far as implementing the ISS approach is concerned, single-union representation is preferable to no union representation. Employees are better able to participate in many important decisions by the means of such representation.

The company needs to establish an LMCC (labour-management consultative committee) with the single union, and all information can then be disclosed to employees through the LMCC. The LMCC plays a crucial role in helping in the area of sharing information and power (responsibility). The strong points of the LMCC are that it establishes an organizational information system and facilitates feedback as well as the sharing of information in an organization, thus stimulating an employee-based information system. This is an informal information system generated by employees that serves two purposes: it satisfies employees' work-oriented needs and provides an informal communications system.

Conclusion

We have argued that the concept of the ISS approach is an improvement upon the conventional ideas of human resource management as well as on the stereotypical views of Japanese management. Also, the approach is a useful strategy when implementing new factory systems, particulary those organized by Japanese electronics companies overseas.

This research is a very limited one and cannot therefore provide data attesting to the universal validity of such an approach. However, certain general implications stand out: first, the validity of an overall approach seems to depend on the formal business strategy used by the top management in a company. If top management figures look to long-term profitability, then the ISS approach may be useful. This decision by the top management is crucial, because it can be argued that the ISS type of management system maximises high trust, but it also can be seen to carry considerable risk, not only for the company, but also for the individuals concerned.

Such a system implies commitment. And commitment always implies risk because of the relative autonomy of the people concerned. The argument here is that risk can be met by the greater operational relevance of the business taken within such a system, so that survival of the system is more likely to take place because of the involvement of the people within it. This is, therefore, a system for people who are prepared to face facts and not just see the world they would like to see. It also depends, clearly, on the operational skills possessed by management and the potential of such skills. Such a system is sophisticated, and it places a great burden on management at all levels. A management training programme is essential.

It also theoretically implies that such an approach is a long-term strategy which, in turn, requires a long-term commitment on the part of top management. With the commitment of human resource development for technological and R&D investment, such a system cannot be simply running a production system effectively. Essentially, it must be about growth and change and improvement of the quality of decisions made within a system. The system cannot stand still.

Two questions emerge which can be answered in this research: Firstly, how far are Japanese companies in future overseas plant investments really prepared to follow such an ISS approach? In all of the cases examined, only one Japanese company was pursuing a long-term ISS approach. It is clear that by no means are all Japanese companies prepared to follow this approach. These ideas may not be popular simply because of the risks that may be perceived to be involved. The second question concerns the necessity for an adequate degree of harmony between organizational objectives and the needs and desires of its individual members (Likert 1961). In every healthy organization, there is an unending process of examining and modifying individual goals and organizational objectives as well as considering the methods for achieving them (Likert 1961).

The ISS approach deals with conflict on a constructive basis. Conflict and differences of opinion always exist in a healthy, virile organization, for it is usually from such differences that new and better objectives and methods emerge. Differences are essential to progress, but bitter, unresolved differences can immobilise an organisation (Likert 1961). The central problem, consequently, is not how to reduce or eliminate conflict, but how to deal constructively with it. Effective organizations have an extraordinary capacity to handle conflict (Likert 1961). We know little of this except that there are some famous cases. But what conditions existed to create these few famous examples? Lastly, and perhaps most fundamentally, we need to know much more about the extent to which individuals within such a system will respond to the challenge of developing such an ISS approach.

It is clear that in the past Japanese could draw on traditional loyalties, nationalistic feelings, and responses to paternalistic policies. But these factors are now passing. What is not clear and needs to be studied carefully is how far and what conditions individuals collectively will be prepared to commit themselves to work in such a system. It is possible that this requires a different ownership pattern, such as cooperative or sharing ownership, before it takes place. It is hoped that a further study will be undertaken to answer the above stated questions in the near future.

Appendix 1:
Definition of scoring for evaluating practices

The standards and scores for evaluation:

Score	Do the companies have any policy?	Do the companies actually implement it?
4	yes	yes
3	yes	yes, sometimes
2	no	yes, sometimes
1	no	no

Details of criteria for responding to the questionnaires

Definitions	Score
1. Labour-Management Consultative Committee	
Formal agreement is made with trade union and informal agreement is made with local representatives, and they have been regularly implemented.	4
No formal agreement is made with trade union, but informal agreement is made with local representatives.	3
No agreement is made with either trade union or local representatives, but it is sometimes implemented.	2
No agreement is made with either trade union or local representatives, and nothing is implemented.	1
2. Regular Meetings by Each Committee and Line Members	
Regular department meetings (Function Meeting) and formal meetings with all employees to explain corporate management policy (Policy Meeting) are held.	
Both Function Meeting and Policy Meeting are held regularly.	4
Function Meeting is held regularly, and Policy Meeting is held occasionally.	3
Only Function Meeting held and no Policy Meeting held.	2
No meetings are held.	1
3. Small Group Activities	
Held as normal working practices, and substantial experimental cases are illustrated.	4
Encouraged, but only some experimental cases are illustrated.	3

continued on next page

Appendix 1 contd.

Definiton	Score
Encouraged, but no actual experimental cases are available.	2
No policy and no experiences.	1
4. Motivating Employees' Initiative and Responsibilities in the Workplace (Criteria same as those for Small Group Activities)	
5. Recruiting of New Entrants	
Have a formal policy for normal recruiting practice and employ new entrants regularly.	4
No formal policy, but have some experience in employing them and want to do as much as possible.	3
No experience in employing them, but want to do so if possible.	2
No experience and no policy to employ.	1
6. Job Rotation and On-the-Job Training	
Regulated formally and implemented regularly.	4
Regulated formally and sometimes implemented, if necessary.	3
No regulation, but implemented if necessary.	2
No regulation and no intention to do so.	1

Appendix 2: Evaluation of findings and scoring of five UK companies

ISS Equipment	Co. A 1984	Co. A 1987	Co. B 1984	Co. B 1987	Co. C 1984	Co. C 1987	Co. D 1984	Co. D 1987	Co. E 1985	Co. E 1987
1. Labour-Management Consultative Committee	4	4	4	4	3	3	3	3	4	4
2. Regular Meeting by Each Committee and Line Members	4	4	4	4	3	4	3	4	3	4
3. Small Group Activities	3	3	3	3	3	3	1	2	1	2
4. Motivating Employees' Initiative and Responsibilities in the Workplace	3	3	2	3	2	2	1	1	1	2
5. Recruitment of New Graduates	3	3	3	3	3	3	3	3	3	3
6. Job Rotation and On-the-job Training	4	4	3	3	3	3	3	3	3	3
Total	21	21	19	20	17	18	14	16	13	17

Note: Definition of scores and criteria of evaluation given in Appendix 1.

Bibliography

Cascio, W.F., and Awad, E.M. *Human Resources Management: An Information Approach*. Prentice-Hall, New York, 1981.

Cole, R.E. *Work, Mobility and Participation*. University of California Press, Berkeley, 1979.

———. 'Target Information for Competitive Performance'. *Harvard Business Review*, Boston, May-June 1985, pp. 125–32.

Dore, R.P. *British Factory-Japanese Factory*. University of California Press, Berkeley, 1973.

Fox, A. *Beyond Contract: Work, Power and Trust Relations*. Faber and Faber Ltd., New York, 1974.

Fulkes, F.K., and Moran, H.M. 'Organizing and Staffing the Personnel Function'. *Harvard Business Review*, Boston, May-June 1974, pp. 142–54.

Gruver, R.C. 'Personnel Management in the Small Organization'. *Personnel Administration*, 23 March 1978, pp. 38–44.

Hazama, H. *Characteristics of Japanese-style Management*. Japanese Economic Studies, 1979, pp. 110–73.

Likert, R. *New Pattern of Management*. McGraw-Hill, New York, 1961.

McGregor, D. *The Human Side of Enterprise*. McGraw-Hill, New York, 1960.

Miles, R.E. 'Human Relations or Human Resources?' *Harvard Business Review*, Boston, July-August, 1965, pp. 148–63.

Miller, E.C. 'Consensus'. *Personnel*, May 1977.

Miner, J.B. *Management Theory*. Macmillan, New York, 1971.

Peters, T.J., and Waterman, R.H. *In Search of Excellence*. Harper & Row, New York, 1981.

Pelz, D.C. 'Influence: A Key to Effective Leadership in the First Line Supervisor'. *Personnel*, Nov. 1952.

Pucik, V., and Hatvany, N. 'An Integrated Management System: Lessons from the Japanese Experience'. In *Motivation and Work Behavior*, ed. by R.M. Steers and L.W. Porter. McGraw-Hill, New York, 1983.

Robinson, R.D. *Internationalization of Business: An Introduction*. Holt, Rinehart and Winston, New York, 1984.

Sakuma, M. *Nihonteki Keiei no Kokusaisei* (Internationalisation of the Japanese Management System). Yūhikaku, Tokyo, 1984.

———. 'Strategic Human Resource Management in Japan: A Comparative Study of Information Sharing System'. Ph.D. dissertation, London School of Economics and Political Science, University of London, 1986.

———. *Kokusai Keiei to Nihongata Rōshi Kankei* (Strategy of International Business and Japanese-type Industrial Relations). Yūhikaku, Tokyo, 1987.

Schein, E. *Organizational Psychology*. Prentice-Hall, New York, 1987.

Schuler, R.S. *Personnel and Human Resource Management*. West Publishing Co., Chicago, 1981.

Schuster, F.E. 'Human Resource Management: Key to the Future'. *Personnel Administration*, Dec. 1978.

Shimada, H. 'Japanese Postwar Industrial Growth and Labor Management Relations'. *Keio Economic Society Discussion Paper*, Series No. 5, 1983.

Steer, R.M., and Porter, L.W. *Motivation and Work Behavior*. McGraw-Hill, New York, 1983.

Tsurumi, Y. *Multinational Management: Business Strategy and Government Policy*. Ballinger, New York, 1984.

JAPANESE MANAGERS AND BRITISH STAFF: A COMPARISON OF RELATIONS AND EXPECTATIONS IN BLUE-COLLAR AND WHITE-COLLAR FIRMS

Malcolm Trevor
Policy Studies Institute

With the increasing internationalisation of Japanese business and the continuing discussion of internationalisation within Japanese companies, often focusing on the question of what is the best way to manage local staff in a particular country, the distinction between the blue-collar sector and the white-collar sector is an important one. Much of the research into the management techniques used in Japanese companies overseas and into the reactions of local staff to such techniques, especially in Europe and the USA, have concentrated on the blue-collar sector. This is understandable, insofar as management problems in the two regions are mainly perceived to concern manufacturing; but it has led to an imbalance between the considerable attention paid to blue-collar workers in the West on the one hand and to white-collar employees, and especially to managers, on the other.

The frequent tendency to overlook the differences between these three categories, of blue-collar workers, white-collar staff, and managers, can lead to mistakes in interpreting the outlook and behaviour of local staff. This is a problem for Japanese managers who must work with them every day and lead them in such a way as to achieve the company's goals. For example, some aspects of the local 'culture' identified as characteristic of all employees in Britain, France, and elsewhere may really be characteristic of only one category.

In Japan itself, it would be a mistake to overlook the differences between large, medium, and small firms and their specific types of labour force; just as it would be a mistake to overlook the differences between the tasks of a manufacturing company, a bank, and a sales company, etc.; or the differences between old, established companies with a high degree of formal organisation and newer companies, even large ones, with a more entrepreneurial character. Differences have been identified both in Japan and in Britain between public corporations, or what in Britain are referred to as nationalised industries, on the one hand, and private firms, on the other. These differences are expressed in such different ways as manning levels and employee attitudes and behaviour. In both countries, privatisation is being pursued for the same reason.

The example suggests how unrealistic it is to see all enterprises in a country as the same. Even within the same sector, there are well-known differences between competitors, as the examples of the Japanese motor industry, the electrical and electronics industry, and the trading houses show. Management and enterprises also change over time, as the brilliant study by the late Professor Hirschmeier of Nanzan University and Professor Yui showed in their classic work, *The Development of Japanese Business 1600–1980* (1).

In 1973, the American management writer Henry Mintzberg, in his book *The Nature of Managerial Work*, asked what appears to be a simple question, 'What do managers do?' (2). Many people in Europe and America would probably reply that managers are paid to make decisions and to assume responsibility for them. As in other countries, there are a lot of assumptions about the job of a manager, and it may not be felt necessary to say explicitly what they are. So what do British and Japanese managers think the 'nature of managerial work', to quote Mintzberg again, is? If they have different ideas about the job of a manager, how are these differences accommodated in their daily work together?

The Policy Studies Institute's recent study of management development in a sample of Japanese companies in Britain and Germany (3) developed out of a previous study of Japanese managers and British workers (4). This was because of two of the conclusions. The first was that the experience of Japanese managers, who had been alarmed by horror stories in the media about militancy, etc., among British workers, had been much better than expected (5). The second was that the experience of Japanese managers with white-collar staff and particularly with British managers had been more problematical than anticipated.

Some Japanese managers seem not to have expected problems with British managers. They seem to have felt that the better educated a person was and the higher his or her position in the company, the greater the commitment to the company would be. Blue-collar workers were expected to be 'different', but both British and Japanese managers may have assumed too much that the nature of managerial work is self-evidently the same, even though both had vague ideas about the other's 'culture'. Neither fully appreciated the differences between their respective labour market situations, with all the implications for career paths and the whole way of thinking about what a manager's job is that different types of labour market have.

This mismatch might be expected where Japanese managers without overseas experience are thrown together with British managers without any firsthand experience in Japan and with only stereotypical ideas about Japanese business and society. It has produced some disappointment on the Japanese side and some perplexity on the British. The earlier study also showed that British workers were critical of British managers, who were perceived to be more interested in their own personal careers than in the work and progress of the company as a whole. Such managers were said to be less than enthusiastic about the new styles of management introduced by the Japanese and to want to go back to 'the bad old days', if they got the chance. In other words, British blue-collar workers were actually more enthusiastic about the new Japanese management styles than some British managers were.

Here one obvious point, so obvious that it is seldom mentioned in the literature, must be made. It is that there is no career rivalry between Japanese managers and British workers, but that there is career rivalry between Japanese managers and British managers. It is the old problem of what the career prospects for local managers are in foreign firms of any nationality where there are expatriate managers, especially the more numerous the latter are. It is a problem that has been found in multinational firms of many nationalities.

Can a local manager be promoted to head of the organisation? How many expatriates in Japanese firms in Britain are there, and does their occupation of managerial positions effectively put a ceiling on local promotion? Japanese banks and trading companies in London typically have about one third Japanese personnel. All are managers, except for a few trainees and female clerical staff, who are mostly locally recruited and employed as local staff only. There is no known example of a local manager being promoted in the wider organisation outside the UK. This is not necessarily surpising because the international spread of Japanese companies is more recent than that of the Western multinationals, but it should be remembered when discussing managers' careers and their views of managerial work, and their ideas should not be looked at out of context.

It is not just because they are Japanese that these firms have a high proportion of expatriates: it is because they are Japanese companies in the commercial and financial sector. In Japanese manufacturing companies in Britain and in sales and distribution companies, there are far fewer expatriates: typically, not more than 10 per cent. To put it another way, Japanese commercial and financial companies in the UK are more centralised than manufacturing or sales companies. Manufacturing and selling involve more direct contact with local people and local markets. Selling, for instance, requires local personnel with knowledge of the market, usually gained from experience with a British company, and the ability to approach British purchasing managers in the right way. Most Japanese blue-collar operations in Britain are unionised, but union relations are usually handled by local managers. Almost all Japanese manufacturers, together with the large sales companies, have a British personnel manager, typically an IPM (Institute of Personnel Management) qualified 'professional'. The differences between the jobs of British and Japanese personnel managers will be discussed below.

The Policy Studies Institute management development study investigated in depth one Japanese manufacturing company, one sales and distribution company, and one trading company in the UK. The manufacturer and the trading company had been researched in the previous worker study, and the sales company was known from other contacts. British and Japanese managers were asked to give details of their education, training, qualifications, job assignments, promotions, and, where relevant, changes of employer. How far they saw themselves, and their colleagues, as either 'generalists' or 'specialists' was then discussed, and this question was used to open up the whole discussion of the nature of managerial work.

We would obviously like to study management development in Japan itself, but an international study has two advantages. First, it enables different models of organisation and of managers' assignments and careers to be compared. Second, it enables one to collect empirical data on the daily working relationships between British and Japanese managers. If there are problems in companies with such mixed management teams which do not exist in Japan, such a study can investigate possible solutions. It can likewise discuss whether there are practical benefits for British companies in the Japanese approach, and, if so, how far it is realistic to try to adopt it.

Our research was done in Britain, and there are important differences between British and American societies, the role of business, and the importance of management in society, etc. At the same time, there are significant similarities in such relevant areas as job descriptions, functional specialisation, off-the-job training, individual career paths and job mobility, 'professionalism', especially among groups like accountants and lawyers, the existence of effective professional associations, formal organisation, and a great part of the thinking about management. In the background are comparable financial systems and labour markets and similar ideas about free-market competition, which directly affect managerial work because of time horizons, and the assessment of managers and their performance, which are both more short-term and more formalised than is usual in Japan. One Japanese manager who has commented on this point and on the harmful effect on the company of short-time horizons is Mr. Morita of Sony.

There is support in the literature for a view of Anglo-American models of organisation and managerial work. 'Professionalism, as it has developed in Britain and the United States, is characterised by an isolation of separable tasks and jobs to be claimed as the specialist domain of members of each profession. . . . The institutional and value systems of professionalism are highly developed in Britain but . . . there has been no debate in Germany about whether management is a profession, ought to be one, or can justify a claim to professional standing' (6). A delegation from the British Institute of Management was surprised, and alarmed, to find that 'the word "professional" in any discussion with German managers generally proved to be an obstacle to understanding the role of manager'; although, as the author remarks, 'If we judge an industry's professionalism by the integrity of its end products, the Germans are professional by anybody's standards' (7). The example shows how mistaken it is to look at management in all Western countries as the same.

Similar remarks can be applied to the Japanese case, where there is also an absence of business schools like in Germany and an absence of Anglo-American ideas of 'professionalism' in the narrowly defined sense of the word. An article in *Harvard Business Review*, written with American readers in mind, urged managers to look at 'Germany's world-class manufacturers' and their management (8).

One Japanese trading company manager in London wrote that the British chartered accountant 'probably feels stronger loyalty to his professional body, such as the Institute of Chartered Accountants, than to the company he works for. . . . This kind of self-identification with a profession very seldom exists in Japanese society. . . . The training of the manager in Japan is mostly carried out in-house and on-the-job. . . . The manager's function is related primarily to his relationship with the people whom he is to manage' (9).

A Japanese researcher, with British and American experience, contrasts the 'strictly functional' authority of Western managers with the 'basically personal' authority of Japanese managers. In his view, the Japanese manager 'is more efficient in terms of a "generalist" than in terms of a "specialist": his effectiveness consists essentially in providing his subordinates with the proper work climate' (10). The concepts of the 'generalist' and the 'specialist' were used in our study to try and determine how far they were realities for managers or how far they were principles, or even myths.

The researcher just quoted states that in Japan, 'Line-staff organisation . . . is readily accepted in theory but remains denied in practice. . . . Mostly sooner than later . . . a staff function ends up in the line organisation. Here . . . interdependence is expected, and accountability is diffused all over the organisation'. Japanese managers in Britain, expecting demarcation among blue-collar workers but not among managers, are shocked when they hear the popular phrase, 'That's not my job', from managers and by what they see as local managers' wilful and irrational refusal to share information with colleagues and subordinates. But then Japanese managers in the major corporations have a high degree of job security in the one organisation, within which it is rational to do any task assigned and where the seniority element means that Japanese managers need not watch their backs for subordinates who threaten their own position to the same extent (11). They are not, like British managers, exposed to an external labour market in which they must be conscious of what constitutes their value and determines their career development.

The case of accountants was mentioned, who in companies in Japan are not generally independent 'professionals', able to move from firm to firm. The same is true of, for instance, personnel managers. To quote the same Japanese researcher again, personnel managers in Japan are 'not expected to be professionals of personnel administration'. In Britain, they would typically be members of the Institute of Personnel Management, following a recognised specialism, with a qualification validated by the examination of this professional association and with a corpus of intellectual knowledge at their disposal. Because of the explosion of qualifications and the increasing tendency for occupations to upgrade themselves to professional status, it is a pattern found in Britain now from doctors and lawyers, on the one hand, to building surveyors and librarians, on the other. Interdepartmental rivalry, the defence of territory, and organisational politics may not be unknown in Japan, but this splitting of functions and of positions has not gone as far as in Britain.

There is now a debate in the UK as to whether separating line and personnel function has been a healthy development. Personnel managers may seek to promote their ideas in the company and line managers may see this either as a threat or as a mistake; but many line managers were said to be glad to be able to leave problems to the personnel department that they themselves did not want to deal with. The theory was that this would help them to 'concentrate on the job'; as if they were not working with people—an idea at variance with the usual Japanese views of managerial work.

The discrepancy between idealistic theories of personnel management in Britain and the actual role that personnel managers are likely to have in practice has been vividly described (12). It must be asked whether the 'professional' IPM approach is not actually making a difficult situation worse by splitting off one more specialised function, when what is needed is an integrated approach, more in line with the Japanese model.

For instance, Lord Sieff of Marks and Spencer, the company regularly praised by Peter Drucker and one of Britain's most successful managers, states that 'good human relations are not something that can be left to the personnel department. . . . The commitment must come from the top. We do not make a rigid distinction between line management and personnel management. . . . The welfare of staff is also the concern of line managers who must be trained in dealing with people' (13). This sounds like a Japanese company president speaking, and one could find several similarities between the approach of Marks and Spencer and that of Japanese companies. But most British companies are not like Marks and Spencer.

In an American view, the return on investment (ROI) criterion 'was developed earlier in this century to help in the management of the new multiactivity corporations. . . . ROI was used as an indicator of the efficiency of diverse operating departments . . . and as an overall measure of the financial performance of the entire company' (14). The aim was to assist 'the financial performance of the entire company', not to promote the 'professional' ethic of accounting in isolation from the business as a whole. The view expressed is that what often happened instead was excessive reliance on ROI by senior executives, who ran companies 'by the numbers' without proper knowledge of divisional operations and technology. Accountants emphasised 'professional' accounting rather than contribution to the company as a whole. It was specialisation of a type that Japanese organisations normally seem determined to avoid.

Two Japanese scholars, concerned with 'mystical or irrational' views of Japanese organisations, have also shown the effects of the financial system on managers and their jobs. In Japan, bank finance plays a major role in company operations, so the 'central coordination of capital flow is less important than in the US' (15). At the same time, the status of chief financial officers in Japan 'has not been as high as compared to the US'. The writers then put the question into context, underlining what has been said about internal labour markets and how training and expertise belong to the company, not to the individual. 'Perhaps the most important benefit of a well-developed internal labour market is the opportunity of enlarging the employee's firm-specific skills and know-how. Internal development of such capabilities is the norm (and benefit) in the Japanese internal labour market'.

Professor Takahashi of Chūō University states that 'at the beginning of the 1950s Japanese managers tried to introduce the American management system whereby the scope and content of jobs (authority and responsibility) of managers and workers were clearly defined. However, Japanese managers came to know that it was quite impossible to define the content or scope of a job objectively, even when authority was formally assigned to it as far as possible, and that it was unrealistic to expect such a change within the context of such Japanese organisational and personnel practices as the lifetime employment system, the seniority system and the group decision-making system. . . . The American system could not be directly introduced but had to be modified. . . . The control and scope of the job is clarified by groups, by sections, and by departments'(16). Applying job descriptions to departments rather than to individuals modifies the whole idea, and it is said that they are very general, if they are in use at all.

A recent Japanese account of the comparative values of British and Japanese managers, by R. Miyajima of the University of Manchester Institute of Science and Technology, quoted Japanese criticisms of British managers' 'professional' type of 'careerism', and specifically for 'regarding the firm they work for as a stepping stone' (16). 'The British style of management was often seen to be status-conscious, territory-conscious, authoritarian, and conservative. . . . British managers were over-concerned with a formal chain of command but little concerned with horizontal communication'—remarks that to an extent echo the criticisms made by British workers.

The 'ideal manager' to the British was a 'cool professional', but to the Japanese it was a 'benevolent father'. From the 'ideal subordinate', the Japanese expected more 'initiative' and active involvement, while the British approach was more 'top down'. Japanese managers in Britain and elsewhere overseas complain of the 'apathy' or 'lack of initiative' of subordinates and at having to give instructions each time they want something done. Local subordinates, who may not have been instructed that they should try to anticipate the manager's wishes, are frustrated because they cannot get a clear instruction or decision and are not sure what they should do. In extreme cases, this can lead to a situation where both the local staff and the Japanese management are waiting for the other to do something, and nothing gets done. For Japanese managers, the implication is that they need to be more explicit and to explain more what they want done than they need to at home. This includes telling local staff about the type of initiative they should show.

For purposes of comparison, it is useful to put forward two models of managers' careers and to see how far they correspond with the findings at Japanese companies in Britain. For the major Japanese corporations, there is the long-term employment 'generalist' model. For British managers, there is the external labour market 'professional' or 'specialist' model. While the Japanese manager is a 'benevolent father' to his subordinates, the British manager must avoid 'invading the privacy' of his subordinates.

Marubeni exhorts its staff to 'acknowledge our individual insignificance and seek strength in our combined efforts . . . avoiding arrogance and exemplifying humility'. Japanese managers must know that their organisations are made up of high flyers, average performers, plodders, and poor performers, but they appear to be following the principle that the sum of the whole is greater than the mere total of its separate parts: maximum performance is to be obtained through cohesion. Many British organisations contain able individuals, but cohesion is frequently low. The top management frequently does not communicate what the company is about and what its overriding goal is; so the organisation is a loose collection of parts and of people 'doing their own thing'.

The differences outlined between British and Japanese approaches to the nature of managerial work lead one to expect problems in operating mixed-management teams, but there may still be some surprises. The three case studies in Britain were of Japanese organisations that were not large in themselves, but which were branches of first-class companies in Japan. Their Japanese managers had been recruited, assigned to departments, and brought up in the management philosophy of corporations of this type. Behind the local operations were powerful resources and a global strategy. Two companies, the first in precision engineering and the other in sales and distribution for a leading electrical manufacturer, had approximately two hundred staff each. The third company, a branch of one of the Big Nine trading companies, had over a hundred staff. Precise numbers cannot be given because of confidentiality.

The character of the three companies differed widely. The engineering company had a policy consciously aimed at creating a community spirit. The wearing of company uniform clothing by all staff, without exception, had been written into the contract of employment. There was a single union agreement and job flexibility. Operators were taught to do their own quality checks and had been made responsible for them. The personnel manager, an IPM-qualified professional, had worked six months on the shop floor, which would be very unusual in a British company. There was one single-status canteen and no status symbols, such as reserved parking spaces for managers. There was, therefore, a high degree of what is often termed 'Japanese management' style and an absence of the job and status barriers characteristic of traditional British companies. The company had advanced rapidly into the market, was expanding its facilities, and was about the only company on the industrial estate actually taking on more employees. The demands of precision engineering and the intention to increase market share underlay its management style. Its mood was optimistic and aggressive.

In contrast, the sales company had an entrepreneurial basis and was less 'Japanese' in management style, although it had about the same proportion of Japanese staff. Its mission was to expand its share of the local market in competition with Japanese rivals. It was the sales arm of an established, conservative manufacturer, and this character was reflected in the relatively 'slow but sure' approach of its Japanese managers, with a fair degree of formal organisation. It contrasted, for example, with another sales company headed by a more aggressively entrepreneurial and 'individualistic' Japanese manager. It was located in an outer suburban area, where land for warehousing is moderately priced and where there is good access to motorways.

Our research in Japan revealed close connections between marketing and product development, consistent with the flexible approach to job boundaries. We also found that Japanese salesmen, unlike in Britain or America, do not get an individual commission: they get the same percentage bonus as all other company employees, based on the overall performance of the firm.

So far, no Japanese sales company in Britain has tried to introduce the same payment system for salesmen, or for other staff for that matter, that it has in Japan—for obvious reasons. The British sales personnel in the company studied were highly individualistic and entrepreneurial, interested in their commissions and future careers. Most had already been salesmen or sales managers in British companies and what had attracted them to the Japanese company was the prospects of advancement in a new company with quality products, financial backing, and the aim of capturing an expanding share of the market.

It was not possible to detect any wish among these white-collar and managerial staff for the single-status system, such as there was in the blue-collar engineering company.

Japanese managers often complain about job changing among British managers and their lack of 'loyalty' to the company. Some evidently expect British staff to have a special feeling about the company because it is Japanese and 'different' and find it hard to understand that for many local staff a job is a job and that it is not important whether the company is Japanese, British, or any other nationality.

Japanese managers may also forget that job changing allows them easier access to qualified personnel than has until recently been the case for foreign firms in Japan, who have had difficulty in recruiting good Japanese staff (17). This has been partly the foreign companies' own fault for not taking enough care over recruitment and career development. Now that foreign firms are increasingly meeting Japanese employees' aspirations by localising their personnel in senior positions, and now that job changing in Japan is slightly on the increase, the possibilities for foreign firms to recruit good quality Japanese staff, even by using headhunters, is on the increase.

The character of the general trading company's London branch again differed from those of the two other companies studied. As a trading house, it handles everything from commodities and manufactured products to financial services and the putting together of complex package deals like plant exports. In spite of the holistic theory, it has a strong departmental organisation, reflecting the completely different businesses it is in. At another trading company in London, the departments were said to be 'kingdoms unto themselves'. Managers' career profiles showed that it was extremely rare for them to be moved from one type of business to another, which must raise questions about the concept of the 'generalist'.

Significantly, the personnel manager himself, who had been working loyally in the job for ten years, had never wanted to enter the personnel department. His hope had always been to enter a business department, where the money is made and where he saw the greatest power and prestige, though some managers think that the support departments, such as credit control, have great power. It is hard to imagine a British personnel 'professional' thinking or behaving in the same way. In both the other companies, the personnel managers were IPM-qualified professionals with the usual previous experience. The sales company personnel manager, whose approach was both firm and diplomatic, had carved out the stronger position of the two.

It is unusual for there to be a Japanese personnel manager with direct control of British staff. A previous study found only one other example, also in a trading company. The reasons suggested are that in both cases the companies decided that what was needed was more a recruitment officer than a personnel manager and that they would be able to control the situation more tightly with a Japanese manager in charge. This may have been one way of dealing with the situation caused by sluggish business. But the cases are exceptional.

The trading company is located in the City of London, in quite a buoyant white-collar labour market, although for older, long-serving local staff with mortgage (housing loan) commitments, etc., the chances of moving to a better job elsewhere are remote. The organisation's sub-divisions are called departments, as in the head office, but because of the smaller overall size of the company, they should really be called sections. Expatriates occupy all senior positions with authority, rather than with just a title, and almost all managerial positions down to and including section manager and assistant section manager level. This does not leave much scope for local managers, who typically tend to settle for security rather than advancement. There is a considerable contrast with the entrepreneurially orientated sales company, which also, of course, has a smaller proportion of expatriates. Job stability does fit the trading company's philosophy, but it makes it hard to appeal to local high flyers, and the situation shows the nature of the localisation problem in the City. The Japanese managers at all three companies studied are all university or college graduates; not all their British managers are, reflecting the smaller numbers of graduate managers in British compared with Japanese firms.

Of the three companies, the sales company is the one that has tackled one problem of functional specialisation, or over-specialisation, most directly (3). The Quality Assurance Principles of the engineering company speak of 'maintaining and improving existing quality standards, using all of the specialist knowledge and managerial techniques at our disposal'. Although following a 'generalist' approach towards flexibility, its Japanese graduate engineers are more highly qualified than their British colleagues, and the use of the words 'specialist knowledge' in the principles is interesting.

The 'basic philosophy' of the sales company, as put forward by its Japanese general manager, emphasises teamwork, punctuality, hard work, flexibility, and non-bureaucracy. Three of the five points—team work, flexibility, and non-bureaucracy—all refer to the blurring of the boundaries of jobs and authority. Punctuality is also interpreted as trustworthiness, a quality of the good team member.

As a statement about job flexibility, contrasting with Anglo-American concepts of 'professionalism' and organisation theory, it is unusually direct and seems to express what most Japanese managers think but seldom say:

I have also discovered job specifications since coming to the UK, which I personally dislike; although fundamentally I recognise the need, and that employees wish to protect themselves . . . if a company and employees are both flexible with regard to job functions, an enthusiastic employee can be supported and helped by the company to move in another direction. Also, the company can request support from employees to help in other areas when necessary, thus saving on recruitment and additional salaries.

Saving on recruitment and salaries is a significant point. The statement encapsulates the philosophy of the nature of managerial work, both in its economic rationale of cost cutting and in its more emotional dislike of job descriptions. It suggests how hard it may be for British and Japanese managers really to see each other's point of view about work and careers and why it is necessary for the 'nature of managerial work' to be discussed in detail in order that managers can work efficiently side by side.

The career profiles of the British and Japanese managers showed expected data on, for instance, Japanese managers' higher educational or technical qualifications and their continuous service with only one company since starting work. The surprise was that Japanese managers were invariably kept in the same job or department to which they had originally been assigned. On the basis of qualifications and job assignments, they could therefore be said to be more objectively 'professional' than the British managers, if 'professionalism' is taken to mean job-related factors rather than status or ideology.

Japanese managers assigned to Britain, on average for between four and five years, receive little advanced warning of when they will be transferred either from Japan or back home. In some companies, there seems to be little or no orientation training for managers sent abroad and seldom any systematic way of passing on their knowledge when they return home. It looks as if the companies are not making the best use of their returnees' experience, and many managers on their first overseas assignment are 'thrown in at the deep end', although companies now have a considerable number of managers with a wealth of practical experience overseas.

Given that the term 'generalist' is less often used in Britain and that what it means is not necessarily self-evident, one might have expected more British managers interviewed during the study to question it. Contrary to the myth, not all Japanese managers described themselves as 'generalists' and all their British colleagues as 'specialists', or vice versa. The mixed replies received suggested that the companies were not just promoting a straightforward 'generalist' ideology and that the concept is more complex than frequently asserted. But the companies were actively promoting flexibility and a non-demarcated way of thinking about managerial work, which they are convinced is necessary for the job and which is an important innovation.

'Japanese management' has no monopoly on the terms 'generalist' and 'specialist', which suggests that they are not just the products of 'Japanese culture' and that it is important to look at how the two terms have been used in British and American contexts. The British Civil Service, for instance, clearly distinguishes between the two, and one study of civil servants had the title 'Specialists and Generalists' (18). A chapter in another study had the title 'The Cult of the Generalist' (19). 'Specialists' in this case meant scientists, engineers, statisticians, etc., qualified in one field and assigned to one area. They are regarded as rather inferior by the 'generalists', who are supposed to be able to make policy decisions in any area, while perhaps being 'specialised' in none of them. In the United States, Whyte's classic study of the 'organisation man' referred to the training systems of the General Electric Company, with its emphasis on the concept of 'the well-rounded man' (20).

It is also commonly observed that the qualities that make a good functional manager or expert at departmental level do not necessarily make a good top manager. There is the problem of breadth of vision and, as is sometimes said in the case of engineers or technicians, the problem of leadership qualities and the ability to get on with people and to motivate them. The American Army principle, for instance, is that 'officers who are to assume higher command . . . and who must function effectively in planning and policy-making positions . . . require development as true "generalists" ' (21).

The study to some extent confirmed the validity of the long-term generalist internal labour market model in Japanese corporations and of the specialist 'professional' external labour market model in the British case. A clear example is the contrast between Anglo-American accountants, with accounting qualifications independently awarded by their own professional association, which is recognised throughout society, and Japanese accounting managers, graduates in economics perhaps and without externally examined qualifications who learn on-the-job in the one company that they typically expect to work for until the age of 55 or 60 how to provide the information that that particular company wants in the way that it wants it and how to make their contribution to the company's overall objectives. The contrast is also between the professional qualifications of the British or American accountants that enable them to get a job in any company whose job specifications they are seen to meet and Japanese accounting department personnel whose knowledge and experience are company-specific and who learn to follow the specific procedures in one company only.

All three Japanese companies studied showed a high degree of stable job assignments among Japanese managers. How then does one evaluate Japanese engineers with a university degree, better qualified than their British counterparts, who stay in the same kind of work in the same firm? Are they generalists or specialists, or are they more professional, in the best sense of the word, than their British colleagues? Is there a difference between a British specialist and a Japanese specialist?

The answer pointed to by the conclusion to the study is contained in the remarks of two different Japanese managers. The first stated that Japanese managers needed both 'speciality and generality for promotion'. The second saw Japanese managers as specialised but flexible, and as more adaptable and with a wider view than British specialists, with their more demarcated attitude and behaviour. As with other apparently incompatible opposites, like competition and collaboration, the companies were perhaps getting the best of both worlds, integrating high levels of specific expertise with a broad view of how this expertise should be applied and how it should be channelled into company performance. One Japanese manager commented on Western job descriptions: 'We don't have them. So I don't know what my job is, what I must cover. It's not clear. If I think it's my job, I will do it'. This is perhaps the 'initiative' referred to earlier.

Professionalism, in the best sense of the word, means doing the job of a manager competently, with all the specialist knowledge and skill necessary, in the way that most effectively contributes to the organisation's aims. At the same time, these aims must be properly formulated by the top management and communicated in a concrete and readily understandable way to all employees. Japanese managers are normally good at communicating the 'vision', or strategic direction, of the enterprise to employees and at motivating them, and at involving employees in teamwork, small group activities, and Quality Circles, etc.

In the UK, some Japanese managers appear not to know that such well-known companies as Jaguar Cars, Rolls-Royce Aero Engines,

Wedgwood, May and Baker, and others have their own Quality Circle movements. While it is easier to introduce Circles, etc., at companies in Japan, because teamwork is an accepted style, it can be done in Britain and other countries, provided that enough training, explanation, and management commitment are given. Many British workers actually want a new management style, which can be introduced in a new company, although it is more difficult in an old one. They are disappointed if their expectations of change, including greater involvement, are not met. Industrial relations in Britain are becoming increasingly concentrated on the plant level, rather as in Japan, and away from the national level. This tendency and the trend in more British companies for Quality Circle programmes and other forms of employee involvement to be introduced should be helpful to Japanese companies and managers.

Some of the differences between blue-collar, white-collar, and managerial staff in Britain have already been referred to. Making a very simple comparison, it can be said the British blue-collar workers are the least geographically mobile category and that for them the local community is important in a way that does not apply so much to the others—and least of all to the managers. British blue-collar workers are in fact rather 'groupish', while white-collar staff think more about their own career paths and prospects. Managers are the most individualistic and most geographically mobile category. They will move from one part of the country to another in pursuit of their careers. This brief outline shows why it is important for Japanese managers who work together in the same firms with them to bear in mind, for example, that British managers are more individualistic than the other two categories, while blue-collar workers value solidarity, camaraderie, and the single-status employment systems promoted in the UK by some Japanese companies.

The situation is always changing, as old industrial firms decline and new high-tech and entrepreneurial firms spring up. A recent development, for instance, was deregulation, the so-called Big Bang, in the City of London on 27 October 1986, which has made companies revise their personnel policies to meet the new labour market conditions.

New companies in the UK do have the chance to innovate and to establish a new style, free from the burdens of the past, 'from day one', as some managers express it. It is important to start in the same way that you want to continue. To give a small example: people will accept company uniform if it is the rule from day one. When this is done at the start, a new habit is created. But one company which mistakenly thought it would be better to introduce company uniforms later on

180 TREVOR

found it was difficult—people were used to a different habit and some were unwilling to change after the habit had been established. It is important for companies to establish their new habits, working practices, or 'culture' right from the first day. Real examples show that these companies have the greatest success because they can introduce the newest and best methods.

Japanese companies in Britain, like other foreign companies, have one problem and also some advantages. The problem is familiarisation, or getting to know the local people and situation. This is preparatory work that must be done, both by companies and by individual managers. The advantage is that a Japanese company setting up in the UK is new. Especially because such companies are widely seen as well managed and successful, people will accept new styles and innovations from them. Several studies, in fact, show that foreign firms in Britain are more successful than local firms because of the way in which they can introduce new management methods. Many people are ready to welcome Japanese companies and their introduction of new and better ways of managing. Provided the companies familiarise themselves with the local situation and tell people clearly what they want people to do, local people will be willing to follow their lead. There is a good opportunity for Japanese companies which should not be missed.

Notes

(1) J. Hirschmeier and T. Yui, *The Development of Japanese Business, 1600–1980*, Allen & Unwin, London, 1981.
(2) H. Mintzberg, *The Nature of Managerial Work*, Harper & Row, New York 1973.
(3) M.H. Trevor, J. Schendel, and B. Wilpert, *The Japanese Management Development System. Generalists and Specialists in Japanese Companies Abroad*, Pinter, London, 1986.
(4) M. White and M.H. Trevor, *Under Japanese Management: The Experience of British Workers*, Heinemann, London, 1983.
(5) Technova Inc., *Japanese Direct Investment in the UK: Its Possibilities and Problems*, Technova, Tokyo, 1980.
(6) J. Child, et al. 'A Price to Pay? Professionalism and Work Organisation in Britain and West Germany', *Sociology*, Vol. 17, No. 1, London, Feb. 1983.
(7) A. Mant, *The Rise and Fall of the British Manager*, Pan, London, 1979.
(8) J.A. Limprecht and R.H. Hayes, 'Germany's World-Class Manufacturers', *Harvard Business Review*, Vol. 60, No. 6, November-December 1982.
(9) Y. Funaki, 'Japanese Management and Management Training', *BACIE Journal*, London, January 1981.
(10) H. Inohara, 'The Personnel Department in Japanese Companies', *Bulletin of the Socio-Economic Institute*, No. 63, Sophia University, Tokyo, 1977.

(11) J. McLoughlin, 'Comfort in Suntory's Happy Song', *The Guardian*, London, 19 October 1982.
(12) K. Legge, *Power, Innovation and Problem-Solving in Personnel Management*, McGraw-Hill, Maidenhead, 1978.
(13) Lord Sieff, 'How I See the Personnel Function', *Personnel Management*, London, December 1984.
(14) R.S. Kaplan, 'Yesterday's Accounting Undermines Production', *Harvard Business Review*, No. 4, July-August 1984.
(15) K. Imai and H. Itami, 'Organisation and Market Interpenetration', *International Journal of Industrial Organisation*, No. 2, North Holland, 1984.
(16) M.H. Trevor (ed.), *The Internationalisation of Japanese Business: European and Japanese Perceptions*, Campus Verlag, Frankfurt/Westview Press, Colorado, 1987.
(17) R.J. Ballon (ed.), *The Japanese Employee*, Sophia/Tuttle, Tokyo, 1969.
(18) E.F. Ridley (ed.), *Specialists and Generalists: A Comparative Study of the Professional Civil Servant at Home and Abroad*, Allen & Unwin, London, 1968.
(19) P. Kellner and Lord Crowther-Hunt, *The Civil Servants: An Inquiry into Britain's Ruling Class*, Macdonald, London, 1980.
(20) W.H. Whyte, *The Organisation Man*, Penguin, Harmondsworth, 1960.
(21) T.J. Crockel, 'On the Making of Lieutenants and Colonels', *The Public Interest*, No. 76, National Affairs Inc., Easton, Pa., Summer 1984.

JAPANESE DIRECT MANUFACTURING INVESTMENT IN FRANCE

Masaru Yoshimori
International University of Japan

Introduction

The image of France as a potential host country for direct investment has not been very favourable among Japanese multinationals. For a long time, France has been associated, in the eyes of most Japanese businessmen, with strong protectionism, particularly directed against Japan, tight government control on foreign trade, foreign direct investment and foreign currency transactions, troubled industrial relations, undisciplined workers, and unpredictable social explosions. The 1982 incident of Poitiers, which caused a drastic import restriction on Japanese VCRs, aggravated such negative perceptions.

Host-country preferences for direct investment projects of 38 large Japanese multinationals operating in Paris from among five EC countries were ascertained by a Japanese business organization (see Table 1). Eighteen chose West Germany as the most preferred country, and eight opted for England, but no firm gave France first priority. Only one firm assigned a second priority to France, and for the majority of respondents, France was the third or fourth choice.

Indeed, the number of cases of Japanese direct manufacturing investment in France has been negligible. In the sixties, only one firm, Pentel, established a production unit there. It was followed by YKK, the zipper maker, with its plant near Lille. These pioneers were followed by Ajinomoto in 1976 and Dai Nippon Ink in 1978. In the sixties and seventies, only five Japanese firms set up local production facilities. Starting in 1982, however, there has been a sudden and continued increase of direct investment. In 1982 alone, six companies, or more than

---

This is a revised version of a paper published in *Management Japan*, Vol. 21, No. 1 (Spring 1988).

Table 1   Preference indication by Japanese firms in Paris for direct investment projects
Question: In which of the following countries would you like to realize a
direct investment project? Please give the rank order of your preference.

	1st	2nd	3rd	4th	5th
UK	8	14	6	2	0
W. Germany	18	10	1	1	0
France	0	1	10	15	4
Italy	0	0	0	5	25
Belgium	4	15	13	8	0

Source: *Nichifutsu Keizai Masatsu no Bunseki* (Analysis of Economic Frictions between Japan and France), Kansai Keizai Kenkyū Center, Aug.
1984.

all the investor firms during the preceding two decades, established
production units. This trend is maintained up to this date with the
average number of six or seven cases a year.

The causes for this impressive turn in situation are multifarious. On
the French side, the failure of the industrial policy founded on the
solution française has obliged the French government to revise radically
its restrictive and selective screening policy on Japanese direct investment. Approval of a joint venture between Toyoda Machine Tools and
the French HES is a case in point. A second possible cause is the high
level of unemployment, exceeding 10 per cent, in the last several years.
This problem has prompted the government to be more receptive to
foreign direct investment in general but to that by Japanese companies
in particular. Benefiting from such a favourable change in attitude,
coupled with various fiscal, financial, and other forms of incentive,
several Japanese multinationals have made direct investments in such
depressed areas as Alsace-Lorraine, Bretagne, and southern France.
A third and probably more significant element is the interest of the
French government and industry to acquire advanced technology from
Japan. This is in line with the government's established policy of *ré-
novation industrielle*, or modernisation of the French industry.

The above shift of the French government as regards Japanese direct
investment culminated in the statement by Laurent Fabius, then Industry and Research minister, during his visit to Japan in July 1984,
to the effect that France will adopt a more receptive stance to Japanese
direct investment, provided that it is beneficial to both countries. To
Japanese businessmen, France offered a large and attractive market
which had been left largely untouched while Japanese multinational
firms were busy setting up their production units in the UK or in West

Germany. Now that direct investment opportunities have been more or less exploited in these two countries, it was logical for the Japanese companies to turn to France.

Direct manufacturing investment was also envisaged in France as insurance against French protectionism. Besides, it was felt easier to export from France, a country which was running chronic trade balance deficits with West Germany and other major industrialised countries. This factor, however, seems to be secondary, as most Japanese firms studied have invested in France not so much to circumvent protectionism as to realize their global strategies.

Because Japanese direct investment in France is a relatively recent phenomenon, it has not been studied, at least not on the same level of detail and comprehensiveness as that in the UK or West Germany. The following is a report on a study carried out with a view to testing some of the basic hypotheses in the areas of Japanese multinational management. One relates to the transferability of the so-called Japanese management or, to be more specific, of the distinctive characteristics of Japanese management behaviour and structure. Second is the localisation policy and its reality. Coupled with this is the problem of headquarters-subsidiary relations.

The field study was conducted between March 1 through 28, 1987, at 13 Japanese subsidiaries, all manufacturing companies operating in France. The interviews were carried out with 18 Japanese chief executives and managers and 12 French counterparts. The interviews were based on a pre-prepared questionnaire. During the process, the interviewees often provided additional views and information beyond the scope of the questionnaire. As a result, the interviews consisted of both structured and open-ended feedback. The average duration of the interviews was approximately two hours, sometimes over lunch or during a factory tour or were interrupted by telephone calls and other contingencies. Hence the smaller number of usable responses.

Some major research findings

(1) Motives for Direct Investment in France
(multiple answers)

As a part of global strategy development	13
To fend off possible protectionist measures	5
Incentives from the French government	2
To counter a competitor's move	0

Contrary to initial expectations, all of the Japanese subsidiaries studied established themselves in France as a step in implementing the firm's global strategies. Five firms mentioned insurance against possible protectionism. French protectionism did seem to play an important role in the motives of Japanese firms in considering France as a host country.

(2) Earnings Situation

	Positive	Break-even	Negative
Annual	4	2	6
Cumulative	3	1	8

Reflecting recent start-up dates, the majority of the firms were still running deficits both on an annual and a cumulative basis. Cumulative break-even position means that the subsidiary has recovered all the initial investment in fixed assets, working capital requirements, and other set-up expenses.

(3) Projected Earnings Position

Annual	Positive in		Actual	
	1 year	2	0.5 year	1
	2 years	2	1 year	1
	2.5 years	1	3 years	1
	3 years	5		
Cumulative	Positive in		Actual	
	2 years	1	1.5 years	1
	3 years	1	2 years	1
	5 years	6	10 years	1
	7 years	1		
	10 years	1		

Five subsidiaries had, as an objective, a maximum three-year period in which to generate the first profits. An equal number of firms were even more ambitious to shoot for a target period of less than three years. In fact, such an optimistic projection was not altogether unreasonable. Three subsidiaries were able to place their operations on a profitable basis within three years; one did so in half a year. Given the strong international competitiveness of Japanese products, it seems relatively easy to realize profitable operations within a short period of time after the start-up.

In cumulative terms, most subsidiaries were trying to recover their initial investment within five years (six firms). One firm estimated that it would take ten years to do so, but this is rather exceptional. One company recuperated its total investment in one and half years. This is the same company which realized the first profits within half a year.

(4) Overall Operating Performance since the Start-up
Better than initially anticipated   5

As initially predicted   3
Worse than expected   1

The subsidiaries were generally pleased with their operating performance compared with their initial forecast. Only one company reported that its performance was below initial expectations.

(5) Overall Operating Performance compared with the Japanese level

Much worse   1
Worse   4
About the same   1
Better   1
Much better   1

By and large, overall operating performance of the subsidiaries is inferior to the Japanese level. This is not surprising, as most of them have recently started their operations and therefore have not yet reached a cruising speed. Three firms which reported same or better performance had been active in France for several years.

(6) Factors Contributing to the Performance

Structure   2
Strategies   6

(product 3, pricing 2, distribution 2, advertising 2, after-sales services 1)

The majority of the respondents believed that their strategies were largely responsible for the performance, with only two stressing structure. This invites an important conclusion, that strategies determine the success of local production, not the structure related to the characteristics of Japanese management, even if they are applied at all.

(7) Comparative Performance with Japan

	Superior to Japan	Equal to Japan	Inferior to Japan
Reject rate	2	5	5
Productivity	0	4	8
Employee turnover	3	7	2
Absenteeism	1	2	9
Loss of workdays due to labor conflicts	0	4	6

'Better than expected' would be the typical reaction of Japanese managers on the comparative performance of their French subsidiaries with the Japanese home-country units. Firms reporting the same or better work-reject rates were more numerous (seven) than those who replied to the contrary (five). Productivity was still not up to the Japanese standards, probably because of the recent start-up of the manufacturing facilities. Employment turnover was very low, and this may be partly due to the same reason. It should be stressed that most subsidiaries were located in the depressed areas of France where the unemployment rate was above the national level. Absenteeism was rather high compared with Japan. (It is recognized that this may not be a valid comparison.) The same would apply to a comparison of the loss of work days due to labour conflicts.

Transferability of Japanese management structure

When a company operates a business unit outside of its home country, it faces the following questions in regard to the way in which the foreign operations are to be managed: 1) the grounds and feasibility of management transfer. Is it desirable and possible to try to transfer specific elements of structure and strategy of the home office and factories? 2) identification of transferable elements. If so, which elements of the home country strategies and structure should be transferred?

To answer the first question, the Japanese firm must develop an in depth understanding of the distinctive characteristics of management in the host country. 'Distinctive characteristics' are always a relative concept and should be identified in relation to the way Japanese firms are managed in Japan. This requires that the Japanese undertake a serious study of management characteristics of both countries in comparative perspective. The guiding policy of such an analysis should be to identify what may be termed comparative advantages of local management as opposed to Japanese management. This process calls for an examination of relative strengths and weaknesses of host country management methods relative to that of the Japanese counter parts.

It is curious that despite a mountain of literature on Japanese management, little effort has been undertaken so far to define what Japanese management is. Terms like Japanese management or Japanese management style have been used without a clear-cut definition of what is meant by them. Even on such key concepts as lifetime employment, it is doubtful that there is reasonable consensus on a definition.

An analytical framework defining the characteristics of Japanese management behaviour is therefore in order. One approach may be to analyse a firm in its interaction with the environment (strategy) and its internal process of adapting its resources in response to the threats and opportunities which the external world presents to the firm (structure).

Table 2   Organisational structure and industrial relations: a Japan-UK comparison

	Japan	UK
WORK		
Work ethic	Source of intrinsic satisfaction	Unpleasant means of earning money
Work atmosphere	Disciplined formality	Relaxed informality
Work unity	Group solidarity	Individualistic; indifferent to others
Job interchangeability	Large	Small
STATUS		
Status security	High	Low
Status difference	Small	Large
HIERARCHY		
Hierarchical relations	Cooperative	Conflictual, competitive
Hierarchical gap	Small due to finer grading	Large
View on position	Prestige	Power and authority
AUTHORITY		
Attitude toward authority	Accepted; considered legitimate; more respect for management prerogatives	Authority challenged and resented; limited managerial prerogatives
Extent of authority/ functions	Broad; extending beyond work relations	Narrow; limited to work relations
Responsibility	Diffuse, unclear	Specific, clear
Sanction	Symbolic sanction of the superior	Sanction against directly responsible
Behaviour regulation	Collective commitment	Individual control
RECRUITMENT AND EMPLOYMENT		
Source	School to company	Individual to company
Relations	Permanent	Contractual
TRAINING		
Outlook	Investment	Cost
Cost	Company-sponsored	State-sponsored
OJT	Important	Less important
In-company training	Extensive and systematic	Less extensive and systematic

Table 2 contd.

	Japan	UK
WORK SKILLS		
Owner	Shared by individuals and belong to firm	Belong to the individuals
Competence validation	By company	By professional associations
Validity of experience	Company-specific	Industry-wide
Objectives	Socialisation, indoctrination (internalisation of company-specific values	working competence; functional skill development
INDUSTRIAL RELATIONS		
Union-company relationship	No fundamental discrepancy in the norms and goals of the union and those of the company	Fundamental incompatability of the norms and goals between the union and the company
Union legitimacy	Union right legitimised and recognised	Less institutionalised
Degree of institutionalisation	More institutionalised	Less institutionalised
Union structure	Company-based single union	Craft-based plural unions
Activity	Active at the company level	Not active at the company level
Financial resources	More resources	Less resources
Defense of the interest	Oriented to the defence of the long-term company interest	Oriented to the defence of the interest of a skill-based group
Union-management consultation	Institutionalised	Not institutionalised
Union-middle management relationship	Conversion of interest	Antagonistic

Source: Based on Ronald Dore, *British Factory–Japanese Factory,* London, 1973.

Strategy is defined as the determination of the basic long-term goals and objectives of an enterprise and the adoption of means of action and the allocation of resources necessary for carrying out these goals (Chandler, 1962). More specifically, strategy is a combination of products and markets selected for the firm. Strategic decisions are therefore concerned primarily with external problems of the firm and with selection of the product mix which the firm will produce and the markets to which it will sell (Ansoff, 1965). Structure refers to the designing of the organization through which the enterprise is administered, i.e., the lines of authority and communication as well as the information and data that flow through these lines of communication and authority (Chandler, 1962). Environment is understood to be all economic, political, and socio-cultural forces but particularly the market situation which is likely to influence the firm's strategies.

It is beyond the scope of this paper to cover all the elements. Only the structural dimension will be addressed. Table 2 indicates characteristics of the structure of Japanese firms as compared with those of Britain. Though this contrast may not be entirely valid for establishing a Japanese-French comparison, it may serve as a starting point. In fact, it may be safely assumed that the traits of French management structure share many commonalities with those of the UK. In order to look into the specifically French characteristics, however, we will review some of the literature relative to the subject.

Characteristics of French management style

'L'entreprise est une monarchie, ou ce n'est rien' (A company is a monarchy, otherwise it is nothing), quipped de Fouche, former chief executive of Paribas, France's largest financial group. Perhaps no other phrase summarizes so well the high degree of power concentration in the hands of French chief executives. Another oft-used expression, *'le patron de droit divin'* (a president by divine right) falls under the same category.

According to research conducted by G. Benguigui, D. Monjardet, and A. Griset on eight industrial firms and two research centers, the majority of the foremen were complaining of not receiving sufficient information to fulfil their tasks and of being subjected to excessive control excercised on them by their superiors. The autonomy of the foremen is substantially limited by such control and also by the retention of information. Under such circumstances, it is difficult for the foremen to perform their task or to make a decision. They are not informed of the basic policy of the top management, and therefore their dependency on the latter is increased. Indeed, 69 per cent of the foremen and other middle managers studied felt that they were poorly informed of the important decisions of their firm, and 70 per cent thought they had no basis on which to understand the objectives of such decisions. This leads to a profound feeling of detachment of the middle management from the top management.

In Guy Groux's *Les Cadres* (1983), M. Bauer and E. Cohen argue that the middle management rarely participates in the elaboration of specific policies, let alone general policies of their firm. Many feel they are excluded from the real process of decision making. This is why an important part of the middle management adopted the attitude of distance and disengagement vis-à-vis the top management and is still more reinforced in the ensuing economic crisis.

Papin claims that centralisation of power in the chief executive officers in French firms entails two negative consequences. Firstly, the chief executive officers directly interfere with the managers of all echelons and with all sorts of problems. Their decisions are not limited to strategic issues but are extended to planning, control, and even to day-to-day management details. They are hostile to participation of subordinates in the decision-making process. Secondly, this power concentration leads to arbitrariness and uncertainty of the decisions. The president, by virtue of his absolute authority, does not need to justify his decisions to anybody, not even to himself. A decision is typically made by him alone or in consultation with a few assistants without proper preparation and therefore under a highly uncertain situation.

The result is that the quality of decision will suffer and that the president himself has to interfere to remedy the shortcomings during the implementation stage. This is the reason why the president is involved in details and short-circuits the hierarchical channel. Since the decision is taken personally by the president, it is at any time open to revision, modification, or cancellation. Under such a decision-making process, the first victim is the middle manager who perceives himself as being insufficiently entrusted with authority and bypassed by the president who deals directly with their subordinates. Since middle management is largely excluded from the process of analysis and elaboration of a decision-making act, potential problems cannot be identified beforehand and come to the surface only when the decision is implemented. The end result of all this is that not only middle management but also the

rank and file become negative, ironical, and critical of such a decision
and even distort and sabotage the implementation work.

G. Hofstede (1983) used the concept of power distance in his comprehensive study of work-related values of 50 nations. Power distance
is essentially the degree of inequality in power and wealth in a society.
The higher on the power distance scale, the more centralised and au-
tocratic is the leadership. France scored the highest power distance
index among the industrialised nations, followed by Belgium, Spain,
and Italy.

In a similar survey on nine European nations and the United States,
André Laurent (1983) found that French managers together with Ital-
ian and Belgian counterparts tend to consider authority as property
of the individual. He concludes that France is indeed the country where
the power for decision making, implementation, and control is most
strongly concentrated in the hands of the chief executive.

The situation described above seems to be a phenomenon widespread
in the Western industrialised nations, though in France the problems
are perceived as more serious. The common root of the difficulties is
the Taylor method of scientific management, which originated in the
USA. For several years, Taylorism has been under mounting criticism
in France. Taylorism practiced in France is essentially identical to
what it is in the USA and other European countries. As is well known,
Taylor's principles of work rationalization are based on the dual division of labour, horizontal and vertical. Horizontal division of labor
calls for execution of an elementary task for which every worker has
more or less the same capability to perform. Put in another way, work
is fragmented into a number of most simple tasks so that even an unskilled worker can deliver the standard level of work performance
with very little training. Vertical division of labour reserves the function
of planning, supervision, and control for the management, and the
role of execution for the workers. Authority and responsibility are clearly defined for individuals and for each layer of management, and the
tasks and standards are specified for each category of workers.

Taylorism has been criticized primarily because it confines middle
and lower management as well as the rank and file to their respective
narrow and specific activities. In fact, this facilitates the control by the
supervisors, as 'the more a worker deploys his intelligence on the production line, the more he is likely to escape from the organization and
from the managerial control'. The price of this system is worker aliena-
tion. Hérve Sérieyx, president of the French Association of Quality
Control Circles, reported a case of a worker who said, 'Every morning

before I start working, I put my intelligence in the locker, and I take it back when I leave the factory at the end of the day'. A group of chief executives, headed by François Dalle of L'Oréal, have been advocating for quite some time the need to reverse this traditional work method under the slogan of *Taylorism à l'envers* (reverse Taylorism).

From the foregoing descriptions on what the French perceive as one of the major challenges of management, it appears that the Japanese model may offer an effective alternative to deal with this problem.

Hypothesis One: *Japanese subsidiaries in France assign a high degree of importance to direct communications between top management and the rank and file.*

Our findings do indicate that most Japanese subsidiaries studied are practicing some form of communication, written or verbal, direct or indirect, throughout the hierarchy.

It is interesting to note, however, that the French top executives in Japanese subsidiaries in France believe much more in direct communication with the rank and file and are indeed practicing it with a stronger commitment and confidence than are their Japanese counterparts. One may even say that as far as the subsidiaries are concerned, the local French executives are the best practitioners of this specific and major element of Japanese management, and not the Japanese expatriates. The following two cases explain the situation.

Case One. This subsidiary belongs to one of the leading Japanese multinationals in the consumer electronics industry. The company's production unit in France was the first major direct investment by a Japanese firm in that country and therefore has been covered extensively by the local press. This subsidiary is probably one of the most successful Japanese multinationals operating in France both in terms of presumably high working morale of the employees and of its financial performance. This manufacturing unit is rather exceptional in the sense that its chief executive is French. He is a passionate believer in direct communications with the first-line operators. He does not say that this is an ingredient of Japanese management but qualifies it as *management par le bon sens*, meaning that it is of universal validity, not specific to Japanese companies.

The French general manager holds monthly information sessions for all employees, in the factory canteen. The first 20 minutes are for his report on the overall situation of the firm, including the competitive position, the market, operating results, and long-term goals and policy.

The factory director then has another 20 minutes in which to brief them on the production results, productivity figures, and other matters related to production management. The last 20 minutes are reserved for questions from the floor. This dialogue lasts more than one hour, which is a good indication that the employees are really involved in the exchange of information. The same briefing session is held three times on the same day in order to cover all the operators, who work three shifts. Since the company has another factory, the whole process is repeated there. This means that the top management spends at least two full days per month at this, not counting the time for preparation.

The emphasis placed on the direct dialogue with the rank and file is evident. The factory boasts of productivity at the level of 95 per cent of a comparable home-office unit in Japan, about the same reject rate, and nearly zero turnover rate. Absenteeism is inferior to the Japanese standard, but is about half of the local average. Other elements of Japanese management practised include salary determination according to the earnings position of the company, a multi-skilled workforce, emphasis on teamwork, egalitarianism, and Quality Control circles.

Case Two. This subsidiary is also in the consumer electronics industry. It is a joint venture where the Japanese company has a minority stake. This factory shares a commonality with the foregoing case in terms of localisation at top management level. The president as well as the factory director are French, and the latter acts as de facto president, as the former is based in Paris away from the factory.

A sociologist by education, the factory director seems to enjoy practical application of organizational and motivational theories in his own factory. Use of sociometrics to determine optimum member structure of work groups is one example. He openly admits that his leadership behaviour is strongly influenced by the Japanese example.

His central belief is that French management suffers from excessive individualism and that *esprit de communauté* is a viable alternative to the problem. This he implements by being physically close to the workers. He has deliberately installed his office adjacent to the factory. The wall of his office facing the factory is made of large window panes so that he can have a panoramic view of the factory from his desk. Conversely, the operators can see him working in the office. Below the window wall on the factory side are installed several sofas for the employees to sit down and relax. The idea is for the factory manager to be able to join them easily when he feels inclined to have informal conversations with them.

Among the Japanese subsidiaries covered by this study, this particular one has adopted perhaps most extensively and intensively what are usually considered to be Japanese management characteristics. Life-time commitment is declared an official policy, and indeed it is not an abstract slogan. During the period shortly after the Poitiers incident, the factory was in a distressed situation because it was deprived of a regular supply of components from Japan. Even during this difficulty, the factory did not discharge a single worker and assured them of employment guarantee. The French general manager appeared on television to protest the government decision, which put the company in great difficulty. He said, 'It is not the prime minister, but I who must pay for the salaries of 150 workers of my factory'.

Salary differentials are maintained at a minimum, the degree of formalisation is low, as there are no written job descriptions or position descriptions for the managers. Emphasis on indoctrination of company goals and norms, decision by broad consensus, and promotion criteria based not so much on technical skill as on tacit endorsement of the potentials of subordinates are some of the management characteristics at the factory.

In comparison with a similar establishment in Japan, the factory reports a reject rate of about the same level for VCRs, higher for audio equipment, a zero turnover rate, and zero work days lost. The French factory manager boasted that many of the woman employees leave the factory and go shopping proudly with their work uniforms on.

In striking contrast to these French managers, the Japanese general managers interviewed, without exception, keep a low profile in implementing such a direct dialogue with the employees. Their typical attitude would consist in saying, 'We don't like to impose our ways in France'. This may be due to the following factors. Firstly, most Japanese general managers do not speak French, at least not fluently enough to speak directly to hundreds of employees at an official meeting. Secondly, they do not like to be seen as overbearing, arrogant, or pushy in trying to reinforce communications from above. Thirdly, such direct contact with the rank and file represents nothing new and exciting to them. They cannot become as enthusiastic about use of direct channels of communication as their French counterparts, for whom it may be an almost revolutionary approach.

Localisation policy and headquarters-subsidiary relations

William Ouchi (1977) presented two models of control: behaviour control and output control. Control is defined by Ouchi as a process of monitoring something, comparing it with some standard, and providing selective rewards and assessments. The basic assumption of behaviour control is that if one behaves as he should know he should (transformation process), he can be certain that the expected performance will be delivered. In the case of output control, such transformation process need not be known at all, but a reliable and valid measure of the desired output must be available. Behaviour control is suitable when each individual's contribution to the output cannot be determined, as in the case of the double plays made in baseball. Output control is possible when individual assessment of output is possible, as in a singles tennis match.

Which control modality is appropriate for the headquarters-subsidiary relations? The headquarters can certainly assess the subsidiary performance with clearly quantifiable criteria, such as return on investment, market share, production, volume, and productivity. Normally, however, a subsidiary is not completely independent of the home office. For instance, it has to purchase finished products from it for resale on the local market or buy components to assemble into complete units. The subsidiary performance, therefore, depends largely on the product design and production cost and other elements of marketing mix developed by the headquarters. Under the circumstances, it is difficult to isolate the subsidiary's contribution from the headquarters in a subsequent assessment process. It is probably for this reason that Japanese firms in general resort to behaviour control.

Egelhoff (1984), based on Ouchi's dichotomic model, undertook a study on the control patterns of US, UK, and European multinationals. His theoretical framework is summarised in Table 3.

From the contrast of two control models, it is apparent that behaviour control fits more easily into Japanese management structure. Indeed, one may even argue that structural characteristics of Japanese corporations are based on behaviour control. In a Japanese company where tasks are assigned to and performed by a team rather than individuals, where lines of job demarcation are fluid and flexible, where managers and the rank and file are evaluated not on a short-term basis but in long-term perspective under the life-time employment system, there seems to be little room for output control. Instead, behaviour

Table 3   Patterns of subsidiary control

	Behaviour Control	Output Control
Control Modality Means of Control at Subsidiary Level	Personal control Parent firm managers filling key positions at subsidiary	Factual control Reporting system based on precise goals
Control Emphasis Monitoring, Evaluation, and Feedback	Process At subsidiary level	Output At parent level
Underlying Premise	Shared understanding and agreement on the goals and the process	Formalization of the goals and the process

Source: Based on William G. Egelhoff, 'Patterns of Control in U.S., U.K. and European Multinational Corporations', *Journal of International Business Studies*, Fall 1984 (slightly adapted).

control provides a much more efficient mode of control under the Japanese organisational context.

Behaviour control by the Japanese headquarters on its foreign subsidiaries is therefore a logical consequence. Under behaviour control, overseas subsidiaries are controlled through personal contacts by the home office manager, rather, by factual control based on data and other written quantitative information. Less home-office control is required as the top-level managerial positions of subsidiaries are filled by expatriate home-office managers. A larger delegation of authority and responsibility is realized under behaviour control with the result that monitoring, evaluation, and feedback over subsidiary performance are done at a subsidiary level rather than at a parent-company level.

The requirement and the degree of formalisation are lower for behaviour control than for output control, as the process and the goals as well as the performance evaluation criteria need not be spelled out as clearly and in as much detail as in the case of output control.

From this theoretical framework, the following set of hypotheses can be made relative to the control modality of Japanese subsidiaries in France.

Hypothesis Two: Low Level of Localisation: *Japanese subsidiaries in France are managed by Japanese managers, and few French or third-country nationals assume such positions.*

Localisation is defined here as appointment of local nationals to the chief executive post or other top-level executive positions for subsidiary management. Japanese multinationals are notorious for their ethnocentric orientation. This fact is sometimes criticised by the European press. In a study by Negandhi (1985) on US, West German, and Japanese multinationals, the majority (79 per cent) of the Japanese multinationals did not employ even a single host-country national in the top management rank, while the majority of American subsidiaries were employing local nationals in such positions, and German subsidiaries were somewhere in between the two extremes.

In our sample of 13 Japanese subsidiaries in France, there are 7 which are wholly owned by the Japanese parent. Of these, only two were run by French chief executives. The Japanese propensity to rely on home-country nationals for subsidiary top management is confirmed by our study too. Six of the 13 subsidiaries gave usable answers on the question related to their localisation policy, which are summarized here:

1) Established policy on localisation
           Yes   5   No   2

2) The localisation policy is announced
           Yes   1   No   5

3) The localisation policy is effectively carried out
           Yes   0   No   5

4) Localisation within the next five years is
           Probable   1   Difficult   5

5) Do you think the local employees are frustrated due to lack of localisation policy or lack of its implementation?
           Yes   0   No   5

The first finding is that there is a large discrepancy between the established policy on localisation and its actual implementation. While five subsidiaries responded that they had a standing policy for localisation, only one officially had declared the policy to the local personnel. What is more significant is that no subsidiary was actually putting the localisation policy into practice. The policy remained essentially a slogan not backed up by deeds. Furthermore, most firms hold that localisation would not be probable in the next five years. Still more interesting is that no subsidiary thought that the lack of localisation would entail lower morale of the employees.

The author recalls a loaded question submitted in writing to him during a seminar organized in a European country by a Japanese multinational firm. Most of the European managers working in the company's subsidiaries were present. The author was presiding over a session for exchanges of views, opinions, and suggestions on all aspects of the subsidiary between the local managers and the Japanese staff. The question was, 'Are we working with the Japanese or for the Japanese?' The dialogue which ensued was not very fruitful, to say the least. One of the European managers who presumably had written the question asked the Japanese executives, hesitatingly, whether and when the declared localisation policy would be effectively realized. A Japanese home-office executive who had flown in from Japan gave an ambiguous answer. The European managers were visibly disappointed, and they probably thought that the Japanese headquarters were paying a lip service to the localisation policy.

During the author's interviews, one of the French managers who had been working with the company for over ten years commented as follows: 'This company does not have any local European top executives at any of its subsidiaries in Europe. I am not happy. If I am not motivated, how is it possible that my subordinates would be?'

Localisation as an empty slogan was also criticized by at least three Japanese expatriate general managers themselves. One of them admitted that localisation policy was developed by the headquarters to enhance their corporate image in Japan.

Case Three. Another Japanese chief executive had to experience a rather dramatic experience over the discrepancy of the localisation policy between the subsidiary and the home office. His French personnel manager had been so dedicated and efficient in dealing with delicate labour union negotiations that he sent him and his wife to Japan ostensibly for training but in fact as a reward for his performance. During his stay in the Japanese home office, he was introduced to the president, who told him that the company was pursuing a localisation policy. The president was probably not talking specifically about the subsidiary but was merely stating a general policy.

The French personnel manager, however, thought that he was going to be promoted to head the subsidiary. He took the president's words as an official commitment for his imminent promotion. Upon his return to France, he hinted to his colleagues and subordinates that he was soon to succeed the Japanese general manager, who would be returning to Japan. Gradually, the Japanese general manager was no longer given regular reports by his managers, and it took some time before he realized what was happening. This was followed by bitter personal and working relations between both. Finally, the French personnel manager left the company. Since then, the position of personnel manager is not entrusted to a French national, and the Japanese general manager assumes the function.

Various reasons were given to the question 'Why is your subsidiary not yet localised?' Most frequent grounds were, firstly, possible communications difficulty with the home office, and secondly, difficulty of finding local managers to fill the executive positions.

Even Japanese general managers who in principle were for the localisation policy after an initial start-up period were generally doubtful if local nationals would be qualified as top executives. The alleged communications problem with the home office rather reveals an insufficient level of internationalisation at the home office level. This does not necessarily mean that the home office does not have a qualified staff capable of communicating effectively in English with local nationals of the subsidiaries. Nearly all the firms studied are Japan's leading multinationals whose international experience extends over two decades. There should be a fairly important reservoir of specialists who have already worked abroad. It may be therefore not a question of possibility but one of preference of the home-office staff as well as the Japanese staff working in foreign subsidiaries. The Japanese staff find it by far easier to communicate among themselves rather than with non-Japanese local managers.

The other reason, that of difficulty of finding qualified local nationals, does not seem to be justified either. According to a French president interviewed, it should be relatively easy to recruit local managers at the top and middle management level. He stresses that Japanese multinationals are highly regarded as stepping-stones to advance one's professional career. The French chief executive continued that his subsidiary had been able to recruit middle managers who accepted a drop in their previous income to join the Japanese subsidiary. Besides, many French managers are potentially interested in a job opportunity in a subsidiary of a Japanese firm, as they are unhappy to be excluded from the decision-making process and to be given only a low level of autonomy, according to the French president.

Hypothesis Three: Larger Autonomy for Subsidiary Management: *Since the Japanese expatriates are supposed to internalise the process and the goals, there will be less need for home-office control, and therefore there will be broader freedom of action for the subsidiary general managers.*

Negandhi's research findings (1985) quoted earlier indicated that the Japanese subsidiaries scored the highest degree of influence in decision making. Expressed in what he termed as an overall delegation index, the Japanese were the highest, 2.89, while the value for the German subsidiaries was 1.4 and for the US counterparts –1.68. Our findings are similar to the above, as the majority of six subsidiary general managers replied that their decision-making authority was sufficient, with only one complaining that it was too limited. Eight respondents, however, said that the headquarters required excessive amounts of reports.

Hypothesis Four: Lower Level of Formalisation: *There will be less formalisation at subsidiaries, as organisational goals and processes are understood and shaped by the subsidiary managers.*

In this respect, subsidiaries in France are basically identical to firms in Japan, which are also characterised by a low degree of formalisation.

1) Tasks, authority, and responsibility for managers are

    Defined by writing   4

    Not defined   5

    In process   1

2) Tasks for white-collar personnel are

    Defined in writing   4

    Not defined   5

    In process   1

Out of nine responding firms, seven worked without operating manuals relative to the subsidiary activities and reporting requirements. Only two subsidiaries were given such manuals from the home office. One of them had six volumes of operating procedures, but this should be considered as exceptional. Perhaps the typical attitude towards operating manuals was expressed by a Japanese general manager, 'We know what we have to do and how we should go about it. Exceptional problems are handled on a case-by-case basis by talking directly with the home office people'.

In contrast and as if to compensate for the low degree of formalisation, the density of communication, both written and verbal, between subsidiary and home office is rather important. One subsidiary manager was calling his home office every day; five were in telephone communications two to three times a week; and one was doing so one or two times per week. Communications by facsimile is also utilized. Though precise information was not obtained, personal contact with the headquarters executives and managers was also important. Two subsidiary general managers receive, on the average, visits from 20 home-office staff per year, one between 30 and 40 from Japan.

Conclusion

This study, though of a preliminary nature, offers three suggestions for the management of foreign manufacturing operations of Japanese multinationals.

(1) Application of specific elements of Japanese management structure by local general managers. It should be stressed again that specific characteristics of Japanese management structure are relevant and meaningful only when they are presumed to help remedy the drawbacks of local managerial behaviour and system. In the French context, one of the most serious challenges is the motivation of the rank and file through participation in information and decision making. This necessitates a frequent and intensive verbal communication directly between the first-line personnel and the top executives to their middle management.

In our study, three local chief executives and a manager have demonstrated outstanding capability as well as a firm and almost religious conviction of the validity of such direct contact. For the reasons indicated already, the Japanese expatriates, at least at the present, seem to be far less equipped to deal with the task.

(2) Implementation of a localisation policy. This leads to our suggestion that French manufacturing activities should be managed by local nationals who share such a belief. The many advantages that will accrue for the Japanese multinationals are summarised in Table 4, together with the conditions required for implementing the localisation policy.

Discrepancy between policy and practice over localisation might provoke serious credibility and a communications gap between the local middle management and the Japanese top executives. Declaring localisation policy without immediate prospects of its implementation can be harmful. Japanese multinationals have three alternatives: they officially announce their localisation policy when the candidates already exist to take up the top executive positions; make localisation conditional on the fulfillment of specific requirements by local candidates; or, thirdly, not make it public at all.

In any case, more transparency and straightforwardness are imperative for the localisation policy, as it usually has an important repercussion on the career plan and expectations of local managers and personnel. The worst situation would be to merely pay lip service to the localisation policy, giving a false impression of forthcoming promotion of local nationals to top management positions.

(3) Balance between autonomy and control in subsidiary-head-

Table 4   Advantages and conditions for localisation of subsidiary top Management

Advantages

1. Enhancement of employee motivation and identification with company
2. Synergistic integration of strengths of Japanese and local managerial structures
3. Maintenance of consistency in the modality of subsidiary management
4. Increased communications effectiveness both internally with the personnel and externally with the government, trade associations, market, press, etc.
5. Reduced cost involved in installation and transfer of Japanese expatriate managers

Conditions

1. Local top executives must be familiar with the comparative advantages of local management and Japanese management characteristics to integrate them into a coherent and more competitive organizational structure
2. Minimum degree of formalisation to define the roles, responsibilities, and authority of local top executives
3. Establishment of more elaborate reporting and control systems to enable the headquarters to grasp the overall subsidiary performance before problems get out of control
4. Use of local executive search firms to recruit local top-level staff
5. Japanese expatriates to serve in an advisory capacity for subsidiaries

quarters relations. By and large, the Japanese approach of assigning a large freedom of activity to subsidiary executives should be maintained. This is one of the major comparative advantages of Japanese multinational management, as has been evidenced by two cases where French top executives developed close contact with the rank and file. Broad subsidiary autonomy and headquarters control are not mutually exclusive. Delegation of authority should be matched by corresponding control so that headquarters is well informed of the subsidiary situation and corrective actions can be taken immediately, if necessary.

In comparison with US and European multinational management, the Japanese approach offers a set of distinct potential advantages. This potentiality, however, is not fully utilized by the subsidiaries studied here. The same would be the case for those operating elsewhere. From the perspective of the structure, the Japanese model offers a viable solution to the problems associated with Taylorism. Intense communication vertically among top, middle, and lower management echelons and between these and the rank and file, on the one hand, and laterally across different functional units, on the other, would be an interesting alternative.

This potential advantage will be fully realized by French nationals, as our case studies have indicated. The Japanese expatriates have a serious handicap in communicating effectively in the French language with the local management staff and the personnel. If such structural potential is given full play, Japanese multinational management, coupled with its already existing strategic strengths, will provide a most competitive approach to global management.

Bibliography

Ansoff, H. Igor. *Corporate Strategy*. Penguin, London. 1965.
Archier, Georges, and Sérieyx, Hérve. *L'entreprise du 3e type*. Seuil, Paris, 1984.
Chandler, Alfred D. *Strategy and Structure*. MIT, Cambridge, 1962.
'Die geschlossene Gesellschaft, Japanische Manager in Deutschland'. *Manager Magazine*, No. 6, 1980.
Dunning, John H. *Japanese Participation in British Industry*. Croom Helm, London, 1986.
ENA. 'Les implantations japonaises en France'. mars 1986.
Groux, Guy. *Les Cadres*. Maspero, Paris, 1983.
'Harmonie mit Hindernis, Japanisches Management in Deutschland'. *Wirtschaftswoche*, 12. 7. 1985.
Hofstede, Gert. 'The Cultural Relativity of Organizational Practices and Theories'. *Journal of International Business Studies*, Fall 1983.
Johnson, Richard T., and Ouchi, William G. 'Made in America under Japanese Management'. *Harvard Business Review*, Sept.-Oct., 1974.
Kujawa, Duane. *Japanese Multinationals in the United States*. Praeger, New York, 1986.
Kumar, Brij N. *Deutsche Unternehmen in den U.S.A.* Gabler, Wiesbaden, 1987.
Laurent, André. 'The Cultural Diversity of Western Conception of Management'. *International Studies of Management and Organization*, Vol. XII, Nos. 1-2.
Merz, Hans-Peter, and Park, Sung-Jo. *Japanisches Management in der Bundesrepublik Deutschland*. Express Edition, Berlin, 1986.
Negandhi, Anant R. 'Management Strategies and Policies of American, German and Japanese Multinational Corporations'. *Management Japan*, Spring 1985.

Negandhi, Anant R., and B.R. Baliga. *Tables Are Turning: German and Japanese Multinational Companies in the United States.* Oelgeshlager, Gunn & Hain, Cambridge, 1981.

Ouchi, William G. 'The Relationship between Organizational Structure and Organizational Control'. *Administrative Science Quarterly*, March 1977.

Park, Sung-Jo et al. (eds.). *Transfer des japanischen Managementsystems.* Express Edition, Berlin, 1985.

Reitsperger, Wolf. 'Japanese Management: Coping with British Industrial Relations'. *Journal of Management Studies.* Jan. 1986.

Takamiya, Susumu, and Thurley, Keith (eds.). *Japan's Emerging Multinationals.* University of Tokyo Press, Tokyo, 1985.

Trevor, Malcolm. *Japan's Reluctant Multinationals: Japanese Management at Home and Abroad.* St. Martin's Press, New York, 1983.

Tsurumi, Yoshi. 'Best of Times and Worst of Times: Japanese Management in America'. *Columbia Journal of World Business*, Summer 1978.

'Un syndicat chez moi? Jamais!' *L'Expansion*, 8–21 Nov. 1985.

White, Michael, and Trevor, Malcolm. *Under Japanese Management,* Heinemann, London, 1983.

PERSONNEL MANAGEMENT OF JAPANESE SUBSIDIARIES IN WEST GERMANY

S.J. Park
Free University of Berlin

Introduction

This paper is a summary of the empirical research on the 'Personnel Management of Japanese Subsidiaries in the Federal Republic of Germany', which was conducted from early 1986 to April 1987 (1). A rather comprehensive study (1985–86) (2) on Japanese subsidiaries prior to the above mentioned disclosed that the strategy of personnel management of Japanese companies in Western Europe appeared to be a focus worthy of further profound scrutiny.

The main accent of the study (1986–87) was placed on the question of to what extent the transfer of personnel management peculiar to Japanese big enterprises, in particular, the concept of human resources development strategy, had materialized in Japanese subsidiaries in Germany. In line with this, we firstly concentrated on the strategy of Japanese subsidiaries of how to assure and maintain regular workers (similar to *honkō*). The analysis of this point was true of recruitment practice, manpower training, and other measures of manpower integration. Secondly, it is needless to say that the strategy of personnel development has to be adjusted to local labour market conditions with a view to avoiding criticisms that the Japanese stick to a pure form of Japanese personnel policy. Additionally, the motivation and tie of local (German) employees to the company are based on a mechanism in Germany which differs considerably from Japanese practice. To get an insight into how Japanese expatriates take cognizance of this situation and how they take it into consideration was another objective.

Moreover, we were concerned with collecting information about the division of competence between Japanese expatriates and local managers in Japanese subsidiaries. The focus here was directed towards the strategy of the localisation of personnel. Particular attention was paid

206

Table 1   Japanese subsidiaries studied in West Germany

Sector	Size of employment	Up to 160 persons	201–300	301–500	More than 500
Manufacturing	1		1		
Trading	3				
Sales	1		1	1	
Banking	1				

to the existence of the interface and the structuring of its role as an intermediary between local and Japanese executives.

Nine Japanese subsidiaries operating in West Germany were chosen. Table 1 indicates the range of the sample and the company sizes. Only two manufacturing companies were joint ventures; the others were 'pure' branch offices of parent companies. The size of employment ranged from 60 to 780 persons. The other traits of the nine companies are systematised in Table 2.

Interviews usually took place with staff in the general management department. In the case of two trading companies and the bank, only Japanese expatriates were available, while other companies enabled local as well as Japanese executives to be researched.

Some remarks on the samples seem to be adequate: the main goal of two manufacturing plants in the form of a joint venture consists in providing their parent companies with (semi-) fabricated products. Accordingly, they do not have a sales department. Further, their common trait, which was made explicit, was that the adopted localisation policy of manufacturing in Europe, in order to avoid protectionism from the EC, resulted in the increase of the value added share in Germany, but this does not necessarily imply that Japanese parent companies were increasingly turning to the use of local technology and equipment.

There are considerable similarities between the trading companies. All of them were subsidiaries of Japanese general trading companies and were built up in the 1950s. Meanwhile, they showed rather moderate growth rates. Most of them were concentrated in the Dusseldorf region, with at least one branch office in Hamburg. The range of their trading products covered capital-intensive goods, including chemical and paper products, as well as labour-intensive goods, such as food products and textiles. The three sales companies were opened at very different points of time and have shown remarkably high growth rates. The regional concentration of the nine researched companies is in Dusseldorf, Hamburg, and Frankfurt. Frequently, they are represented

Table 2　Characteristics of Japanese subsidiaries studied

Item	Manufacturing		Trading				Sales		Banking
Sector companies	A	B	C	D	E	F	G	H	I
Opening	1974	1983	1958	1959	1956	1963	1970	1980	1970
Japanese capital share (%)	40	65	100	100	100	100	100	100	100
Economic growth	middle	low	extremely low	stagnant	stagnant	strong	strong	strong	middle
Branch	consumer electronics	consumer electronics	general trading	general trading	general trading	fine mechanics	electronics	electronics	banking
Employment size 1984	188	200	85	72	n.a.	335	638	64	58
1986	213	659	76	82	32	385	768	87	n.a.

by another branch office in the same place. Only two manufacturing plants are far from any urban centre, which has nothing to do with any 'policy' making.

Basic characteristics of personnel management practice

We found that the practice of Japanese subsidiaries is far from the so-called typical Japanese type of personnel management, even though it can be admitted that a clear-cut picture of a company on this point largely depends on management principles or on the transnationalisation strategy of its own parent company.

However, two different forms are striking: on the one hand, we have subsidiaries with an extremely high dependence on the parent company and, consequently, on its personnel policy decisions. On the other hand, some subsidiaries are equipped with quite a broad decision-making competence concerning business and personnel policy. According to the degree of centralisation of decision making and, to be more concrete, that of integration of the local decision-making competence into the global market strategy of the parent company, we might be inclined to classify the practice of Japanese subsidiaries into ethnocentric, or polycentric or geocentric, management. Due to the lack of comparative analysis with the practices of Japanese subsidiaries in other countries, we confined ourselves to a rather 'vague' distinction between centralised or decentralised personnel management from the standpoint of the parent company:

Centralised personnel management: trading companies C, D, E

Decentralised personnel management: production companies A,

B; sales (F, G, H); bank (I).

The empirical investigation disclosed that all the trading companies were extremely highly centralised in personnel policy, while decentralised personnel management could be found in other fields. The high degree of centralisation of personnel management can be seen somewhat 'paradoxically' in contrast to the fact that Japanese trading companies are operating on a worldwide scale. In particular, their basically negative attitude towards the German staff (employees) with regard to their technical qualifications is quite apparent, which may be presumably attributable to the extreme complexity of daily business operations as well as the subsequent absolute necessity of constant contact with the parent company. The lower significance of local personnel is reflected especially in the perception of Germans of a very low degree of commitment on the part of the Japanese company concerned, and above all in an extremely disharmonious corporate ambience. These facts give birth to doubts about the seriousness of efforts by Japanese expatriates to increase localisation of management personnel.

Regarding the other aspects of decentralised personnel management, it may easily be assumed that the strong influence of local executives with their pertinent competence in the formation and development of the whole personnel management can be exercised very efficiently. We should, however, admit that much depends on how the personality and individual motivation of local managers make use of their personnel policy decision-making capacity. However, the sole fact that local managers do accede to the top decision-making level of Japanese subsidiaries (in the case of companies A, B, F, G, H, and I) is clear evidence of the seriousness with which Japanese subsidiaries put the localisation policy of personnel into effect. Furthermore, this endeavour corresponds significantly with the decreasing share of Japanese expatriates in the top management of Japanese subsidiaries.

Thus, we can arrive at the conclusion that the increase in the degree of localisation of personnel management results in the increase of local executives' influence, and the transfer of Japanese personnel management to subsidiaries in Germany was thus becoming superfluous. This means that one should speak of 'international' rather than 'Japanese' personnel management in such decentralised subsidiaries (3).

Low relevance of the hypothetical construct 'interface'

The second topic to be dealt with was the problem of 'interface'. We conceived of the interface as a neutral position and informal function with regard to mediation between local employees and Japanese expatriates.

We were interested to know who (at which hierarchical level) was fulfilling the interface function and how this positioning was changing in the meantime. It was additionally presumed that different employment structures (*Belegschaftsstrukturen*), in the sense of a peripheral or standard worker status, were evolving among Japanese expatriates or local employees.

The most interesting fact was that our investigation led to a useful distinction between an enterprise-internal interface and a concern-internal interface. The latter refers to the cooperation and competence distribution between the parent company and its subsidiaries. In the case of trading companies with centralised management where an extremely clear-cut structure has already evolved, the control was excercised by Japanese parent companies through expatriates. In companies with rather decentralised management (manufacturing, sales, banking), a different situation was observed. German subsidiaries were partly given broad autonomy. In general, the Japanese general managers (*Geschäftsführungsmitglied*) or, in the case of solely German general management, the German managers (A) perceived the interface-function vis-à-vis the parent company. Serious difficulties in the co-operation between the parent company and its subsidiaries very seldom arose. This means that the formation and functioning of a concern-internal interface is being pursued in terms of the selection of expatriates almost exclusively on the side of the parent company.

Of crucial importance, however, is the question of an enterprise-internal interface. Our research did not verify the hypothesis as regards the enterprise-internal interface. The localisation of the interface does not primarily depend upon its hierarchical position, but on its (respective) nationality, which implies that the interface for expatriates is a Japanese executive, the interface for the local staff a German one.

In case of conflicts, each side's interface is impelled to solve them through its own channel.

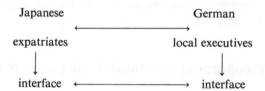

German executives as well as Japanese executives perceive interface-function here. No influence can be expected from the informal structure which has been shown in the meantime, nor in the case of the shrinking relative proportion of expatriates.

Consequently, there is by now no indication of a transfer of the interface function from Japanese expatriates to German local executives. That is to say that the personnel structure does not play any role because basically all Japanese expatriates belong to the category of core workers (employees) of the parent company, this situation not being true of German local staff. No correlation exists between enterprise-internal interface and the possible proper consideration of this interface in the framework of a comprehensive personnel policy of development planning.

In sum, the hypothetical construct concerning the interface has proven to be practicable to a limited extent. Summarising the enterprise-internal and concern-internal aspects, the following picture can be imagined:

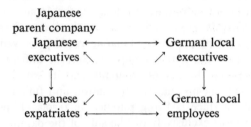

According to the difference in types of enterprises, there is a different weighting of interrelationships: in the case of trading companies strongly dominated by Japanese management and with a low degree of importance of German local staff, the interface structure deserves no consideration; the concerns of the German local staff are perceived as having minor importance in the cons ciousness of Japanese management. Wide autonomy in corporate decision making is, however, attributed to them by nearly all the other firms: in short, they have a relatively high degree of independence from the parent company. However, it remains unanswered to what extent this judgement corresponds with reality (4).

Lack of the concept of personnel development planning

Our research also revealed that no company possessed a basic concept or strategy of personnel development planning. Obviously, most of the companies researched had introduced certain rules and principles, which partly imply some elements of personnel development planning and which could be conceived of as a sort of personnel policy concept under certain circumstances. However, this practice was usually confined to daily and short-term management operations.

What are the reasons for the lack of a personnel development concept which, on the contrary, is so consistently underlined as peculiar to Japanese management? The main reason which was very frequently mentioned was rapid economic change which makes the working out of personnel development planning impossible. The other reason is the relatively small size of the company concerned. The third factor may be that, due to the labour market situation in Germany, there is little motivation for Japanese personnel planning or its adaptation to the supply of (highly) skilled manpower available in the local labour market, as well as the frequent job changing of German workers, which prevent enterprises from carrying out basic internal personnel training.

The above-mentioned adjustments of Japanese subsidiaries in West Germany to local conditions and needs refer to the internationalisation, or Europeanisation, of Japanese management, at least in the companies with decentralised management. To put it in more concrete terms, Japanese subsidiaries have practised no consistent personnel development policy based upon Japanese management. One can consequently raise much doubt about the broadly described thesis of a positive attitude toward sthe transfer of Japanese personnel management to Japanese subsidiaries abroad (5).

Notes

(1) In the meantime, this study was published by Susanne Kitscha, Martin Küchle, and Hans-Peter Merz, as *Personalmanagement japanischer Niederlassungen in der Bundesrepublik Deutschland*, Frankfurt/New York, 1988.

(2) Cf. Hans-Peter Merz and Sung-Jo Park, *Japanisches Management in der Bundesrepublik Deutschland*, Berlin, 1986.

(3) Cf. H. Demes, H.-P. Merz, S.J. Park, *Japanische Unternehmen in der Bundesrepublik Deutschland*, Social and Economic Research on Modern Japan, Occasional Papers No. 55, Berlin, 1984.

(4) It was reported in a seminar on Japanese (-German) enterprises in West Germany that some different types of interfaces have already evolved.

Toyota: German executives as interface in the four functional departments

Minolta: German top executives equipped with international business experiences and some training in Japan, however, without Japanese knowledge; some supervisors (Germans) in sales department

Kao: Interface function applies to technology and legal matters, however, not to communications function

Sony: Japanese as interface sent from the parent company.

(5) Cf. H. Demes, H.-P. Merz and S.J. Park, 'The Japanese Personnel Practices in Germany: A Case of Misunderstanding', *Euro-Asia Business Review*, May 1985, pp. 20ff.; H.-P. Merz, *Personalpolitik japanischer Unternenhmen in der Bundesrepublik*, Berlin 1987 (Diss.). JETRO's survey arrived at a different conclusion concerning the personnel management of Japanese companies in Europe. See JETRO, *Japanese Manufacturing Companies Operating in Europe*, 2nd Survey Report, Tokyo, 1986.

HOW JAPANESE WORK OUT AS BOSSES IN GERMANY

H.J. Heise
The Executive's Counsel

This paper presents the results of an empirical study of personnel management and business administration in Japanese companies in West Germany, based on the experience of German executives working in these companies. Two problem areas were chosen for study in a project that began in 1986 and was completed in 1987: (1) recruitment—how Japanese subsidiaries in Germany rate different methods of staffing, and (2) problems in transnationalisation—personnel management and business administration (1).

An open and structured questionnaire was used as the guideline for interviews, which averaged four hours. A total of 23 (25) German sales and/or marketing managers of 23 different Japanese subsidiaries in West Germany were interviewed. Their work experience at the subsidiaries ranged from one to 26 years, and their ages from 26 to 52 years. In educational background, there were more than half who had apprenticeship backgrounds rather than university or polytechnic training. (See Appendix 1.) The subsidiaries themselves were manufacturers of a variety of goods, from cameras and motorbikes to office equipment and chemicals. Company size ranged from those staffed by less than 50 to those between 200 and 500 employees. (See Appendix 2).

The employment interview

The majority of the managers interviewed (65.2%) rated very poorly the Japanese managers' ability to run a professional interview. Thus, the majority of these managers chose to join the Japanese company not as a result of a professional and convincing interview but in spite of a poorly conducted employment interview.

214

Table 1   Accuracy of information given by the Japanese management during employment interview (%)

	Completely correct	Partially correct	Reasonably accurate	Partially incorrect	Completely incorrect
Planned orientation period and training (N=20)	15	20	10	35	20
Possibility to discuss with the Japanese management actions to be taken and plans related to the department of the German manager (N=22)	9.1	31.8	40.9	13.6	00.0
Managerial style (N=21)	4.8	19.0	28.6	38.1	9.5
Dependence on parent company to make decisions (N=19)	0.5	31.6	15.8	26.3	15.8
Qualifications of subordinates (N=18)	11.1	33.3	16.7	22.2	16.7
Organizational climate (N=17)	17.6	5.9	41.2	11.8	23.5

The respondents were asked to assess, in retrospect, the information given to them by the Japanese during the interview, regarding the accuracy of that information on a scale of 1 to 5, i.e., level 1 being 'completely correct' and level 5 'completely incorrect' (see Table 1). The responses differed regarding the interviewees' length of working experience at these subsidiaries. However the assessment of the respondents who had seven and more years of experience did not differ greatly from those with only one to six years of experience.

The following information was determined as being primarily correct:
 – the duties of the respondent;
 – the personal authority to make a decision;
 – colleagues' qualifications;
 – opportunity of the respondents to discuss their plans and activities with the Japanese management;

- the number and function of Japanese staff in the German subsidiary;
- future economic development of the Japanese subsidiary in West Germany.

The following information was assessed as being accurate but with some reservations:

- extent and frequency of reporting;
- qualification of the subordinates;
- opportunity of the respondents to discuss the plans and activities of their Japanese management;
- working atmosphere (attitude of the staff towards the corporation and its goals);
- actual financial situation of the Japanese subsidiary in Germany.

With a great deal of reservation, the following information was assessed as being correct:

- management style of the Japanese;
- dependence on the parent company to make decisions;
- planned orientation period and training.

It is noteworthy and surprising that the specific elements of Japanese management, such as the possibility to discuss management decisions and dependence on the parent company, were presented so poorly to many of the German executives that they did not consider themselves as having been well informed. This might be caused by the difficulty of the Japanese in explaining their management style in the way it is experienced by foreign personnel.

If the information about the future tasks of a local manager is incongruent with the subsequent reality, the candidate will have made a decision for a particular job based on inaccurate information. Therefore, he may have decided to take a job and join a company that he will not find. If he had known the reality beforehand, he might not have accepted the employment offer.

Within the first 12 months after joining, 34 per cent of the respondents seriously considered leaving the company. Among those managers interviewed with less than 7 years experience in a Japanese subsidiary, 42.8% seriously considered leaving the company within the first 12 months.

Assessing the staff

The ability of the Japanese managers to assess local staff and job candidates was severely rated by the respondents. Questions were posed

Table 2   Capability of Japanese managers to assess personal characteristics of local staff and job candidates, as rated by German executives (%)

Staff Category	Excel-lent	Good	Satis-factory	Less than satisfactory	Poor	Totally insuf-ficient
Staff ($N=19$)	5.2	15.8	21.1	21.1	31.6	5.3
Group leaders ($N=19$)	5.3	5.3	26.3	26.3	36.8	0
Department managers ($N=21$)	4.8	9.5	14.3	33.3	38.1	0
Sales representatives ($N=22$)	0	13.6	22.7	22.7	27.3	13.6
Regional sales managers ($N=21$)	0	9.5	23.8	28.6	33.3	4.8
'Specialists' (EDP, advertising, product management) ($N=21$)	0	5	5	30	35	25

Table 3   Capability of Japanese managers to assess job-related qualifications of local staff and job candidates, as rated by German executives (%)

Staff category	Excel-lent	Good	Satis-factory	Less than satisfactory	Poor	Totally insuf-ficient
Staff ($N=17$)	5.9	5.9	41.2	17.6	35.3	0
Group leaders ($N=18$)	5.6	22.2	16.7	33.3	22.2	0
Department managers ($N=21$)	4.8	23.8	23.8	23.8	19.0	4.8
Sales representatives ($N=22$)	0	18.2	31.8	13.6	31.8	4.5
Regional sales managers ($N=21$)	0	19.0	19.0	14.3	42.9	4.8
'Specialists' (EDP, advertising, product management) ($N=21$)	0	4.8	33.3	14.3	28.6	19.0

concerning assessment of personal characteristics (Table 2) and job qualifications (Table 3).

In all of the six staff categories, between 58 and 90 per cent of the respondents rated the capability of Japanese managers to assess personal traits as from less than satisfactory to completely unsatisfactory. The shortcomings in the assessment of personal characteristics of specialists are very obvious.

In five of the six staff categories, the rating capabilities of Japanese managers for job-related qualifications were better than their rating capabilities of personal characteristics. It is not surprising to see that they received better results concerning these ratings because they are not as culturally determined as in the case of personal characteristics.

Relations between expatriate and local staffs

More than 50 per cent of the respondents rated their Japanese bosses poorly in their knowledge and understanding of the German executives' job, while 40 per cent felt that their understanding was good or very good. The empirical data clearly underline the findings of other research concerning the conviction of local managers of Japanese subsidiaries about this deficiency of their leaders. Tsurumi states, for example: 'American subordinates test their chief executive's ability to lead, decisively resolve problems, and seize opportunities. Unfortunately, most Japanese chief executives fail this test' (2).

The lack of competence of Japanese superiors in the knowledge and understanding of the job of the respondent is possibly an explanation for the perceived weak-to-average pressure exerted by Japanese executives for better performance (see Table 4).

The support offered by Japanese superiors in the event of difficulties was also surveyed. Out of 24 responses, we find that support was given

Table 4   Do Japanese superiors exert pressure on local managerial staff? (%)

	None	A little	Mod-erate	A lot	A great deal
Managerial staff (N = 24)	25	20.8	29.2	16.7	8.3
Managerial staff with one to six years experience in the firm (N = 14)	7.1	21.4	42.9	21.4	7.1

in various degrees: great, 28 per cent; moderate, 28 per cent; some, 28 per cent; and none, 16 per cent. Still, 62.5 percent felt that more support could have been given. The reasons for this were various and fall into the following general categories: the Japanese management was indecisive, wished to avoid conflict, or lacked knowledge. Also, their primary interests seem to lie with the parent company and with sales (but not in other aspects). The support given by the Japanese superiors to their German managers is on the whole problematic, not only regarding the amount of support but also its quality.

Decision making and motivation

The Japanese decision-making process had negative effects on the necessary motivation of German managers and their staffs and on the execution of actions decided upon. Out of 23 responses, 34.8 per cent felt that there was little or no motivation and that a negative working environment was created; 47.8 per cent felt little motivation; 8.7 per cent felt some motivation; and 8.7 per cent felt considerable motivation.

Our study confirmed empirically the findings of other authors concerning the Japanese decision-making process in overseas subsidiaries. For example, Kobayashi states: 'Japanese managers in their overseas operating units often lack the confidence and ability to make on-the-spot decisions. In asking the parent company for approval, the speed of decision-making is rather slow' (3).

In German and Japanese management, the motivational efforts go in different directions. Out of 23 responses, 17.4 per cent perceived a clear contradiction in motivational efforts, which resulted in a weakening of the achievement of corporate goals. Some mutual support with frequent contradiction was felt by 43.5 per cent; frequent mutual support with some contradiction was felt by 17.4 per cent; and 23.7 per cent felt a strong mutual support.

Management authority

Leadership as experienced by the subordinate German managers is mainly determined by the possession of 'exclusive' information by the Japanese management, which is not available to the subordinate German managers. This was experienced by 87.5 per cent of the respon-

Table 5   Type of authority of Japanese managers (%, $N = 24$)

	Never	Seldom	Often	Always	Occasionally
Formal	29.2	4.2	16.7	12.5	37.5
Based on professional competence (intelligence, know-how)	12.5	29.5	25.0	4.2	29.2
Selective (exclusive) information	0	12.5	50	0	37.5

dents who said that this happens occasionally to frequently. The formality and competence of expatriate managers as viewed by 24 German managers are given in Table 5.

Using 16 attributes (4), we were able to obtain the following picture of the Japanese superior of the German managers:

He is mainly friendly (79.2%)   accepting (75.0%)
               cooperative (70.8%)   optimistic (70.8%)
               supportive (66.7%)   pleasant (60.9%)
               capable/efficient (54.2%)

He is also mainly tense (66.7%)   frustrating (62.5%)
                    insecure (58.3%)   distant (54.2%)
                    guarded (54.2%)   chaotic (54.2%)
                    nonproductive/unimportant (54.2%)

The Japanese superior is seen by more than 50 per cent of the respondents as being warmhearted and interesting; the other half see him as cold and boring.

If we look at the ratings of the Japanese superior by their local subordinates (who have 1 to 6 years work experience in Japanese companies in Germany), it is evident that there is little deviation in the percentages regarding the positive remarks. Only the attribute 'capable/efficient' is reduced from 54.2 to 50 per cent.

Of the negative ratings the trend is more pronounced: tense (78.6%, compared with 66.7%); distant (71.4%, compared with 54.2%); reserved (71.4%, compared with 54.2%).

Basically, the employee has the possibility to inform his superior concerning perceived negative attributes or to choose a behaviour which conveys this message and hope that this will effect a change in the Japanese superior.

Regarding the attributes 'tense', 'insecure', 'distant', and 'reserved' given by the respondents, one may presume that such efforts by the subordinate German managerial staff will have little impact because of differences in cultural assessments of these attributes. Moreover, such an attempt even by German subordinates of German managers would be extremely difficult and problematic.

Regarding the attributes 'chaotic', 'unimportant', and 'frustrating', the difficulties are basically the same, but these shortcomings could be more easily conveyed to the superior, because they are more factually related. The impact of this negative assessment of Japanese managers by their German staff makes it evident that the situation is difficult to remedy.

Conclusions and recommendations

We have identified the recruitment of managerial staff, personnel management, and business administration of Japanese subsidiaries in West Germany as being very problematic. It was the intention to show that the occurrence of problems between German and Japanese management is not only a question of bi-cultural differences, but also that these problems indicate shortcomings in the managerial qualifications of the dispatched managers. This situation, however, can be remedied.

A study involving German middle management shows just how difficult this attempt is. It shows that job satisfaction does not increase to the same degree for all members of staff just because certain working conditions have changed. Moreover, the changes must be tailored to the individual's needs, and he has to perceive this as an improvement, if job satisfaction is to increase. The values of employees and their expectations of management are important factors to be considered for effective leadership.

We pointed out above the problems that Japanese managers have in grasping the personal characteristics of a German staff, as well as the difficulties they have in recognizing factors that motivate subordinate local management. The following are recommendations for Japanese management:

(1) Train Japanese managers to be sensitive to the motivational needs of German employees.
(2) Use executive search companies experienced in working for Japanese companies in Europe to relieve the problems in the recruitment of managerial staff and in their personnel assessment. Any management problem can ultimately be reduced to a question of human resources.

(3) The founding and use of advisory boards could be promising for Japanese subsidiaries in West Germany, provided the members of such boards have sufficient experience in dealing successfully with the general problems discussed in this paper.

Advisory boards can be created freely and are not required by law. The company can determine freely the legal status as well as the rights and obligations of the board members. The practice by various companies is manifold and can be adjusted to the individual needs of a company. General experience shows that in companies with a large number of senior managers, the advisory board mainly has a 'control' function, whereas in smaller companies with only a few senior managers, the advisory board provides consulting services and advice. A large number of companies who have an advisory board attach a high value to such a body.

Notes

(1) An earlier paper on this topic was presented in December 1985 at the Policy Studies Institute: 'How to Eliminate Risk in Recruitment: Some Reflections on Executive Search and Personnel Policies of Japanese Subsidiaries in Germany'.
(2) Yoshi Tsurumi, 'The Best of Times and the Worst of Times: Japanese Management in America', in Yoshi Tsurumi, *Japanese Business: A Research Guide with Annotated Bibliography*, New York, 1978, p. 109.
(3) N. Kobayashi, 'The Japanese Approach to "Multinationalism" ', in M.T. Skully, *A Multinational Look at the Transnational Corporation*, Sydney, 1978, p. 123.
(4) The attributes are in accordance with F.E. Fielder, *A Theory of Leadership Effectiveness*, New York, 1967, p. 51.

Appendix 1: Data on respondents

Length of working experience:
    1– 3 years: 30.4% 11–14 years: 13.0%
    4– 6 years: 30.4% 15–26 years: 17.5%
    7–10 years: 8.7%

Respondents' age:
    26–39 years: 17.4% 45–49 years: 30.4%
    40–44 years: 30.4% 50–52 years: 21.8%

Respondents' education:
    Graduates (university or polytechnic): 34.8%
    Apprenticeship: 65.2%

In what language do the respondents speak to their Japanese superiors?
87% in English   13% in English and German

Appendix 2:
Data on subsidiaries where the respondents worked

Kind of industry
office equipment, watches, consumer electronics (hi-fi, video, TV), medical equipment, transport machinery, pharmaceuticals, cosmetics, computers, household appliances, cameras, motorbikes, controls, chemicals.

Length of time in West Germany
35% more than 5 years   65% more than 10 years

Company size (m = million)
34.8%   less than DM 50m sales   21.7%   DM 100–250m sales
34.8%   DM 50–100m sales   8.7%   over DM 250m sales

Number of staff
30.4%   less than 50 employees   30.4%   100–200 employees
26.2%   50–100 employees   13.0%   200–500 employees

Sales in 1984–85
87.0%   growing   0 %   decreasing
13.0%   stagnating

Sales forecast
60.9%   growing   0 %   decreasing

Production facilities
91.3%   no local production plant   8.7%   local production plant

Japanese managerial positions in these companies
87.0%   Japanese managing directors and/or Japanese controllers
13.0%   neither Japanese managing directors nor Japanese controllers

Part III
European Management in Japan

SWIMMING AGAINST THE TIDE? THE STRATEGY OF EUROPEAN MANUFACTURING INVESTORS IN JAPAN

Hafiz Mirza, Peter J. Buckley, and John R. Sparkes
University of Bradford

The outward urge (1)

The last two decades have witnessed the internationalisation of the Japanese economy at a spectacular pace (see Table 1). In the 1970s, this process was especially evident in the rapid expansion of visible and invisible trade (both exports and imports); but in the 1980s, partly as a consequence of this trading success, the baton has passed to international investors and financial institutions. Table 1 shows that long-term capital outflows from Japan (be these direct investment, portfolio investment, or international bank loans) have soared over the period between 1980 and 1986. This expansion overseas is increasingly aggressive, e.g., in 1986, Japanese takeovers in the USA exceeded US$2 billion in value (2), and there is no sign of a slowdown. The Export-Import Bank of Japan predicts a further expansion in outward foreign direct investment (3); and the outflow of long-term capital from Japan during 1987 (at US$170 billion) boosted the stock of such foreign assets by 36 per cent (the 1986 stock was US$476 billion (4).

Of course, the surge in Japanese capital outflows is not unique, and a cursory examination of the net international capital flows of nine industrialised economies (Table 2) reveals that some countries are investing abroad at a very rapid pace (5). However, it is also clear that Japan is in a league of its own (6), with a net long-term capital outflow of US$284.6 billion during the period between 1980 and 1986. This situation is due to a variety of factors including (a) the appreciation of the yen by 61 per cent between 1980 and 1986 (Table 1); (b) a high savings rate combined with non-expansionary economic policies in the domestic market; (c) an increased institutional and corporate awareness of overseas opportunities which can be exploited through recently acquired international managerial experience; and (d) the

227

Table 1   The internationalisation of the Japanese economy
(US$ billions, except where stated)

Item	Value				Expansion (%)[a]	
	1970	1980	1985	1986	'80/70	'86/80
Visible trade						
Exports	19.3	129.8	174.0	205.6	572	58
Imports[b]	18.9	140.5	129.5	126.4	643	−10
Net	0.4	−10.7	44.5	79.2		
Invisible trade						
Exports	4.0	31.5	45.6	53.5	687	70
Imports	5.8	42.8	50.6	58.0	638	36
Net	−1.8	−11.3	−5.0	−4.5		
Foreign direct investment						
Outward	0.4	2.4	6.5	14.1	500	488
Inward	0.1	0.3	0.6	1.8	200	500
Net	0.3	2.1	5.9	12.3		
Foreign portfolio investment						
Outward	0.1	3.8	59.7	102.1	3,700	2,587
Inward	0.3	13.1	16.7	5.4	4,267	−59
Net	−0.1	−9.3	43.0	96.7		
International bank lending.						
Outward	0.6	2.6	10.6	9.2	333	254
Inward	0.1	−0.2	−0.1	−0.1	. . .	. . .
Net	0.5	2.8	10.7	9.3		
Accumulated external Japanese assets and liabilities						
Assets	na	159.6	437.7	727.3	na	356
Liabilities	na	148.0	307.9	547.0	na	270
Net	13.0[c]	11.6	129.8	180.3		
Comparative information						
GNP ($)	203.1	1,040.1	1,331.5	1,963.2	412	89
GNP (¥ tr.)	73.1	240.1	317.3	330.8	2,298	38
World Trade	186.0	1,985.0	1,922.0	2,110.0	967	6
Exchange rates						
¥/$[d]	357.6	226.7	238.5	168.5		
Effective[e]	73.8	100.0	127.1	161.0		

Sources: Bank of Japan, *Economic Statistics Annual*, 1986.
IMF, *International Financial Statistics*, Yearbook 1986 and May 1987.
Daiwa Bank, *Monthly Research Report*, June 1987.
Mitsui & Co., *Mitsui Trade News*, May/June 1987.
GATT, *International Trade*, 1981/1982.
GATT, *Focus*, April 1987.

Notes: a: [(Value 1980 − Value 1970)/Value 1970] × 100. Similarly for 1986/87.
b: CIF values. c: 1973 value. d: period averages. e: Effective exchange rate against a basket of currencies (based on the IMF's MERM model).

Table 2   Japanese internationalisation in a comparative perspective, 1980–
1986[a]

(US$ billions)

Countries	Net International Flows of Long-Term Capital			
	Direct Investment	Portfolio Investment	Other	Total
Canada	−25.1	35.2	−3.8	6.3
France[b]	−3.0	26.6	−23.3	0.3
Germany	−21.6	48.1	−19.0	7.5
Italy[c]	−3.4	−5.9	24.2	14.9
Japan	*−40.1*	*−152.8*	*−91.7*	*−284.6*
Netherlands[c]	−17.3	0.8	−10.8	−27.3
Sweden[c]	−5.8	−4.3	−11.0	−21.1
UK[d]	−22.3	−62.9	−14.4	−99.6
USA	55.3	179.4	−80.2	154.5

Source: IMF, *Balance of Payments Statistics*, May 1987.
Notes: a: 1980 to 1986 inclusive. b: Figures for France are up to the 2nd
quarter, 1986. c: Figures for Italy, Sweden, Netherlands to 3rd
quarter; d: UK to 1st.

Table 3   The world's 30 largest banks ranked by assets, 1986
(US$ billions)

Bank	Assets	Bank	Assets
Dai-Ichi Kangyo	240.74	Sumitomo Trust	125.15
Fuji	213.47	Nat. Westminster	122.86
Sumitomo	206.12	Taiyo Kobe	116.51
Mitsubishi	204.79	Barclays	116.41
Sanwa	192.29	Mitsui Trust	116.05
Citicorp	191.35	Société Generale	
Industrial Bank		Long Term Credit	116.01
of Japan	161.61	Bank of Japan	115.52
Crédit Agricole	154.40	Bank of Tokyo	115.25
Banque Nationale		Daiwa	102.83
de Paris	141.87	Bank America Corp.	102.20
Tokai	138.45	Yasuda Trust	101.34
Norinchukin	136.92	Dresdner	101.18
Crédit Lyonnais	132.07	Chase Manhattan	
Mitsui	132.04	Corp.	94.76
Deutsche	131.80	Union Bank of	
Mitsubishi Trust	127.37	Switzerland	93.72
		Paribas	93.24

Source: *Euromoney*, June 1987.

continuing strength of Japan's economy and major commercial institutions. One example of this international prominence is given by Table 3, which shows that Japanese banks have edged US and French institutions out of their former pre-eminent positions (as ranked by total assets): the top five banks are Japanese, and they also occupy 17 of the top 30 places.

The hollow economy

Yet Japan's internationalisation is not entirely of its own planning, and the government and business community are only too painfully aware of the inherent dangers. Manufacturing firms, in particular, have been driven abroad by the Scylla and Charybdis of increasing low-cost competition from the newly industrialising countries (7) and a dollar in free-fall against the yen:

> Businessmen and government officials, sounding plaintively like their counterparts in the US Rust Belt, stew about the 'hollowing out' of their industries. They have a point. Fully 20% of the country's manufacturing will take place overseas by the turn of the century, vs under 5% today. . . . As a result, manufacturing employment is heading inexorably downwards (8).

The concept of a 'hollow economy' in which manufacturing plays a minimal role was first introduced by *Business Week* (9) in an analysis of the deindustrialisation of the USA. Japanese companies hope to avoid the pitfalls encountered by their counterparts elsewhere, but the pressure to secure foreign markets (e.g., via massive manufacturing investments in the USA) and reduce costs (by investing in the developing countries of Latin America and Pacific Asia) remains intense. In 1986, over half of the 100 largest Japanese companies (10) saw their sales fall, and a third recorded a decline in profits (albeit only seven of these, mainly in steel and shipbuilding, actually suffered a loss).

Despite the difficulties of the country's domestic manufacturers, foreign companies continued to invest in Japan. The bulk of foreign direct investment in Japan (of which three-quarters is in manufacturing) has arrived since 1980 (11), in effect during a period contemporaneous with Japanese foreign expansion. The annual flow of inward FDI tripled to US$1.8 billion between 1985 and 1986 (Table 1), clearly manifesting considerable commitment by foreign companies to the

Japanese economy. According to JETRO, as the Japanese economy spreads its wings:

> US and European multinational businesses are expanding their investment in Japan (R&D investment also [sic]) in such high-tech fields as electrical machinery, electronics and pharmaceuticals. Investment in the financial and securities fields is also on the increase (12).

Given that Japanese manufacturing companies are moving abroad under intense competitive pressures, are foreign multinationals moving into calamity? Or is there a method in their madness? This paper will try to shed some light on such questions by exploring some of the results of a continuing study of European companies with a manufacturing presence in Japan.

Salmo Europar profiled

The project referred to above (the 'Bradford Study') has a current sample size of 28 European parent companies with at least one manufacturing affiliate in Japan, though many companies have several such affiliates. The methodology of the research involves the questionnaire-based interview of executives at each parent company *and* also of executives at their affiliates in Japan. Information was collected on a great many aspects of European companies' strategy and experience in Japan (13, 14), but this paper will examine only some of the results.

Table 4 gives details of foreign investors in Japan. In total, European companies comprise only about a fifth of all foreign direct investment in Japan by value, but their share of annual inward investment is increasing: in 1985, this share was almost a third—and was probably greater in 1986. A comparison of columns 2 and 3 of Table 4 (see table note 'c') indicates that the 28 parent companies (and 79 affiliates) in the Bradford Study represent a fair share of European companies with manufacturing bases in Japan. (The total number of European affiliates established in Japan is of the order of 1,100, but most of these are not involved in manufacturing.) The firms interviewed were domiciled in nine different West European countries (seven EC member countries), roughly in proportion to the scale of each country's manufacturing presence in Japan. The table also shows that there is a concentration of manufacturing investments in two broad industrial categories:

Table 4   A profile of foreign investors in Japan

Country or Industry	Total Value of Inward FDI 1950–85[a] (US$ Mill.)	Total No. of Manuf. Affil's., 1972–86[c]	Bradford Study	
			No. of Parent Co's.	No. of Affiliates[b]
Belgium	6.8	na	2	4
Denmark	12.3	2	4	5
France	137.5	11	3	15
Germany	250.4	17	4	17
Italy	na	na	2	5
Netherlands	166.4	4	3	9
Sweden	84.9	7	2	10
Switzerland	377.5	12	3	4
UK	318.5	8	5	10
Other Europe	74.0			
USA	3,040.6	109		
Other Countries	1,778.3	7		
Commerce	773.6			
Construction and Real Estate	41.3			
Transportation/ Communications	20.1			
Warehousing	43.5			
Other Services	275.8			
Others	526.9			
Manufacturing	4,566.1	177	28	79
Ceramics	113.5	4	1	
Chemicals[d]	2,162.7	66	14	
Machinery[e]	1,447.6	61	11	
Metal Products	408.3	10	2	
Textiles	31.4	2		
Petroleum and Pet. Products	606.2	2		
Rubber	36.7			
Food	157.8	7		
Others	208.0	25		
Total	6,247.2	177	28	79

Sources: MITI, Bank of Japan, Bradford Study.
Notes: a: Approvals/notifications. b: All parent companies in the study
          are involved in manufacturing in Japan, but this does not apply
          to all of their affiliates. c: Only affiliates with 50 per cent or more
          foreign ownership. d: Includes pharmaceuticals. e: Includes all
          machinery: general, electronic, precision, etc.

chemicals and machinery. The firms in the Bradford Study roughly fit this pattern.

Strategy by consecutive reasoning (15)

The motivations underlying the 28 parent firms' manufacturing investments in Japan are complex, but despite the heterogenous nature of the sample (in terms of source country, industry, size), it is possible to establish a general framework of strategic intent. This is perhaps best analysed by discussion in terms of three inter-related sub-categories of strategy:

1. The bottom line. In one form or another, the single most important reason for entering the Japanese market was almost universally the size and potential of the country's market (Table 5). Of course, this was frequently qualified by contingent factors, e.g., import barriers, need to expand market share, need to service specific customers, but the primacy of Japan's market remains. The same conclusion, hardly surprising since Japan constitutes over 10 per cent of the world economy, is confirmed in recent surveys by the Nomura Research Institute (Table 9, categories 1 and 2) and JETRO (16). At this level, the decision to manufacture in Japan is defined largely on the basis of cost: tariff barriers and transportation costs (e.g., for bulky machinery and plant) are positive influences, while global economies of scale (on 'commodity' chemicals) tend to reduce the likelihood of local manufacturing.

However, there is always an element of service provision in the marketing of manufactured goods, and the need to tailor products to the specific tastes and requirements (indeed whims) of Japanese cus-

Table 5 The single most important reason leading to manufacturing investment in japan.

Reason	Number of Parents
1. Japanese market size, rate of growth, or potential[a]	15
2. To cover world market	8
3. To control marketing efforts in Japan	2
4. Defensive reasons	2
5. Technological reasons	1
Total	28

Source: Bradford Study.
Note: a: Includes difficulty of market access due to barriers, etc.

Table 6   The target market of European investors in Japan

Category	Number of Parents
1. Industrial customers only	12
2. A range of customers[a]	11
3. Not known	5
Total	28

Source: Bradford Study.
Note: a: Of which three or four companies are almost entirely consumer-market oriented.

tomers was frequently sufficient justification for establishing a manufacturing base. One interesting finding of the Bradford Study is that about half of the sample companies are orientated solely towards industrial customers (Table 6). Three factors jointly explain this bias: the highly competitive Japanese market permits only firms with advanced technological expertise or other advantages to survive; industrial customers are easier to locate (especially given the complex distribution system), and these customers are demanding in regard to specifications and quality. The last point tends to enforce a Japanese presence.

Another factor is that the firms in the Bradford Study tend to take a long-term view. The potential rewards of the Japanese market are deemed to be sufficiently great to justify low profits while the affiliates are (or were) establishing a firm local foothold. Japan's current difficulties are seen to be short-term ones of readjustment, while the potentialities of Japanese liberalisation are seen as immense (17).

2. **Presence effects and the insider.** Though the size of the Japanese market is sufficient to warrant attention and some cost and service considerations may determine the establishment of local manufacturing facilities, these factors do not explain the full range and extent of manufacturing FDI in Japan. The Bradford Study suggests that much of the explanation for this FDI lies in the considerable externalities obtained from a presence in Japan.

(a) *Presence effects.* One way of looking at these effects is by dividing the barriers to trading in Japan into three types. The first type is simply tariff (and similar) barriers which can be surmounted by jumping the tariff wall, as discussed above, or making an impact at inter-governmental and international fora. A second type is non-tariff measures (NTMs), which are introduced by national authorities or business organisations (e.g., standards and specifications, both mandatory and voluntary) and are either complied with (as many in the

Table 7   "Reverse" transfer of technology and expertise.

'Does your presence in the Japanese market stimulate the home company to make better or more competitive products?'[a]	Number of Parents
Yes	15
Not yet, but expected to	5
No	6
Not known	2
Total	28

Source: Bradford Study.
Note: a: For example, through technology or skill transfer.

sample chose, sometimes to their advantage) or countered with a great deal of fuss. The fact that companies can exploit NTMs to their benefit may warrant a local investment. Finally, there are non-tariff barriers other than NTMs (NTBs) which, in the case of Japan, include language and culture; patriotism and a degree of xenophobia; and distinctive business ethics. According to the sample of firms in the Bradford Study, a local presence was frequently beneficial in such cases. For example, customers are more willing to purchase goods from European firms producing in Japan because such firms are regarded as being near-Japanese; better qualified personnel are more willing to work for foreign firms with a track record of commitment to the Japanese economy (a recent study lends credence to this view) (18); and a local presence is a considerable boon for establishing links with Japanese firms; relationships are long-term and between friends.

(b) *Learning effects.* Most firms believed that their manufacturing presence in the Japanese economy helped them to produce better products (Table 7), though some argued that such benefits were not uncommon in other markets. Some firms designed better products simply because of the adaptations to production methods dictated by the exacting requirements (especially in quality) of Japanese customers. Others said that they had learned from Japanese production methods per se, often in factories run with Japanese joint venture partners (19), and the skills/techniques most frequently cited as acquired were better quality and inventory control. It was also the view of most firms that Japanese productivity performance was higher than that in Europe, but this was usually qualified by the point that 'productivity' was not the right term for comparison purposes. The output per person may by higher, but only because Japanese employees continue work until they complete a task, often unpaid (20) (Table 8).

Table 8   European views on relative productivity performance

'Japanese productivity is':	Number of Parents
Higher than European productivity	11
The same as European productivity	5
Lower than European productivity	4
Don't know	8
Total	28

Source: Bradford Study.

(c) *Insider benefits.* There are considerable benefits to be gained by being considered part of the Japanese domestic scene. Few European investors could claim to be anywhere close to such an exalted position, but local production is considered an essential credential. At the fringes, some firms are beginning to be accepted as members of Japanese corporate associations, while others are making use of cheap Japanese finance in their international operations. Many firms referred to Japan as an 'information paradise' and are able to use information gained in Japan throughout the globe. The Nomura study (Table 9) confirms the importance of information: 28 out of 72 European firms refer to this as a reason for their considering investment/expansion in Japan.

(d) *The potential of the re-structured Japan.* There is little doubt (except in Japan!) that Japanese companies will emerge from their current plight as formidable competitors:

> The factories that remain could be world-beaters. Japanese companies are slashing costs and diversifying aggressively into advanced, premium-priced products and are pouring money into better manufacturing techniques. Some of the biggest exporters have slimmed down enough to operate profitably at 140 yen to the dollar. Toyota Motor Corp., for example, is said to be cutting the time it takes to bore engine blocks from 1 minute to 30 seconds. . . . Japanese business spending on civilian R&D as a percentage of the economy remains significantly larger than that of the US and the gap is widening (21).

Many of the advanced technologies of the future will be developed in Japan, particularly in the information-related industries (Table 10). Though the Bradford Study did not address this question directly, it is clear from the responses of executives in both Europe and Japan that a local manufacturing and R&D presence was regarded as essential for future competitiveness—and even survival—since this enabled

Table 9   US and European companies' motivations underlying the establishment of new bases or expansion of existing bases (Non-financial companies only)

Reasons given (Multiple responses included)	Number			%		
	USA (A)	Europe (B)	Total (C)	USA (A/D)	Europe (B/D)	Total (C/D)
Market						
1. The scale and growth prospects of East Asia/ Pacific Basin market	32	45	78	52.5	62.5	58.2
2. The scale and growth prospects of the Japanese market in particular	44	50	95	72.1	69.4	70.9
Industrial, corporate						
3. The presence of many multinationals	6	5	12	9.8	6.9	9.0
4. Rival corporations have already entered Japan	9	8	18	14.8	11.1	13.4
5. Many of the affiliated group corporations have already entered Japan	1	4	5	1.6	5.6	3.7
6. The presence of good candidates for joint venture partners	27	39	67	44.3	54.2	50.0
7. The presence of suppliers of quality components	10	16	26	16.4	22.2	19.4
Business resources						
8. Ample supply of quality labor	5	8	13	8.2	11.1	9.7
9. Concentration of information (on Asian market, advanced technology, etc.)	15	28	44	24.6	38.9	32.8
10. Availability of sophisticated technology	9	26	36	14.8	36.1	26.9
11. Ready capital procurement	8	10	19	13.1	13.9	14.2

continued on next page

Table 9 contd.

Reasons given	USA	Europe	Total	USA	Europe	Total
Conditions						
12. Political, economic, and social stability	33	33	67	54.1	45.8	50.0
13. Preferential treatment in the context of industrial policy	2	3	5	3.3	4.2	5.7
14. Hedge against exchange risks	4	7	11	6.6	9.7	8.2
15. Transportation and communication center of East Asia/ Pacific Basin	17	18	36	27.9	25.0	26.9
16. Surmount export barriers to Japan	16	24	40	26.2	33.3	29.9
17. Other	6	1	7	9.8	1.4	5.2
Total number of firms (D)	61	72	134			

Source: Nomura Research Institute's 1986 study of companies with an inclination to enter Japan.

Europeans to remain near (if not in) the forefront of new technological developments. This view is also clear from the Nomura research (Table 9, category 10).

The strategic long run. A number of commentators, including Ohmae (22), have recently argued that rapid technological change, increased competitiveness, and escalating production costs are forcing international companies into new strategic decisions. On the one hand, firms are increasingly stressing a presence in the three major loci of the industrialised world (Europe, Japan, and the USA) in order to ensure security of supply and market (and exchange threat with other major companies), and, on the other hand, it is suggested that firms increasingly establish collaborative agreements to reduce costs and mutual risks (23).

The Bradford Study does provide some support for these hypotheses. Table 11 shows the present share of Japan in the global networks of the sample firms. Most firms were of the opinion that their share of the Japanese market had to be expanded. This view was frequently expressed in terms of a 'triangular concept' of the world market, which necessitated having a manufacturing presence in the three major power bases of the world economy, Europe, Japan, and the USA (see also the second category of Table 5) (24). In a world economy in crisis, with the possibility of increased protectionism and a division of the globe into 'blocs', such an insider role has considerable merit.

Table 10   MITI information technology development projects

Project name	Description, elements, working name	Budget (¥ billion), duration
Material and device technology		
New functional devices	Three-dimensional integrated circuits, super lattice devices, biodevices	7.8 (FY 1981–86)
High-speed science and technology computation system	Very high-speed devices	23.0 (FY 1981–89)
Optoelectronic integrated circuits	OEIC	10.0 (FY 1985–95)
Applied synchrotron radiation technology	SOR (X-ray lithography)	14.3 (FY 1985–95)
Information processing technology		
Fifth-generation computer project	Artificial intelligence, natural language processing, machine translation, man-machine interface	About 20.0 until FY 1986 (FY 1982–91)
Software technology development	Technology to integrate software environment	(1982–)
High-speed science and technology computing system*	High-speed processing, large-capacity high-speed memory, decentralized processing machines, other	23.0 (FY 1981–89)
Data-base system for mutual computer operation	Multimedia, decentralized data base, other	15.0 (FY 1985–91)
Machine translation system with neighboring countries	Machine translation	6.25 (FY 1986–92)
Electronic dictionary for processing natural languages	Fifth-generation computer language concept and knowledge base	Minimum 14.3 (FY 1985–94)
Industrial software production system	Sigma project	25.0 (FY 1985–89)
Telecommunications technology		
Data-base system for computer interoperability*	Data transmission software, promotion of OSI, establishment of interoperability conformity	15.0 (FY 1985–91)

continued on naxt page

Table 10 contd.

Project name	Description	Budget (duration)
Basic measuring technology for coherent optical communications	Laser technology, high-efficiency, high-density, high-modulation system	4.3 (FY 1985–91)
Space technology		
Resources exploration observation system	Composite open radar, engineering sensor, high-speed, large-capacity transfer technology	23.0 (FY 1984–90)
Utilization of space observation	Develop space-environment testing device	5.7 (FY 1985–92)
Application systems		
Medical treatment support system	MEDIS	Undecided (FY 1982–88)
Robots for hazardous tasks	Image recognition, other	20.0 (FY 1983–90)
Advanced information processing-type image information system	Advanced HI-OVIS	4.8 (FY 1985–90)
Commissioned R&D on medical and welfare equipment	CT scanner, nervous disorder diagnosis, medical treatment support system	(FY 1976–)
Electrotechnical laboratory projects		
Materials	Electronic material, magnetic and amorphous materials, other	
Electronic devices	High-speed devices, new functional devices, other	
Pattern information	Voice, image recognition, bionics, other	
Computers	Information processing, storage, input-output technology, other	
Software	Program language, network architecture, other	
Control	Information system control technology, other	
Microwave and electronics	Laser, optoelectronics technology, other	
Information technology in extreme environments	Space environment technology, other	

Source: Seiji Hagiwara, 'Creating Tomorrow's Information Technology', *Journal of Japanese Trade & Industry*, No. 3, 1987.
Note: * Items straddle technological fields.

Table 11 Sales in Japan as a share of European firm's global sales

Share	Number of Parents
Up to 2%	3
2–4%	7
5–10%	11
11–15%	2
Over 15%	1
Not known	4
Total	28

Source: Bradford Study.

Table 12 Ownership arrangements of the affiliates of European manufacturing investors in Japan

Arrangement	Number of Affiliates
100% European participation*a*	22
Majority European participation	10
50:50 European-Japanese participation	30
Minority European participation	9
Not known	8
Total	79

Source: Bradford Study.
Note: a: Not necessarily a single European parent company.

In terms of collaboration between European investors and Japanese firms, the results of the study are more mixed. As Table 12 shows, most affiliates in Japan are joint ventures, and this tendency is also apparent from Table 9 (category 6). However, this preference for joint ventures is more readily explained in terms of their facilitating rapid access into a market which is difficult to penetrate. Having said this, a number of 'world-scale' companies in the sample are clearly establishing close collaborative links with Japanese counterparts, links involving joint production, joint research, cross-licensing, and a variety of other forms. These and other firms, nevertheless, remained cautious; after all, the Japanese *keiretsu* have a century of experience in inter-company collaboration! But a recent publication by JETRO identifies a large number of Euro-Japanese collaborative agreements of various types (25).

Concluding remarks

Most executives regarded their manufacturing presence in Japan as

Table 13   The perception of success in Japan at the European headquarters

	Number of Parents
Very Successful	12
Successful	8
Satisfied, but more can be achieved	7
Unsuccessful	1
Total	28

Source: Bradford Study.

successful (Table 13), but this opinion was normally expressed in terms of success (i) in comparison with other foreign competitors or (ii) relative to their modest objectives in a market that requires long-term commitment. In general, this commitment was secure, though some affiliates were concerned regarding the attitude of their European parents. The most abiding impression emerging from the Bradford Study is that a base in the Japanese economy is frequently viewed as being strategically crucial, especially since the reshaped Japan of the future will be even more competitive than today. However, caution is also a key word, since Japan is a difficult market to enter and, moreover, there are lucrative opportunities elsewhere in the world economy. Nevertheless, apart from the 'nuts and bolts' reasons for manufacturing locally, strategic necessity makes an insider presence in Japan absolutely vital for many firms.

Notes

(1) With apologies to John Wyndham.
(2) See 'Takeover Artists Learn the Moves', *Business Week*, 3 August 1987, p.16.
(3) See Seiichi Tsukazaki, 'Japanese Direct Investment Abroad', *Journal of Japanese Trade and Industry*, No. 4, 1987.
(4) See Daiwa Bank, *Monthly Research Report*, June 1988.
(5) Frequently the investment is to the USA.
(6) Table 2 is highly aggregated, but even when the figures are disaggregated, Japan is still far ahead.
(7) Indeed, the low-cost competition could be from anywhere—including Europe.
(8) 'Fear and Trembling in the Colossus', *Fortune*, 30 March 1987, p. 32.
(9) 'The Hollow Corporation', *Business Week*, 3 March 1986.
(10) *Business Week*, 3 July 1987.
(11) The year 1980 saw the full liberalisation of the regime controlling the inflow of foreign direct investment.
(12) JETRO, *White Paper on World and Japanese Overseas Direct Investment (summary)*, Tokyo, February 1987.
(13) The questionnaire was 16 pages long.
(14) The full results will be forthcoming in the following book: Peter J. Buckley, Hafiz Mirza, and John R. Sparkes, *Success in Japan: How European Firms*

Compete in the Japanese Market, Basil Blackwell, Oxford, 1988. There have been a number of reports and articles on other aspects of the Bradford Study. These include *European Affiliates in Japan*, a report submitted to the Japan Foundation, 1984; 'Key to successful investment by foreign companies', *Investors Chronicle*, 19 September 1986; 'A note on Japanese pricing policy', *Applied Economics*, Vol. 19, No. 6; and 'Direct Foreign Investment in Japan as a means of market entry: the case of European firms', *Journal of Marketing Management*, Vol. 2, No. 3, 1987. In addition, there has also been a more specific study of British firms based on a postal questionnaire: *British Companies' Investments in Japan*, report submitted to the Great Britain-Sasakawa Foundation, 1987.

(15) With apologies to John Keats.
(16) JETRO, *op. cit.*, page 6.
(17) See 'Dismantling the Barriers in Tokyo', *Banker*, June 1987.
(18) See The Institute for International Business Communication, *Foreign Affiliates in Japan: The Search for Professional Manpower*, Tokyo, 1987.
(19) It is not uncommon to find the manufacturing production taking place on the existing site of the Japanese joint venture partner.
(20) But many executives did note the superior talents of a Japanese team working together.
(21) 'Remaking Japan', *Business Week*, 13 July 1987, p. 39.
(22) Kenichi Ohmae, *Triad Power: The Coming Shape of Global Competition*, Free Press, New York, 1985.
(23) On cooperation between firms, see Peter J. Buckley and Mark Casson, 'A Theory of Cooperation in International Business', *Management International Review* (forthcoming) and F.J. Contractor and P. Lorange (eds.), *Cooperative Strategies in International Business*, Lexington Books, D.C. Heath and Co., Lexington, Mass., 1987.
(24) Many executives took a wider definition of the 'Japan' part of the triangle, frequently including Korea, Taiwan, and other parts of Pacific Asia.
(25) JETRO, *Cooperations Between European and Japanese Firms: Cases of Industrial Collaboration*, Tokyo, 1986.

MANAGING SUBSIDIARIES OF GERMAN COMPANIES IN JAPAN: SOME FINDINGS ON ADAPTATION STRATEGIES

B. Kumar and H. Steinmann
University of Erlangen-Nuremberg

Introduction

To the extent that German (multinational) companies are increasingly investing directly in their own production and sales subsidiaries in Japan, subsidiary management is becoming a crucial issue for them. The basic problem involved is that German companies in Japan are faced with extremely different cultural conditions from what they are used to at home. Obviously, this calls for adapting subsidiary management to local requirements. But at the same time, the attempt must be made to standardise subsidiary management according to German parent company strengths and policies. After all, it is only on the basis of these resources that these subsidiaries can hope to achieve a competitive advantage over Japanese firms who have an edge over foreign investors by being in their home market.

Finding the right balance between 'local adaptation' and 'standardisation' is a difficult task. Deficiency in the adaptation of management can cause friction with local norms and alienate the subsidiary in its environment (1). Our interviews in Japan show, for instance, that German firms must adapt Japanese leadership styles of communicating intensively with local subordinates. Failure to do so has often led to conflict between expatriate and local staff (2). On the other hand, too much adaptation (or too little standardisation) can distort the firms' specific advantages. For instance, several studies show that German products generally have a good image in Japan, in fact, better than all other nations competing in that market (3). It is therefore advisable to use this competitive advantage by standardising product attributes like brand name and quality standards in accordance with parent company specifications. According to most studies, the balance should generally be in favour of standardisation (4).

In this paper, we shall investigate on these lines the management pattern in Japanese subsidiaries of German (multinational) companies. By relating to management effectivity, the successful mode of operations will be identified.

The conceptual framework

The adaptation spectrum

In order to simplify the analysis, we shall investigate the two-dimensional management pattern defined by 'local adaptation' and 'standardisation' along a one-dimensional adaptation spectrum (i.e., standardisation is equivalent to no or low adaptation). Postulating the adaptation needs of subsidiary management only makes sense when one thinks about firms as open systems that interact with their environment. Therefore, corporate behaviour must be analysed within the context of a social system. The effectiveness of any management style can be understood only within the environmental framework of the people who are doing the managing or being managed. On this basis, we can assume that the degree of adaptation actually practised in subsidiary management will depend on how subsidiary managers perceive the difference between the parent country and host country cultures. Accordingly, we can theoretically assume three modes of management on the 'adaptation spectrum':

(1) The degree of adaptation practised tallies with the perceived differences between home and host country cultural influences. This will be the case when the subsidiary responds to market and social forces in a manner that meets the imposed constraints or what is almost totally required by economic and legal necessity in the host country. Firms in this case hardly have a choice other than to abide by legal and economic rules and institutions. Not adapting to these norms would mean dysfunctionality (*'mode of social obligation'*) (5).

(2) The degree of adaptation actually practised is greater than the perceived differences between the home and the host country. In this case, subsidiary management is adapted to general local practice, although from the viewpoint of the German company a more standardised (not necessarily more efficient) mode would also have been feasible. Apparently, local companies' evaluation of cultural influences is different; therefore, their response is different from what the foreign

subsidiaries might be able to practise. The reason for a different perception of relevant cultural influences lies in the fact that foreign subsidiaries of multinational companies with their intercultural backgrounds are more sensitive to social change in the host country than local firms. Their evaluation of environmental differences between home and host country also accounts for a shifting of norms (towards the former's culture). Therefore, they are in a position to offer management solutions which, although not presently practised by local firms, would be compatible with the (changing) host country culture. But when, in spite of having this possibility at hand, foreign subsidiaries still rather opt for prevailing local practice, they do so in order to keep down their foreign image, especially when the gain from 'taking a step ahead', i.e., making alterations before changing social norms are cemented as a part of the cultural system, is not really pertinent ('*mode of social acceptance*').

(3) The degree of adaptation practised is smaller than the perceived difference between home and host cultural influences. In this case, foreign subsidiaries deliberately behave differently (standardise more) than what present (and changing) host country norms and management practice are perceived to dictate. By reacting differently, foreign subsidiaries strive to compensate for their handicap of 'foreignness' or even get a definite lead vis-à-vis local enterprises. The assumption is that local groups often will be accommodating towards a foreign subsidiary and its non-conforming management, which in the end may even turn out to be more efficient than prevailing practice. As different studies on international management have shown, even local companies in due course often adopt such 'alien' practices. Foreign subsidiaries thus have a 'change agent' function ('*mode of social reponsiveness*').

The influencing factors

As far as modes of adaptation are subject to choice (i.e., [2] and [3] above), they will be determined by two basic factors (6):

(1) Parent company skills: When subsidiaries can count on sufficient parent company skills and resources which give them a definite competitive advantage over local firms, e.g., in products and technology, they will find it easier to practise the mode of social responsiveness.

(2) Structural elements of a subsidiary: Here, three issues are crucial (*ceteris paribus*):

Entry pattern: Subsidiaries which have been established via acquisition of existing local firms will have a higher tendency to adopt the mode of social acceptance. On the other hand, de novo ventures will find it easier to go in for social responsiveness. As various studies show, it is relatively difficult for management in take-overs to give up traditional styles in favour of new ones.

Ownership pattern: Subsidiaries in the form of joint ventures will have a greater tendency towards adopting the mode of social acceptance. On the other hand, wholly owned subsidiaries have more favourable conditions for the mode of social responsiveness. It appears that local partners in joint ventures exert pressure towards behaviour congruent with local norms.

Nationality of chief executive officer: Subsidiaries headed by parent company expatriate managers will tend more towards the mode of social responsiveness, whereas local chief executive officers will prefer the mode of social acceptance.

The empirical research and sample

The investigation was based on a questionnaire survey conducted by the authors in spring 1987. Questionnaires were sent out to chief executive officers of all companies in Japan (177 total) which, according to our own judgement, we identified in the Directory of the German Chamber of Commerce (Japan) as being subsidiaries of German enterprises. As of late spring, we received 52 completed questionnaires (30 per cent response rate). Tables 1 through 5 show some characteristics of the sample. Besides this survey, we conducted interviews in fall 1986 in Japan among some 30 German and Japanese executives who were involved in the activities of Japanese subsidiaries of German companies in one way or another. They included expatriate and local managing staff, bankers, consultants, lawyers, and distributors.

Table 1   German subsidiaries in Japan by number of employees

No. of employees (1986)	No. of subsidiaries ($N = 52$)*
1–under 25	11
25–under 50	11
50–under 100	8
100–under 500	10
500–3,000	10

Note: * Missing = 2

Table 2   German parent companies by number of employees

No. of employees (1986)	No. of answers (N = 52)*
0–under 1,000	9
1,000–under 5,000	16
5,000–under 15,000	6
15,000–under 50,000	8
50,000–250,000	11

Note: * Missing = 2

Table 3   German subsidiaries in Japan by annual turnover

Turnover in billion yen (1986)	No. of companies (N = 52)*
Up to 0.5	2
0.5–under 2.0	12
2.0–under 10.0	14
10.0–under 50.0	10
Over 50.0	11

Note: * Missing = 3

Table 4   Branches of industry

Industry	No. of subsidiaries (N = 52)
Banking	5
Commerce (consumer goods)	6
Commerce (industrial goods)	6
Food/Foodstuffs	2
Engineering (mech., auto., etc.)	9
Electrical	9
Chemical/pharmaceutical	14
Misc. (consumer goods)	1

Table 5   Type of activity of Japanese subsidiaries

Activity	No. of subsidiaries (N = 52)*
Production/sales/service/	18
Sales/service	33

Note: * Missing = 1

Some findings

Mode of management in Japanese subsidiaries

To establish the mode of management in Japanese subsidiaries of German companies according to a concept we need to ascertain (1) the actual degree of adaptation practised in management functions and areas and (2) the perceived degree of differences between German and Japanese management and cultural norms. To find out the actual pattern of adaptation practised in the subsidiaries, we used a 5-point Likert scale. The respondents were given detailed guidance on apprehension of the question posed, which had the following text:

> Managing subsidiaries of German companies in Japan means adapting to local conditions, e.g., long meetings in bars after office hours with subordinates, attending family functions of employees. It also means standardising according to parent company policy, e.g., using same brand name and technology as in Germany. Is your management in Japan more adapted or more standardised? Please check the following items by putting a mark (x) on the scale which you think applies to you.

This question was posed with respect to ten management areas and issues. A low score meant high adaptation, a high score less adaptation (more standardisation).

To ascertain the perceived divergence between home and host country cultures, we asked respondents to evaluate statements comparing management practise in Japan and Germany on a general level. The statements pertained to the same ten management areas, e.g., 'When compared with Germany, advertising is more important in Japan (e.g., more often, better quality)'.

A five-point Likert scale was used for evaluation: (1) = I strongly agree; (5) = I strongly disagree. Agreement (low score) meant that the respondents perceived divergence in the particular area. In this case, adaptation was expected. Non-agreement (high score) meant that the respondents perceived no divergence, and in this case no adaptation was expected.

The findings (Table 6) of our survey can be summarised as follows: On the whole, management in subsidiaries of German companies in Japan follows the mode of social responsiveness. By and large, subsidiary management contains more elements of standardisation based on parent company skills than elements of adaptation. However, the

Table 6   Mode of management in Japanese subsidiaries of German companies ($N = 52$)

Management areas/ issues	Adaptation score: Median 5-point scale[+]	Score of perceived differences: Median 5-point scale*	Diff. △ (mode of management)
Product quality (e.g., durability, finish)	2.333	1.440	+0.893
Service (e.g., delivery, after-sales service)	1.619	1.203	+0.416
Pricing/price policy (e.g., price calculation)	1.762	2.150	−0.388
Distribution (e.g., no. of intermediary outlets)	1.478	1.323	+0.155
Advertisement (e.g., media selection	2.500	2.580	−0.080
Brand policy (e.g., brand name, appearance)	3.800	3.100	+0.700
Financial management (e.g., relationship to banks, crediting)	2.313	2.250	+0.063
Purchasing policy (e.g., supplier relationships)	2.550	2.090	+0.460
Personnel management (e.g., selection, re- cruiting, motivation)	1.350	1.640	−0.290
Production management (e.g., mechanisation, quality control)	2.250	2.826	−0.576
Mean score	2.20	2.060	+0.140

Notes: [+] The smaller the score, the larger the adaptation (smaller the standardisation).
* The smaller the score, the larger the perceived difference.
△ Positive values indicate 'mode of social responsiveness' (Rn).
  Negative values indicate 'mode of social acceptance' (Sa).
  Zero indicates 'mode of obligation' (O).

mean score of + 0.14 indicates that the level of standardisation and implementation of non-Japanese patterns beyond the environmentally feasible margin is not high. Rather, the subsidiaries are very cautious in introducing new patterns. And even these 'new' styles of management have a low 'innovation' level, as indicated by the average adaptation scores in Table 6.

There is quite some variation between the individual management functions and areas. The highest degree of the mode of social responsiveness was practised in connection with product policy: Product quality and brand policy show a score of +0.89 and +0.70, respectively. The highest degree of social acceptance was demonstrated in the area of production management, followed by pricing policy and personnel management.

The smallest divergence ($\triangle$) between perceived difference regarding host and home country cultural influences and actual practiced adaptation was in advertising (-0.08). This indicates that in this area, Japanese subsidiaries of German companies have least scope of choice. Conforming to perceived environmental pressure is an economic or even a legal necessity. There was, however, no case of total social obligation. It seems that the Japanese environment in this sense almost always leaves scope for choice, even though it may be very small.

The role of influencing factors

As mentioned earlier, an important factor influencing the mode of management is the competitive advantage the subsidiary has over local firms. We questioned the respondents as to how they compared the level of their technology, production facilities, and products with those of Japanese competitors. Table 7 shows our findings.

Table 7 Perceived competitive advantage of Japanese subsidiaries of German companies ($N = 52$)

Comparison of technology, etc., by respondents (vis-à-vis Japanese firms)	No. of respondents (%)
We are better	24 (46)
Quite the same	25 (48)
A little inferior	3 (6)

Table 8 Entry strategy of responding subsidiaries ($N = 52$)

Type of entry	No. of respondents* (%)
Via acquisition of existing Japanese firms	6 (11.5)
De novo venture	45 (86.5)

Note: * Missing = 1

252   KUMAR AND STEINMANN

Table 9   Ownership pattern of responding subsidiaries ($N = 52$)

Type	No. of respondents* (%)
Fully owned subsidiaries	30 (58)
Joint Ventures with Japanese partners	18 (38)
Both types	3 (4)

Note: Missing = 1

As to the relevant structural elements of the responding subsidiaries, Tables 8 and 9 show the pattern.

Our results with respect to entry strategy incidentally confirm the general observation that foreign firms only in rare cases enter the Japanese market via take-overs (Table 8). Apparently, German firms also face the problem that Japanese owners are reluctant to part with companies, among other reasons because of a felt social commitment to interest groups (employees, customers, bankers, etc.) (7).

Regarding ownership patterns, our results confirm the general preference of German companies abroad to establish 100 per cent-owned subsidiaries (Table 9). More than half of the Japanese subsidiaries were fully owned by the German parent companies. The preference for unambiguous control is the main motive for choosing this strategy. Even among the joint ventures, majority holdings by German parent companies outnumber minority participation by 14 to 4.

Finally, the nationality of the chief executive officer (CEO) was considered an important influencing factor. Our findings show that the overwhelming majority of CEOs were German expatriate managers (Table 10).

After having looked at the characteristics of the variables, we now turn to investigate their influence on the mode of management as described earlier. The score depicting the mode of management (Table 6) was correlated with each of the influencing factors (Table 11). The findings show that only in a few number of cases is there any significant

Table 10   Nationality of CEO in responding subsidiaries ($N = 52$)

Nationality	No. of respondents (%)
German	36 (69)
Japanese	10 (19)
Third country	6 (12)

Table 11 Role of influencing factors in the mode of subsidiary management
(N = 52)

| Management areas/issues | Influence of variables* | | | | |
	Mode of mgmt.: Sa/Rn	Competitive advantage of subsidiary	Entry strategy	Owner- ship strategy	Nation- ality of CEO
Product quality	Rn				
Service	Rn	0.25*			
Pricing	Sa			0.26*	
Distribution	Rn	0.25*			
Advertisement	Sa				
Brand policy	Rn			0.32*	
Financial mgmt.	Rn		0.22*		
Purchasing policy	Rn		0.24*		
Personnel mgmt.	Sa				
Production mgmt.	Sa				

Note: * Spearman corr. coeff. p ≤ 0.05
Sa = social acceptance; Rn = social responsiveness

relationship. The striking features of these sparse connections are as
follows:

(1) Mostly those functional areas were affected by the variables,
which showed the mode of social responsiveness. Both service and
distribution patterns in the subsidiaries are influenced by the firms'
competitive advantages. Explicitly, subsidiaries who responded as being superior to local firms (Table 7) had a higher degree of social responsiveness in these two areas than subsidiaries who perceived themselves as being equal or inferior.

(2) Financial management and purchasing policy were both affected
by the choice of entry strategy. Specifically, subsidiaries which were
de novo ventures (Table 8) showed a higher score of social responsiveness in these two areas than take-over subsidiaries. Finally, subsidiaries
which were fully owned (Table 9) showed higher social responsiveness
in the area of brand policy than joint ventures.

(3) Pricing is the only management issue which is practised in accordance to the mode of social acceptance and is affected by one of
the variables, i.e., ownership strategy. Subsidiaries which were joint
ventures showed higher scores for social acceptance in pricing than
fully owned subsidiaries.

(4) The nationality of the chief executive officer does not seem to
play any role in the mode of subsidiary management. German expatriate CEOs can implement social acceptance just as well as their

Japanese counterparts; and the latter are in a position to practice social responsiveness just as much as the former. Obviously, both have
had enough socialisation in Japan and in the parent company respectively in order to be able to realize the advantages of both modes of
management in the subsidiary.

Mode of subsidiary management and success of operations

Our findings show that the return-on-investment as reported by the
Japanese subsidiaries averaged 15 per cent over the five years between
1981 and 1986. The variance was very high, however, with four firms
reporting 0 per cent and eight firms 20 to 70 per cent profitability.
In spite of a relatively high average, the responding subsidiaries considered their own success as being just about fair (Table 12). Apparently, they had set themselves a very high level of aspiration in Japan.
The highest degree of satisfaction was achieved with respect to sales
growth; the lowest in connection with market share.

Nevertheless, looking at the reported success as a whole, the responding subsidiaries seem to be optimistic about future trends. By
far, the majority of firms do not regret having started operations in
Japan and in fact would do so again (Table 13).

Table 14 shows how the mode of management relates to the success
of subsidiary operations. In most cases, there was no significant relationship between the mode of management and the success of operations in the subsidiaries. However, the few correlates give some interesting results:

(1) The mode of social responsiveness in the areas of product quality,
service, and distribution seems to affect success in terms of return-on-
investment, sales growth, and market share. Subsidiaries with higher
social responsiveness scores in these fields also showed higher success
ratings.

Table 12   Perceived success according to different criteria ($N = 52$)

Success criteria	Success rating (average over the past 5 years) (Median of a 5-point scale)
Return-on-investment	2.53
Sales growth	2.29
Market share	2.84

Note: 1 = very good; 2 = good; 3 = so-so; 4 = poor; 5 = bad

Table 13 Overall success of Japanese operations ($N = 52$)

Question:	Based on your experience, would you once more start a subsidiary in Japan or give a similar recommendation to a parent firm?

Answers	No. of respondents* (%)
Yes, under all circumstances	35 (67)
Yes, but under different circumstances	13 (25)
No	1(2)

Note: * Missing = 3

Table 14 Mode of management and success in Japanese subsidiaries of German companies ($N = 52$)

Management functions/ issues	Mode of mgmt. Sa/Rn+	Success criteria*		
		Return-on- investment	Sales growth	Market share
Product quality	Rn	0.296*	0.367*	
Service	Rn			0.307*
Pricing	Sa			0.313*
Distribution	Rn			0.25*
Advertisement	Sa	0.374*		0.308*
Brand policy	Rn			
Financial mgmt.	Rn			
Purchasing policy	Rn			
Personnel mgmt.	Sa			
Production mgmt.	Sa	0.28*	0.45*	

Notes: * Spearman corr. coeff. $p \leq 0.05$
+ Sa = mode of social acceptance; Rn = mode of social responsiveness

(2) The mode of social acceptance in the areas of pricing, advertisement, and production management seems to affect success in terms of return-on-investment, market share, and sales growth. Subsidiaries with higher social acceptance scores in these fields also showed higher success ratings.

(3) The success of the responding subsidiaries implies both modes of management: social acceptance and responsiveness styles. None of the success criteria really depended on only one of the management styles. One could also say that a good mixture of adaptation and standardisation in management seems to be the appropriate strategy in subsidiaries.

Discussion

The attempt to elaborate on the content of social acceptance and social responsiveness as established in our findings would mean discussing the practice of management within the Japanese cultural context and also in the context of the German firms' specific characteristics. In this paper, we can do this only in exemplary form based on our interviews.

According to our findings, distribution was an area where the mode of social responsiveness was the management style practised in the subsidiaries of German companies. However, as the degree of social responsiveness is small (Table 6), we can assume that the departure from Japanese patterns is marginal, with the German firms' specific advantages adding some innovative elements (Table 11).

Basically, the Japanese distribution system in most branches of industry is characterized by the existence of many more intermediary steps (e.g., agents, wholesalers) than in Germany, where manufacturers as far as possible try to sell directly in order to allow greater margins for themselves and also to maintain their own influence on sales right down to the customer.

According to our interviews in Japan, the subsidiaries of German companies generally, though often reluctantly, adapt their selling policy to the local system because relationships between manufacturers and distributors are often very traditional and breaking them would mean sacrificing goodwill in the market. Besides, such relationships also offer advantages, such as financing (8). But in spite of such adaptation, many German firms, especially in the industrial good ssector, have decided to also introduce their home company selling pattern, the main feature being independent intermediary outlets supported by company representatives in preparing sales strategies and service. The company's sales staff is trained in the German parent company and specializes in product handling and service. This method has proven especially advantageous in firms with a highly specialized product line (9). Such distribution patterns can be considered as an example of the mode of social responsiveness. Local Japanese methods have been 'enriched' by innovative elements based on the German firms' specific skills, thus giving the subsidiaries an edge over local competitors.

As our findings show (Table 6), the mode of social acceptance, i.e., conforming by the company's own choice to prevailing cultural norms and values (even though introducing new patterns would also be compatible in view of changing norms), was practised in the area of personnel management. As our interviews in Japan indicate, this mode could be established in connection with directing and motivating Japanese subordinates. It is well known and has been documented in many studies that interpersonal relationships in Japanese society have a strong element of 'groupism' (vis-à-vis individualism) (10). Management style in Japanese companies accounts for this, for instance, in the so-called *ringi* system where decision making involves many people from various hierarchies. Even responsibility is shared, and motivating subordinates means satisfying group needs rather than individual aspirations (11).

In most of our interviews in Japan, German expatriate managers and also Japanese subsidiary managers noted a change in Japanese society to the effect that 'groupish' attitudes in interpersonal relationships were on the decline in favour of individualistic thinking, especially among the younger generation. One German manager commented: 'The Japanese are becoming more and more like us in this respect!' With this apprehension of cultural change, it is then plausible to assume that actually motivating employees in German subsidiaries in Japan could be similar to that in the parent company, where individual incentives and achievement determine leadership style. Indeed, some firms we visited had definite plans to introduce such management styles in the near future.

But for the time being, most firms we visited (still) stressed groupism as the basis for leadership, just as the local Japanese companies did. Even though individually based subordinate-supervisor and peer relationships were considered viable, especially among the younger employees, on the whole, preference was (still) given to traditional systems.

Our findings have shown that in some cases the mode of subsidiary management is affected by the structural elements of the subsidiary (Table 11). Take, for instance, the case of purchasing policy which showed signs of social responsiveness and a correlation with entry strategy. It is well known that in Japan the purchasing system is characterized by strong ties between buyers and suppliers, with the latter being very much dependent on the former. According to a 1981 MITI survey, about 66 per cent of all small- and medium-sized Japanese firms have long-term binding relationships with large customers.

Our interviews in Japan have shown that subsidiaries which are de novo ventures have problems finding good suppliers because of this binding. No reputed supplier would risk making deliveries to a German company when it is bound by moral obligations to Japanese competitor firms. In many cases, they are forbidden to do so by contract. Subsidiaries established via acquisition, on the other hand, do not have such problems, since the traditional suppliers of the Japanese

258 KUMAR AND STEINMANN

company which has been bought are taken over by the subsidiaries. Incidentally, this is the important advantage of good acquisitions in Japan, if and when available.

In this situation, de novo subsidiaries have to develop new supply economies themselves. According to our interviews in Japan, many German firms find it essential to offer local suppliers terms and conditions which, when compared with those offered to them by Japanese customers, are very lenient. For instance, these subsidiaries have given suppliers financial and development assistance without strict contractual binding. In some cases, even the commitment for holding larger inventories, which is very common in Japan, has been relaxed in favour of the supplier. One German president of a large German chemical corporation commented in the following manner: 'Our relationship to our suppliers is that of a partnership. Japanese firms often treat their suppliers like slaves'. Japanese supplier firms have responded to a new type of relationship (social responsiveness) with affirmative action and loyalty in delivery.

Summary and conclusion

Our analysis has shown that subsidiaries of German companies in Japan follow management styles which in the context of Japanese cultural influences are both adaptive (social acceptance) and non-forming (social responsiveness). The modes differed according to the management areas and problems. Personnel management and production management were areas with relatively high social acceptance. Product quality and brand policy were marketing issues where high social responsiveness prevailed.

In spite of the different styles prevalent, no particular style contributed more to the success of the operations than any other. On the contrary, it seems that both styles are relevant for success to the same extent.

As far as the influencing factors are concerned, the competitive advantage of firms and entry and ownership strategies do seem to have an effect on management style. However, it was not prevalent in all cases; and what is more important is that the effect seems to be significant only in connection with the mode of social responsiveness.

Based on these results, we can conclude that

(1) German companies wishing to establish subsidiaries in Japan should be prepared to adapt management to the Japanese context

and also to implement their specific skills in certain areas. Explicitly, German expatriate managers must be acquainted with Japanese cultural norms affecting management. Japanese executives must be given training in German parent companies on firm-specific skills and philosophies.

(2) In areas where a management style of social responsiveness is considered essential, more attention must be given to competitive skills and the structural variables of the subsidiary. In other words, social responsiveness styles are easier to implement on the basis of competitive skills, de novo ventures, and wholly owned subsidiaries.

(3) The nationality of the CEO has practically no importance for the mode of management. Small- and medium-sized German firms especially, which are short of qualified managers, can very well do without assigning expatriate managers to Japanese subsidiaries, at least from the point of view of management.

Notes

The research reported in this paper was supported by a generous grant from DFG and the Hans-Frisch-Stiftung (University of Erlangen-Nuremberg). We also owe gratitude to this foundation for making it possible to present our paper in Tokyo. The survey was conducted with the kind assistance of the German Chamber of Commerce (Tokyo), to whom we owe thanks.

(1) The issue of 'local adaptation' and 'standardisation' has been discussed under various headings in international management literature, e.g., J. Fayerweather, 'A Conceptual Framework for the Multinational Corporation', in W. Wacker, H. Haussmann, and B. Kumar (ed.), *Internationale Unternehmensführung*, Schmidt Verlag, Berlin, 1981, pp. 17–32; Y. Doz, *Strategic Management in Multinational Companies*, Oxford University Press, Oxford, 1986.
(2) B. Kumar and H. Steinmann, 'Management and Conflict between Japanese and German Executives in Subsidiaries of Japanese and German Companies', *Annual Report of Economics* 12, Niigata University (Dec. 1987), pp.111–20.
(3) H. Simon, *Markterfolg in Japan*, Gabler Verlag, Wiesbaden, 1986.
(4) This was shown in connection with the US subsidiaries of German firms. B. Kumar, *Deutsche Unternehmen in den USA—Das Management in amerikanischen Niederlassungen deutscher Mittelbetriebe*, Gabler Verlag, Wiesbaden, 1987. For a basic treatise on the underlying hypothesis, see J. Fayerweather, *International Business Management: A Conceptual Framework*, McGraw-Hill, New York, 1969.
(5) In accordance with S.P. Sethi, N. Namiki, and C. Swans, *The False Promise of the Japanese Miracle*, Pitman, Boston, 1984.
(6) Kumar, *op. cit.*
(7) B. Kumar and H. Steinmann, 'Akquisition als Markteintrittsstrategie.' Deutsche Unternehmen in Japan', *Blick durch die Wirtschaft*, 10.7. 1987; E. Batzer and H. Laumer, *Deutsche Unternehmen im Japangeschäft—Markterschliessungsstrategien und Distributionswege*, IfO, München, 1986.

(8) For details, see Kumar and Steinmann, 'Akquisition', *op. cit.*

(9) See, e.g., the case of 'Trumpf GmbH' in Batzer and Laumer, *op. cit.*

(10) S. Marsland and M. Beer, 'The Evolution of Japanese Management: Lessons for U.S. Managers', *Organizational Dynamics*, Winter 1983, p. 49; G. Hofstede, *Cultures Consequences*, Sage, Beverly Hills, 1980.

(11) *Ibid.*

CONCLUSION

Malcolm Trevor
Policy Studies Institute

In his introduction to the theme of the Tokyo Conference, Shibagaki referred to the long-running argument over 'culture' versus economic rationality in attempts to account for the nature of business activity in different societies: an activity which shows considerable variety both in the ways in which it is managed, as evidenced by the (too?) much discussed question of management style, and in terms of performance or results.

Unfortunately, the debate among both managers and wider opinion has been slow in progressing beyond a number of well-worn and value-laden stereotypes. As Yoshimori in his paper observes, 'It is curious that despite a mountain of literature on Japanese management, little effort has been undertaken so far to define what Japanese management is. Terms like Japanese management or Japanese management style have been used without a clear-cut definition'.

A number of reasons for the failure to proceed more rigourously can be identified, and it needs to be remembered that this failure can have serious practical as well as intellectual consequences. It can affect any European or Japanese company which, like the German companies in Japan described in the paper by Kumar and Steinmann or the Japanese companies in a variety of countries discussed in the papers by Yoshihara and others, are confronted daily with the question of how to operate or adapt in an environment different from what they are used to at home and where their familiar assumptions may not apply.

The first reason simply concerns the relative newness of the subject. In the absence of either enough empirical work or awareness of specific detail, discussion at a general level unrelated to case studies inevitably leads to the use of sweeping generalisations, which have the attraction of providing an easy means of accounting for what is a more complicated, changing, and less tidy reality. Clearly, there is much to be

261

done here, and it is to be hoped that the sort of work presented in this volume will contribute to an improvement in the situation.

The problem might appear to be a primarily academic one, but as anyone who has addressed groups of businessmen knows, managers are just as likely to have stereotypical views of a Japanese or a European environment. Managers, at least in a British or American context, are also prone to chase after simple solutions to their problems, in spite of the reiterated warnings of writers like Peter Drucker that there is no panacea or 'secret' that will act as a 'patent medicine'. While there is obviously no substitute for first-hand experience in whatever overseas environment a manager is assigned to, proper orientation before he takes up his post in a local subsidiary can help him adapt better and function more effectively. Yet one wonders how many companies provide adequate orientation training before assigning managers overseas.

Part of the newness of the subject relates to the need for greater international exchange and more comparative work. Those who took part in the conference valued the opportunity for the exchange of information and cross-fertilisation of ideas, which it is very much the aim of the Association to promote.

At the same time, there is the different problem of the coverage of the various research areas and how to reach a comprehensive definition. In the well-known fable of the blind men and the elephant, examination of different parts, such as the trunk, the feet, and the back, led to very different conclusions. Similarly, as the range of papers in the present volume shows, it is theoretically possible to reach very different conclusions about Japanese as well as European management, depending on the field of study.

Looking at large companies in Japan, for instance, might lead to the conclusion that 'lifetime' employment was indeed the major 'pillar' of Japanese management (instead of an institution that probably applies to 30 per cent of all employees at most); while looking at small firms, not to mention the labour market for casual employment in such areas as construction and stevedoring, would not lead to the same conclusion about employment stability and 'loyalty'. Studying large established corporations might again give a picture of a high degree of formal and bureaucratic (not in the bad sense of the word) organisation that would be lacking in more entrepreneurially oriented and especially smaller and owner- or entrepreneur-controlled firms. Likewise, restricting oneself to blue-collar manufacturing areas would be likely to produce different findings in relation to levels of efficiency and cost reduction from what would be the case in white-collar and

office areas. Even on such a basic question as the use of financial resources, the continual search in manufacturing for even the smallest
cost savings, which in practice figures largely in the work of Quality
Circles and similar movements, contrasts with the highly liberal use
of funds on prestige occasions and for business entertaining.

Given these problems, it is not hard to see why so many accounts
fall back on over-generalised notions such as 'culture', but, to take the
last case referred to above, for example, how far is it legitimate to talk
of 'cultural traits' like thrift? Indeed, the continued failure to find an
agreed definition of 'culture' and to agree what use, if any, the concept is has been even more notorious than the failure to define 'Japanese management'. Perhaps, after all, it is better in the meantime to
concentrate on observable phenomena, such as normative or value-
laden thought and behaviour, which some people seem to equate with
'culture', even though this is not explicitly stated.

Thus, in looking at decision making, for instance, it would be possible to separate out the rationality or otherwise of the decision itself,
the way in which it is reached, and how the two impinge on one another.
Instead of leaping to the conclusion that a certain type of decision
making represented 'Japanese management', it would be necessary to
investigate empirically how decisions in Japanese organisations were
reached, whether by top down, bottom up, middle up, or any other
method.

In practice, what has tended to happen is for attention to concentrate on one type of large firm in Japan. This has led to the creation of
a single, and distorted, model for all Japanese firms, based on an
amalgam of practice, especially personnel management practice, in
these leading, established, and financially powerful companies. But
they do not represent the whole economy. As examples in the real
world show, it is possible for an economy to be efficient in agriculture
and distribution and poor in manufacturing, and vice versa. Where
does this lead deterministic generalisations and stereotypes?

Max Weber spent much of his career trying to understand the interaction between what he termed expedient (*zweckrational*) behaviour
and value-laden or value-rational (*wertrational*) behaviour in relation
to economic activity; particularly why 'the spirit of capitalism' had
developed in parts of Europe, rather than, at least earlier on, in China
or India. Unfortunately, Weber did not write a major work on Japan,
and his treatise on China has no more than one reference to the Japanese case, but he did raise most of the questions to which it seems we
are still trying to find the answers.

Speakers at the conference addressed these issues at both the conceptual and empirical levels. Abo, for instance, used Parsons's concepts of universalism and particularism to discuss the behaviour of Japanese firms overseas, while Shenkar et al.'s paper on Quality Circles in Israel gets away from the idea of Circles as something 'unique' and helps to locate them in the context of other approaches to work organisation and job enrichment.

Given the conspicuous international spread of Japanese companies in recent years and the much lower level of involvement of European companies in Japan, consideration of the problem of adaptability is again predominantly in one direction. But it is good to have two papers in Part III on the mirror image; one giving more contextual data and the other more data from the level of company management of, in this case, German subsidiaries in Japan. The remarks on commonly neglected points like supplier relations and what these mean for foreign subsidiaries in Japan are particularly suggestive and help to show that it is not just the obvious points like 'communication' that are the problem. The career issue, too, in the recruitment of Japanese nationals by European or other foreign companies in Japan has been known for some time but could benefit from more research. For many European researchers, there are unfortunately practical difficulties of time and money in doing research in Japan, but to judge from the level of awareness among European managers of Japanese business, there is a pressing need for more to be done. European managers could benefit from the discussion of Ohmae's 'Triad' concept and why, apart simply from selling, it is important for a company to have a presence in Japan.

The empirical papers provide a wide range of data on the management practices of Japanese companies overseas and how they interact with local staff. Differences in the respective inward investment situations and the custom and practice of the various host societies should help to allay the stereotype of the 'West' and to give a more accurately differentiated picture of the situation. The differing reactions to Japanese management approaches of European blue-collar, white-collar, and managerial employees are discussed and the reasons for the different reactions within the same society analysed. Yoshihara in particular takes up the point that there are in any case two different employment systems in Japanese companies in Europe: one for home country staff, amounting to full and 'permanent' membership of the organisation, and another for local staff, equivalent to temporary employment in Japan.

Since recruitment into one of these two categories is on a different basis, with recruitment into the 'permanent' stream in Japan not surprisingly being carried out with great care, it follows that subsequent

treatment is different. The points specifically referred to include communication, as discussed in Sakuma's paper, and such major issues as
pay, training, and promotion. Under the present arrangements, both
expatriates and local staff are following a rationale in their attitudes
towards career paths and employers, as the French example in Yoshimori's paper so dramatically demonstrates; although in Japanese subsidiaries in Europe, and elsewhere, with a mixed workforce the difference between the respective rationales leads to a situation of the 'one
bed, two dreams' type. Both rationales have a value-laden and at times
emotive side, but there is no need to fall back on a mystique to explain
them. The evidence of career dissatisfaction in the empirical studies
from European countries presented at the conference speaks for itself.

This brings the argument to the crux of the matter, which is not just
about ideas, values, or management styles per se, but about the labour
market. Just as German firms in Japan in the case study presented have
to adapt to some aspects of the local labour market structure, custom,
and practice, so Japanese firms in Europe must confront the possibility
of job changing: something that refers to managers even in first-class
companies in a way that the companies are hardly compelled to confront at home. The fact that people in Western European labour markets in conditions of high unemployment nevertheless feel that they
are free to move, theoretically at any time, can only make the problem
appear more intractable. Clearly, a cost element is also involved, as a
free labour market will tend to push up the price of scarce special skills,
as with dealers in the City of London, for example.

Whether the dual employment system in Japanese companies in
Western Europe is seen as the 'fault' of the companies themselves or
of the local staff rather depends on other factors. Some criticisms and
counter-criticisms represent no more than the tip of the iceberg: the
iceberg itself being the difference in labour market mobility and in the
industrial structure. This has many implications, which this is not the
place to go into, such as the longer-term orientation of business in
Japan, compared with the UK and USA in particular, and the difference
in the power of shareholders. Just what structural differences can mean
for performance is brought out in Ikeda's paper on manufacturer-
supplier relations.

Naturally, the situation is not static, but fluid, with the Japanese
economy facing the 'pincer movement' described in the paper by Mirza
et al. of slower economic growth, the high yen, protectionism, and
competition from the NICs. Here, Okumura's example of Matsushita
radios almost entirely composed of parts from Malaysia, Taiwan,
Singapore, etc., is relevant. Kumar and Steinmann's paper also quotes

a German manager in Japan on the increasing similarity between the attitudes of young Japanese and what is common in Western Europe: a convergence which has already had some effect on job mobility in Japan, although nothing like to the extent of creating a Western European type of labour market, particularly as companies as well as job seekers and employees are actors in this situation.

As far as Japanese companies in Europe are concerned, one needs to remember that manufacturers who arrived in the 1970s and 1980s are mostly at an early stage in their development cycle; and the same is true of, for example, the securities companies in London that have been restructuring themselves to take advantage of the recent deregulation. It will be interesting to watch how they evolve over time, and how decentralised, or 'localised', in terms of personnel and managerial authority, they become. What might this mean for the companies in Japan themselves? Rather than being examples of the interaction of stereotypical 'cultures', they will continue to be the location of the interaction of economic, technical, social, and political variables in a manner that one would have to be a bold determinist to predict with confidence. As such, they will continue to be important objects of study, with a significance for business strategy and the means of implementing it that still need to be brought home to European practitioners.

INDEX